OFF CENTER

OFF CENTER

The Republican
Revolution and
the Erosion of
American
Democracy

With a New Afterword

Jacob S. Hacker
and Paul Pierson

Yale University Press
New Haven and London

Set in Galliard type by SPI Publisher Services.

Printed in the United States of America.

Library of Congress Control Number: 2006928580

ISBN-13: 978-0-300-11975-6
ISBN-10: 0-300-11975-5

A catalogue record for this book is available from the British Library.

The paper in this book meets the guidelines for permanence and durability of the Committee on Production Guidelines for Book Longevity of the Council on Library Resources.

10 9 8 7 6 5 4 3 2 1

CONTENTS

OFF CENTER

INTRODUCTION

When President George W. Bush took the stage to deliver his State of the Union Address in 2005, he had plenty of cause to celebrate. To begin with, he was on the podium, having emerged victorious in a bitterly fought election that saw him escape the embarrassing fate of his father, who had been defeated after a single term. Yet the larger reason for celebration was all around him—in the regal House chamber he faced. Flanking Bush were Vice President Dick Cheney, Bush's conservative policy czar, and Speaker of the House Dennis Hastert, the head of the Republican-controlled House of Representatives. In the audience was House Majority Leader Tom DeLay, the ultraconservative Texan known as "The Hammer" who had pushed through a controversial redistricting plan in Bush's home state, padding the Republicans' House majority. In the audience, too, was Senate Majority Leader Bill Frist of Tennessee, who had helped the GOP increase its margin in the Senate to fifty-five seats, to the Democrats' forty-four. As Bush outlined his plans for the long-standing conservative goal of partially privatizing Social Security, the air of triumph in the room was unmistakable: A new order had taken root. A conservative governing coalition, balanced on a razor's edge of partisan control, had seized the reins of power and was now dramatically remaking the laws of the land.

The feeling of accomplishment was certainly warranted. The president and congressional GOP have not always gotten what they wanted, of course. But given the closeness of the political divisions in the nation and the general public skepticism that many of their key aims have provoked, their success in achieving their principal goals has been nothing short of remarkable. Indeed, fitting historical parallels are elusive. The New Deal of FDR and the Great Society of LBJ are the analogies for which today's commentators most often reach. And yet both FDR and LBJ had crushed their campaign opponents, enjoyed vast Democratic margins in Congress, and ridden a wave of overwhelming public support for the government activism they championed. None of this holds true today. Far from marshaling overwhelming party margins, Republicans—including President Bush—exercise power by virtue of successive election victories that are as close as any in American history. And far from eliciting broad public support for their actions, the GOP has eked out victories on issue after issue—from tax cuts to Medicare reform to environmental policy—on which Americans' views of what they are doing range from dubious to downright hostile.

According to the conventional wisdom about American politics, this shouldn't be possible. Our system of government is supposed to thwart the ambitions of slim majorities. Our political leaders are supposed to obey the dictates of surveys and focus groups, afraid to run afoul of the all-powerful oracle of public opinion. Our parties are supposed to be weak, fragmented, and ineffective. Our electoral structure is supposed to encourage two major parties vying for the center, not a majority party heading for the fringes. Our framework of frequent elections is supposed to ensure that politicians who stray too far from their constituents' wishes end up in the dustbin of political history.

Today's governing Republican majority can justly claim that it has defied these normal laws of political gravity. It has ruled with the slimmest of majorities and yet overseen a major transformation of America's governing priorities. It has been locked in tight competition with its political rivals and yet shown little inclination to tack to the political center. It has strayed dramatically from the moderate middle of public opinion and yet faced little public backlash. Again and again, it has sided with the extremes. And much more often than not, it has come out on top.

This book explains why. It shows that those who run our nation are committed to ideas and laws that are at odds with the moderate center of

American opinion. It explains why our nation's political leaders have veered so far right and why the normal mechanisms of democratic accountability have not been able to bring them back. And it explores how the interwoven forces that have created this troubling state of affairs can be overcome. America's great democratic experiment is under assault. Restoring its health requires understanding how those that hold the reins of political power in the United States have succeeded in pushing American government so far off center.

Misery of the Moderates

Every governing coalition has its critics. What is notable about this governing coalition is who has issued the most powerful expressions of discontent: moderates within the Republican fold disaffected by their party's continuing rightward lurch. This is all the more surprising because, as this book will make clear, it is the unmatched coordination and cohesion of ruling Republicans that have allowed them to spin the straw of slim majorities and popular skepticism into the gold of electoral and policy victories. No previous governing coalition has played the media with greater skill. No previous governing coalition has so thoroughly staunched the leaks through which internal feuds spill into the newspapers and airwaves. And yet, the first four years of George W. Bush's presidency yielded not one or two but three fierce critiques from former high-level policy insiders: ex-Treasury Secretary Paul O'Neill; Christine Todd Whitman, former administrator of Bush's Environmental Protection Agency; and John DiIulio, head of the president's Office for Faith-Based Initiatives.[1]

O'Neill, Whitman, and DiIulio have much in common. Each is a political moderate. Each is an experienced public servant, devoted to crafting what he or she sees as good public policy. And each describes a Washington political world in which deliberation is kept to a minimum and policy is systematically and relentlessly subordinated to hard-right political goals. Like the most damning testimony of witnesses in a criminal trial, O'Neill, Whitman, and DiIulio finger the same culprits and describe the same crime. All activity in contemporary GOP circles, they testify, is focused on pushing policy as far right as possible while delivering tangible benefits to the ruling party's most deep-pocketed and extreme supporters.

DiIulio's testimony is the bluntest. "There is no precedent in any modern White House for what is going on in this one, a complete lack of a policy apparatus," DiIulio told the reporter Ron Suskind in late 2002. "What you have is everything—and I mean everything—being run by the political arm. It's the reign of the Mayberry Machiavellis."[2] In a stunning confessional memo, DiIulio wrote: "Staff, senior and junior, . . . consistently talked and acted as if the height of political sophistication consisted in reducing every issue to its simplest, black-and-white terms for public consumption, then steering legislative initiatives or policy proposals as far right as possible."

Whitman is more guarded than DiIulio, as behooves the woman who headed Bush's reelection campaign in New Jersey. But in her recent book, *It's My Party, Too: The Battle for the Heart of the GOP and the Future of America,* she comes out swinging. "The Republican Party at the national level," Whitman writes, "is allowing itself to be dictated to by a coalition of ideological extremists . . . groups that have claimed the mantle of conservatism and show no inclination to seek bipartisan consensus on anything." Calling on fellow GOP moderates, Whitman insists that "we must bring the Republican Party, and American politics more generally, back toward the center."[3]

Then there is the former Treasury secretary, who resigned after two years of unsuccessfully trying to rein in many of the Bush administration's rightward moves on economic policy. O'Neill resists overarching generalizations, but his recounting echoes that of Whitman and DiIulio. Following the midterm elections in 2002, for example, he expressed concern about the mounting budget deficit and questioned a push for yet larger tax cuts for the wealthy. In O'Neill's account, even the president was momentarily unclear about the need for this step. "Didn't we do the investment package already?" he asked at one meeting. Karl Rove, Bush's closest political adviser, then insisted, "stick to principle"—by which he meant slash the dividend tax and accelerate the high-income rate cuts of 2001. A week or so earlier, O'Neill had met with Vice President Cheney to warn against another aggressive round of tax cuts for the well off. Cheney's reply was short and sharp:

"Reagan proved that deficits don't matter. We won the elections. This is our due."[4]

Welcome to the new world of American politics.

Unequal Polarization

To many political analysts, a single word captures this brave new world: *polarization*. Commentators ranging from prominent journalists like David Broder to astute scholarly observers like Princeton political scientist Nolan McCarty all seem to agree that the great problem in American politics is that the parties are drifting ever further apart, with the political center an increasingly large and empty space between them.[5] American politics has become an endless cycle of revenge and retribution. With rival camps of extremists dug into their trenches, exchanging fusillades across a political no-man's-land, the key to success in politics—in the words of the journalist E. J. Dionne, Jr., author of *Why Americans Hate Politics*—"has been to reopen the same divisive issues over and over again."[6]

Though the rise in polarization is undeniable, the conventional lament misses crucial aspects of the change. It suggests a transformation that is somehow equal on both sides, as if the two parties had run away from each other at the same speed. In fact, as we shall see, the move from the center has been spearheaded and driven by the Republican Party. Over the same era in which conservatives have risen to power, they have moved further and further from the political center. Nothing remotely close to this massive shift has happened on the other side of the spectrum, much less among the great bulk of ordinary voters.

No less important, for all the hand-wringing, contemporary discussions of polarization too often suggest that not all that much is at stake. Our politics is less civil, true. But ultimately, in American politics, extremists are not supposed to win the pitched battles they fight. Given the checks and balances built into our institutions, moderates should usually hold the balance of power. In this common view, the worst that polarization can bring is stalemate, as the parties find it harder to agree. But when government does act, it does so only because sensible politicians have at least momentarily reclaimed the middle. As former

Minnesota Republican Congressman Vin Weber recently observed at a large conference on partisan polarization that brought together academics, journalists, and politicians (itself a revealing indicator of the ubiquity of concern about polarization): "It's not at all clear to me what [polarization] has done in terms of the governance of the country. . . . [T]he cultural differences that are driving a lot of polarization in the country are more evident in the rhetoric of the candidates and officeholders than they are in the policy outcomes we're seeing out of the United States Congress."[7]

Yet just as polarization has been unequal in its effects on Republicans and Democrats, it has been inconsistent in its effects on public policy. Polarization has certainly made it harder for the parties to agree, and sometimes gridlock has indeed reigned. Yet, as the testimony of disaffected moderates in the Bush administration suggests, it is not just political rhetoric that has become more extreme. It is the governance of the nation itself. Somehow, ruling Republicans have found a way to do what Democrats, when they held the upper hand in similarly close political fights, either would or could not: put in place policies that are far from the moderate center.

Polarization is a major and growing problem. But the problem is not just polarization. It is *unequal* polarization—unequal between Democrats and Republicans, unequal in its effects on the governing aims of liberals and conservatives, and unequal in its effects on American society. Over the past twenty years, the economic gap between the middle and the top has grown enormously.[8] Recent events strongly indicate that the gap in effective political power has, too.[9] With money more important in politics than ever, with the organizations that once protected the interests of the middle in broad decline, Republicans have showered their attention and largesse on the most privileged elements of American society and worried little about potential fallout. Agreement is often elusive in today's polarized climate. And yet it always seems most elusive when government action is necessary to protect ordinary citizens.

Polarization is real, but it is not the real puzzle. What makes the shift of American politics off center so puzzling is that Republicans have achieved a number of big policy changes in spite of increasing polarization—and in spite of evident public concern about many of them. This book explains how and why Republicans have so often successfully pursued this improbable yet far-reaching campaign.

American Politics Transformed

The winds of change have swept through every cranny of American government. But perhaps the most transformative have been in Congress. In the nation's vaunted legislative body, the moderate center is on life support. Democrats are shut out. Republican leaders aggressively control the agenda of debate and the alternatives members of Congress get to consider. Veteran Congress-watcher Norm Ornstein, a resident fellow at the conservative American Enterprise Institute, says that "it is the middle-finger approach to governing, driven by a mind-set that has brought us the most rancorous and partisan atmosphere that I have seen in the House in 35 years."[10]

Majority Leader Tom DeLay exemplifies the tough new strategy of the Republican congressional elite. From the concerted attempt to impeach President Bill Clinton in the late 1990s to his successful effort to remake the Texas electoral map to bolster the GOP congressional majority in 2004, DeLay has inverted Prussian military strategist Carl von Clausewitz's famous observation that war is simply the continuation of politics by other means. In the new Republican Congress, politics is war by other means.

And yet, the rightward shift of the nation's leadership, evident in every branch of U.S. government, is as much a symptom as a cause of the transformed nature of American politics. DeLay's crusade would go nowhere if those who signed on to his ideological cause believed they risked losing office as a result. In the textbook vision of American politics, ordinary voters ultimately call the shots. So long as both parties need to court swing voters, and so long as such voters have basic information about what politicians are up to, then voters do not have to do anything more than vote for the candidate they like to discipline politicians. The need to court middle-of-the-road voters—or at least to escape their wrath—will by itself keep politicians roughly in line with public sentiment.

In a metaphor that nicely captures this view, the political scientist James Stimson and his colleagues describe politicians as "keen to pick up the faintest signals in their political environment. Like an antelope in an open field, they cock their ears and focus their full attention on the slightest sign of danger."[11] True enough, but in American politics today, middle-of-the-road voters are not the formidable predators of days gone by. Rather, they are more like wounded prey, lacking both the knowledge and the power that once made politicians pay consistent heed. Politicians keep their ears cocked, but the main threats they listen for come from their party's leaders and their partisan base.

In an age of big government, voters need to know more than ever to make informed judgments. But thanks to personality-focused elections, run through a news media that provides increasingly little in the way of substantive information, most voters find it hard even to learn the basics. Political elites know this well. They now shape the issues of debate and structure laws and policies in ways that make it exceedingly difficult, even for the attentive and well informed, to know how they will be affected by what government does. It is a devastating one-two punch. Take away the old sources of information, like traditional news organizations, widespread voluntary organizations, and locally grounded political parties. Then craft rhetoric and policies to make it difficult for even the well informed to know what is going on.[12]

Knowledge and power are, of course, intertwined—and ordinary voters have seen both ebb over the past thirty years. Middle-class Americans have seen their paychecks rise only modestly, while the richest Americans have witnessed dramatic increases in their income and wealth. Middle-class Americans have watched as the organizational and financial resources that ordinary voters can bring to bear in politics have atrophied, even as American politics has become much more responsive to organization and wealth.[13] To be noticed, voters increasingly need to be highly mobilized or highly wealthy or both. Instead of assiduously courting the ordinary voter, political elites cater to business groups and the well heeled, increasingly confident they can circumvent the hapless run-of-the-mill citizen on Election Day.

The shift has been abetted by our rickety electoral structure, which gives those who finance campaigns and the highly energized partisans who vote in primaries increasing power to shape who gets elected. The biggest change is the rise in safe seats. As recently as a decade ago, a quarter or more of congressional seats genuinely were in play in any given election. Today, virtually none are. Thanks to the increasing power of incumbency, combined with sophisticated partisan gerrymandering, most House districts are almost completely safe for one party or the other, and Senate elections are also less competitive than they once were. This leaves favored candidates to worry almost exclusively about pleasing their partisans.[14]

At the same time, the parties—and especially the Republican Party—have grown much more involved in campaign finance, and much more adept at targeting their resources to maintain partisan unity and power.[15] Unconcerned about challenges from the other side of the aisle, protected by the resources of the party (and fearful of losing the favors of powerful groups and leaders), most members of Congress today find it far better to be a loyalist than a maverick. And so most voters sit on the sidelines watching a political blood sport that plays out with little concern for what the moderate center of opinion thinks—except as that moderate center represents a modest obstacle to be evaded.

The Race to the Base

"Go West, young man" was the slogan of the nineteenth-century frontiersman. Today's Republicans receive a similar battle cry: "Go Right, young politician." Not all Republicans are as conservative as Tom DeLay, but almost all of the newly elected ones are in the general ballpark. From the early 1970s to the present, according to reliable ideological measures, the party has tracked consistently to the right.[16] New Republicans are almost always more conservative than old ones. Existing Republicans generally move right as they age. The center of the party was once roughly where the Arizona maverick John McCain now stands—that is, far to the left of its current conservative core.

What is the great force that pulls Republican politicians to the right? In a word, the "base." The base is the party's most committed, mobilized, and deep-pocketed supporters: big donors, ideological activist groups, grassroots conservative organizations, and, increasingly, party leaders themselves. The base has always had power, but never the kind of power it has today. With money more important in campaigns than ever, the base has money. With the political and organizational resources of ordinary voters in decline, the base is mobilized and well organized. With most congressional seats safe for one party or the other, the base has the troops to influence the typically low-turnout primaries that determine who goes to Washington. "Who says you can't have it all?" a catchy ad campaign once asked. Increasingly, the Republican base does.

And when you have it all, politicians pay attention. As American politics grew more candidate-centered, with each political aspirant running his or her own independent race for office, the standard assumption was that the parties and their political bases mattered less.[17] But the opposite has turned out to be closer to the truth. Without independent wealth, those who want to run for office need money, and money flows through party coffers and closely affiliated organizations. Even if money is not a barrier, candidates need activist allies and ground troops. And to get them, they need certification from conservative political organizations.

The base has the troops, and it does the certification. Are you a true tax-cutter? Better convince Americans for Tax Reform and other anti-tax groups. Committed to moral revitalization? Make sure the Christian Coalition and Focus on the Family think you are, too. Eager to roll back restrictions on gun ownership? Let the National Rifle Association know and hope it agrees. A true Republican? The congressional GOP might have something to say about that—and a lot of money, if you really are.

The base has fewer tools for making already-established incumbents toe the conservative line (though occasionally, by threatening a primary or withholding money or perks, it puts a scare into those deemed less than fully loyal to the conservative cause). But the base has an impressive and growing arsenal for recruiting and certifying new entries into the Republican fold. Incumbents may be able to thwart electoral defeat; but they cannot thwart mortality, ambition for higher office, or sheer political fatigue. And so, with every new recruit, with every new election, the pull of the base increases, the ascendance of the hard right grows—and the power of moderate voters to ensure that American politicians abide by their wishes erodes.

The Unexpected Centralization of American Political Power

The base has pulled the Republican Party to the right from the bottom. The new breed of Republican elites that now dominates Washington has pulled it to the right from the top. In doing so, Republican leaders have benefited from a dramatic shift in the American political system: the increasing coordination and centralization of GOP political elites. In the 1970s and 1980s, political scientists and pundits alike talked about the "fragmentation" of politics—the breaking apart of established institutions, the undermining of old sources of authority. We were told that political leaders had to "build coalitions in the sand," that getting politicians to join up for common causes was akin to "herding cats."[18] Today, these complaints ring anachronistic. American political institutions are still fragmented. But a set of informal and formal institutions has emerged in the past decade—particularly on the Republican side of the aisle—to make the sands of politics much firmer and the cats that need herding much more compliant.

The most visible sign of the shift is the growing power that party leaders wield in Congress, especially the House of Representatives.[19] The congressional leadership now enjoys extensive authority to decide which issues get debated and which alternatives get considered. It now eagerly uses so-called closed rules to limit debate and quell minority input. It now regularly yanks committee chairs and other perks away from wayward members. Party leaders were once thought of as maître d's gently steering members of Congress toward the right table and ensuring they got what they needed. As anybody who has watched Tom DeLay at work can attest, they are not maître d's today.

The centralization of Congress is, however, only part of the move toward greater Republican coordination. From the base of the grassroots up to the pinnacles of power in Washington, D.C., the informal ties that bind conservatives have grown tighter and denser. The Republican base is the foundation of this remarkable structure of political authority, but the glue that binds the structure is a small group of elites—figures like Karl Rove, Tom DeLay, Dick Cheney, and anti-tax activist Grover Norquist, head of the advocacy group Americans for Tax Reform—whom we term the "New Power Brokers." These New Power Brokers share two key characteristics. They sit at the intersection of multiple worlds of influence, at the nexus of money, mobilization, and authority. And they are fiercely committed to the conservative cause.

The New Power Brokers make things happen in the new world of American politics. They cut deals, establish connections, organize lobbying, mobilize activists. They are not all-powerful, to be sure. Much of their influence flows up from the remarkable unity of the party on behalf of which they labor. But their ability to coordinate political action is nonetheless unprecedented in recent American politics. More important, it is far greater than the capacity for coordination enjoyed by their opponents. In politics, all power is relative, and relatively speaking, the New Power Brokers are powerful indeed.

Backlash Insurance

The New Power Brokers and the Republican base emit a powerful gravitational pull to the right. But this alone does not explain why moderate voters have seen their influence decline so greatly. The hard right may love a candidate. But if the majority of voters don't want to buy what it is selling, then all its efforts will be for naught. In the conventional view of American politics, elections are the ultimate check on candidates' fates—a check that eventually drives all politicians toward the center. The extreme right may have many cards, but the median voter has the trump card.

Yet it turns out that conservative political elites have a trump card of their own—what we call "backlash insurance." Backlash insurance describes an assortment of strategies and procedures that party leaders use to keep quavering moderates in line and shield party loyalists against political retaliation by moderate voters. The most powerful of these tools are agenda control and policy design—the choice and framing of issues and alternatives, and the construction of policies so that ordinary voters have difficulty correctly understanding policy effects or attributing responsibility for them.

Students of politics, even professional ones, frequently take for granted the agenda of political debate—as if everyone agrees what issues should be debated and what alternatives should be considered to address them. This is a profound error. The great political scientist E. E. Schattschneider once observed: "There are billions of potential conflicts in any modern society, but only a few become significant. . . . [T]he definition of the alternatives is the supreme instrument of power. He who determines what politics is about runs the country."[20] One does not have to believe in a cohesive power elite pushing all conflict to the side to recognize that the power to set the terms of debate is a hugely important mechanism of influence. As we shall see, it is a mechanism that the increasingly coordinated GOP establishment has skillfully used to shift American governance to the right.

The increased coordination of conservatives has not only allowed them to set the American political agenda. It has also enabled them to deploy the second major component of backlash insurance: the careful design of public policies to highlight some effects and beneficiaries and downplay others. Political observers too often forget that policies are not just the product of political discussion and conflict; they are also a major influence on them. The design of public policies shapes not just who gets what from them but also how the actions of government are perceived and how political actors and the public respond to those actions over time.[21] And shaping these perceptions and responses is what Republican leaders, with the benefit of increased coordination and agenda control, have skillfully done.

In Chapter 2, for example, we show that the hugely expensive tax cuts of the first Bush term were all designed with a keen eye toward public perceptions and future political battles. Americans were fearful that the tax cuts would threaten other governing priorities they deemed more important—so advocates of the tax cuts designed them in ways that consistently masked their true long-term cost, delaying the biggest cuts, insisting that all the cuts would be magically rescinded in 2011, and failing to fix problems in the tax code that would require further tax cuts in the years ahead. Americans were opposed to giving disproportionately large tax cuts to the well off—so advocates of the tax cuts loaded the benefits for the middle class up front while deferring the much larger benefits for the rich until later, when the public spotlight would be focused elsewhere. Americans wanted the tax cuts limited to what could be funded without risk to other priorities, such as health care, education, and Social Security—so advocates of the tax cuts threw in a range of policy tricks, from exploding time bombs to unrealistic phase-outs, that they knew would create huge political pressure from the rich and powerful for more and more tax cuts down the road. In short, advocates of the tax cuts didn't see policy simply as a way of delivering benefits or affecting the economy. They saw it as a way of achieving and locking in courses of government action at odds with what large majorities of Americans believed in.

This story contains an irony that is often mistaken for a contradiction. Republicans have succeeded so handsomely not in spite of but because of big government. While railing against big government, they have taken advantage of its complexity and opaqueness in their aggressive effort to transform what government does. As is often noted, usually with a "gotcha" thrown in, the size of public spending under President Bush has *not* fallen, even as tax revenues have plummeted and deficits have soared. Conservatives may well be intent on "starving the beast," as tax-cutters have portrayed their goal.[22] But so far the beast seems relatively unfazed. And while Republicans are reducing the beast's daily rations, they are asking it to take on more responsibilities, too—from new subsidies for corporations and rich investors to new drug benefits for the aged to trillions in potential borrowing to establish private accounts within the Social Security system.

Some say this means the Republican Revolution never happened.[23] The truth is more complex. Although Republicans have not starved the beast in the short run, they are putting it on a very specific diet that is transforming the role of government in American life. This special diet is not principally aimed at making government larger or smaller, at least in the short term. It is aimed at tilting the balance of benefits and protections away from ordinary Americans and toward the well off, the well connected, and the Republican base. Commentators too often miss this because they too often look at slogans rather than policy details—at the phrase "drug benefit" rather than the reality of what the GOP drug benefit actually does. But when the details are in view, it becomes clear that Republicans are eager and willing to use government to achieve their ends. The rub is that the ends that they are seeking are often at odds with core beliefs of the American people.

And the rub will only get worse. The Republican innovation has been to separate the pleasant business of cutting taxes from the unpleasant business of slashing popular programs. But if Republicans continue on their present course, the unpleasantness *will* arrive. And it will be especially painful to those who rely on the valued social and economic programs that come under the knife. Yet, thanks to the GOP's own safety net of backlash insurance, Republicans have good reason to believe that the resulting political fallout will not interfere with their efforts to build a permanent majority and restructure American government.

Backlash insurance is one of the most innovative and successful products developed in decades. It allows party leaders to protect vulnerable incumbents who might otherwise balk at running with the party herd. It lets prominent politicians claim that they are helping the little guy when they are really stepping on him to reach the big guys. It lets Republicans race to their base without constant fear of alienating the center. Backlash insurance is a boon to the Right. It is also a threat to democracy.

Democracy under Siege

Democracy—literally, rule of the people—takes many concrete forms, from the direct democracy of town hall meetings to the representative democracy of elected officials with defined roles.[24] Our complaint is decidedly not with representative democracy. We see no substitute for it in making most of the decisions that national governments confront. Nor do we believe that every departure from public opinion, or every attempt to respond to intense minority interests, is a breach of democratic ideals. We agree with the esteemed economist Joseph Schumpeter that the essence of democracy is that political leaders "acquire the power to decide by means of a competitive struggle for the people's vote."[25] To be sure, this competitive vision of democracy is incomplete; basic political rights are also essential, and direct democracy is sometimes necessary and valuable. But the competitive model is deeply appealing, for it shows how ordinary citizens can discipline extraordinarily powerful public figures, just as ordinary consumers in a competitive marketplace can discipline extraordinarily large private corporations.

But for competition—whether political or economic—to work, it must be fair. Basic information must be available and accessible, and "consumers" must have real and effective opportunities to reject "products" on the basis of that information. The argument of this book is that America's political market no longer looks like the effectively functioning markets that economics textbooks laud. Rather, it increasingly resembles the sort of market that gave us the Enron scandal, in which corporate bigwigs with privileged information got rich at the expense of ordinary shareholders, workers, and consumers.

We make this argument not as partisans but as professional political scientists deeply concerned about the health and future of our nation's democratic institutions. In today's political climate, we recognize that this statement will strike those who disagree with our politics as disingenuous—a cloaking of a partisan grudge in the mantle of public spirit. (As the philosopher Thomas Hobbes once wrote, "They that are discontented under monarchy call it tyranny.")[26] We make no pretense that we have any affection for the substance of the Republicans' domestic agenda. But many of our complaints about the current direction of American politics should strike a chord across the political spectrum. Our concerns, after all, are echoed in moderate Republican voices, including those who have seen the new political system from the inside. Moreover, some of these concerns have already sparked efforts at reform by Republican state governors—a move we applaud in principle but worry about in practice, as the final chapter explains.

The goal of effective democratic accountability is not partisan. Oliver Wendell Holmes expressed his own democratic spirit by stating, "If my fellow citizens want to go to Hell, I will help them. It's my job."[27] We share the sentiment. The problem we are concerned about is not that America's political elite is heading in the wrong direction, though we believe it is. It is that this elite is increasingly pulling American government away from its citizens. The problem is not conservative policymaking. It is off-center policymaking—policymaking that starkly and repeatedly departs from the center of public opinion but that the normal institutions of democratic accountability have not been able to bring back.

We are not arguing that political elites are ignoring public opinion. In fact, they have never paid more attention to it or had greater capacity to chart its every ripple.[28] Yet they are using their knowledge of public opinion not to respond to the public's wishes and concerns but to blunt the tools that citizens use to hold them to account. For democratic competition to work, voters need to be able to find out what politicians do and how it affects them, and they need to have the opportunity to effectively cast judgment on those politicians at the ballot box. These prerequisites of democracy have weakened in recent decades, and the nation's governing elite has worked to weaken them further.

The cords of accountability have weakened because the electoral map has sorted into safely Republican and Democratic districts. They have weakened because of rising incumbency advantage. They have weakened because of the growing importance of money in the electoral arena. They have weakened because of the growing inequality of resources and organization between the rich and the rest. And perhaps most overlooked, they have weakened because of the deliberate efforts of political elites to make it hard for Americans to know what they are up to—to manage and distort information in ways that greatly undermine the sway of ordinary voters.

These efforts have gone well beyond the typical tools of public relations with which students of modern politics are so familiar: focus groups, poll-tested phrases, costly advertising blitzes. Even more than deliberate misinformation—of which there is certainly no shortage—the challenge posed by the maneuvering of today's GOP elite is deceptive policy design. The subject seems uninteresting, we know: Why should we care about policy details? Experts don't always agree on them. Politicians rarely talk about them. The news media all but ignores them. But as the old saying goes, the devil is truly in the details of off-center policymaking.

The devil in the details of recent polices is not complexity, which is all but unavoidable in modern governance. It is policy features that are designed to hide what policies are really doing while deliberately restricting the scope for future democratic choice. As we show in Part I of this book, today's political elites are pursuing policies that often meet these two tests. As just noted, the tax cuts of the first Bush term were designed to obscure their true effects while making it nearly inevitable that more and more tax cuts would be passed down the line—despite little public support for the initial tax cuts, much less further ones. But the tax cuts are not the only example of deceptive policy design. Similar features can be found in the prescription drug bill of 2003, proposals for partial privatization of Social Security, and many other recent measures. None of these features is unprecedented. Their scale and the frequency of their deployment are. And so is their repeated use to target central, long-standing, and popular elements of our nation's policies.

The Argument to Come

It should already be clear that the main target of our critique is *Republican* political elites, not political elites in general. It is true that a number of the trends that we discuss—the growing power of the parties' "bases," the rise in safe seats, the opportunities for manipulation of political rhetoric and policy design—have created opportunities for mischief that can be exploited by either party. And we should make clear that such mischief on the part of either party is equally troubling. The goal of this book is to identify dangers to democracy, not dangers to the Democratic Party.

But as will become clear, the neutral language of polarization, with its implication of equivalence, is a fundamentally misleading description of contemporary American politics. For one thing, Republicans currently hold the overwhelming balance of power in American politics, and for this reason alone they are the political figures who benefit most from the worrisome trends that this book examines. Yet Republicans have also proved much more determined and capable of pushing American politics off center—for reasons we outline in Part II. To put the point in more technical terms, the shift of American politics off center is not symmetrical. It has benefited Republicans far more than it has benefited Democrats. Contrary to the conventional view of polarization, the threat to political accountability today comes not from the "extremes" in equal measure. It comes mostly from the right pole.

It does not, however, come only from George W. Bush, as many liberals now seem to believe. In 2004, the *New Republic* devoted its cover to a drawing of a single arm with "W." cufflinks slamming its hand down on the balance scale of American politics, throwing helpless citizens aside. "The Case against George W. Bush: (Less) Democracy in America," read the headline.[29] But Bush is not the sole, or even the principal, antagonist in our story. Although he has taken advantage of the new landscape of American politics, he did not create it. Nor is he the only elected politician who has seized on the opportunities for off-center policymaking that it has presented.

Instead, we focus much of our attention on Congress. America's Congress is less likely than the White House to attract the television cameras (it is hard to imagine the hit TV series *The West Wing* spawning a sequel entitled *The House Chamber*). And for many Americans, it seems remote and minimally relevant. But a truly formidable amount of power in American politics rests in the nation's Congress. And Congress is where the Republicans' surprising ability to pursue their extreme goals with impunity is most evident. In 2004, as a likeable president masterfully wielding his commander-in-chief credentials eked out a narrow victory, almost all of the little-known but intensely conservative members of the GOP congressional majority coasted to victory without breaking a sweat. Indeed, even if the Republican Party loses the presidency in 2008, most of these ultraconservative Republicans will still be around, and will still be using their enormous power to push public policy to the right—unless the foundations of their growing influence are recognized and redressed.

The story we tell, in short, is not of a powerful president riding roughshod over public opinion and established democratic procedures. It is, in key respects, more troubling. It is the story of a systemic weakening of the institutional bonds that connect ordinary voters with elected politicians to ensure that American politics remains on center.

Looking at how these bonds have weakened also casts doubt on the common claim that Bush and his allies have succeeded largely because of the terrorist attacks of 9/11. Clearly, Republicans in general and President Bush in particular have been bolstered by public concerns about terrorism. And clearly, they have also sought to use the issue of national security to advance their broader policy agenda. (The 2005 "playbook" of GOP pollster—and conservative message guru—Frank Luntz emphasizes a range of imaginative ways to invoke terrorism when discussing domestic issues. On the subject of the budget deficit, for example, Luntz advises Republicans to "start with 9/11. . . . Without the context of 9/11, you will be blamed for the deficit. . . . The trick then is to contextualize the deficit inside of 9/11.")[30]

Yet the larger shifts in American politics that we chart in this book are largely independent of 9/11. Almost all, indeed, substantially predate the terrible attacks on the World Trade Center and the Pentagon. For that matter, so do several of the most striking off-center forays that these trends have helped produce—notably, the concerted effort to impeach Bill Clinton and the tax cuts of 2001.

One of the major reasons to doubt the all-purpose power of the "national security card" is that the same card has rarely helped presidents, or their parties, in the past. Although big political fights over national security are not unheard of, the old adage that "politics stops at the water's edge" contains a good deal of truth. During times of war and crisis, presidents are granted substantial latitude in foreign affairs. Historically, however, this latitude has not carried over to domestic policy. On issues that do not cross "the water's edge," members of Congress have traditionally proved quite eager to act independently and more than willing to obstruct initiatives they oppose. "War presidents" often gain electoral strength (though not always). But neither they nor their congressional allies have historically found it any easier to advance their domestic agendas. In fact, as frustrated presidents from FDR to Truman to LBJ have learned, the inverse has usually proved closer to the case.

In short, although a changed national security climate has facilitated the Republican domestic agenda, especially by widening the electoral "margin of error" enjoyed by GOP politicians, it has served mainly to intensify trends that were already well under way. The question remains: Even if Republicans have successfully turned the "war on terror" into electoral success, how have they managed to keep the divisive aspects of their domestic agenda from distracting public attention from these post-9/11 themes? To answer this question requires understanding how they have repeatedly departed from the moderate center on key domestic issues without acute fear of public backlash or electoral defeat.

Of course, some would deny that off-center policymaking is even possible. This, as we have pointed out, is the common view of American politics. It is also a position held by a sizable share of our profession. In the professional study of American politics, the conventional assumption is that the center is where power always resides.[31] In Congress, power lies at the middle—with the moderates who provide the pivotal votes to pass new legislation. In elections, power again lies in the middle—with the so-called swing voters who sit exactly at the center of the distribution of opinion within the electorate. Politicians and parties might get away with sidestepping moderate public opinion every now and then, but sustained forays off center should crumble under the combined weight of congressional moderates and middle-of-the-road voters.

Yet the center is not holding in American politics, as we show in Part I of this book. In Chapter 1, we demonstrate that Republican activists and leaders are increasingly to the right of most Americans. In Chapters 2 and 3, we show just how much this growing conservatism matters, exploring first Republicans' massive tax cuts (Chapter 2) and then a broad array of additional areas in which Republicans have rewritten the laws of the land to achieve their ultra-conservative goals (Chapter 3).

Part II turns to our explanation for this unsettling state of affairs. Why has America's system of checks and balances, designed to enforce moderation, given way to extremists? In Chapter 4, we uncover the forces that have pulled Republican political elites so far from the middle. In Chapter 5, we explain the increasingly coordinated character of the conservative movement and how it allows Republicans to get away with doing things that few Americans support. And in Chapter 6, we show why Republican leaders have been able to outmaneuver and outgun the traditional "guardians" of the center—voters, the opposition party, the media, and moderate members of the governing party.

We build on these arguments in our concluding chapter, which lays out the case for—and the formidable barriers to—political reform. Taking these barriers seriously, we present a series of prescriptions for restoring the power of the center, beginning with the need for an effective challenge to a ruling elite that, in its positions and its policies, has repeatedly shown contempt for the judgment of the people.

I

ABANDONING THE MIDDLE

1

OFF CENTER

The elected leaders who run our government today are very conservative. On a left-right ideological spectrum in which the left champions a strong role for government in protecting the environment, regulating business, and providing economic security and the right supports a more limited role for government in these areas and champions private property rights, they are generally quite far to the right. They are not just far to the right of the Republican leadership of a generation ago. They are also far to the right of the programs and policy ideals established in the past three to four decades of bipartisan public policymaking. And most important, they are far to the right of the middle-of-the road American voter. Our nation's leadership is off center.

This is our view, but it is not simply our opinion. As we show in this chapter, overwhelming evidence points to a growing distance between the views of ordinary Americans (generally moderate) and those of American political elites (increasingly conservative). This divorce is itself revealing—and troubling. Whatever else elected officials are meant to do once in office, they are supposed to represent (not perfectly, of course, but broadly) the views of the voters in whose name they exercise power. For this reason, we generally expect that our nation's political leaders will try to be ideologically in sync with middle-of-the-road voters. We also expect that they will not shift dramatically in one ideological direction or another unless Americans do, too. We expect these things to hold true, but they do not.

The Great Republican Right Turn

If a modern Rip Van Winkle fell asleep in 1975 and woke up thirty years later, the world would look very different indeed. Cell phones in every hand, computers in every briefcase, a vast and strange territory called cyberspace beckoning with commerce, sin, and knowledge—how strange it all would seem. Yet perhaps the most jarring realization would come when our good-natured Rip logged onto one of those exotic computers for the first time. After marveling at the wonders of cyberspace, he might ask himself what Republicans and Democrats were up to after all those years. And then he would get one of the biggest shocks of all.

Through his sleepy haze, Rip might recall the moderate Midwestern Republican Gerald Ford and the staid conservative party he momentarily led. He might remember that in the early 1970s, Republicans helped push for a bevy of new environmental and consumer regulations, higher Social Security benefits, and national price controls, not to mention a huge increase in social spending for the poor (including a near-miss on a Republican-developed plan for a guaranteed minimum income). And so he might be more than a little surprised to discover that the Republican Party of 2005 defines itself roughly in opposition to all those causes.

Now a party firmly grounded in the South, all but extinct in its old stomping ground of the Northeast, the GOP is headed by a former Texas governor who wants to carve private accounts out of Social Security, make Medicare more reliant on private health plans, and slash taxes while holding the line on social spending. Meanwhile, the party's most bellicose congressional strongman, House Majority Leader Tom DeLay, is against federal regulation as a matter of course, gleefully likening the Environmental Protection Agency—created under Republican presidential rule in 1970—to the Nazi Gestapo.

But you do not have to take our fictional character's word for it. The evidence to back up his perceptions is abundant and clear. The story is the same whether one looks at the party's base of grassroots activists, GOP members of Congress, the president, or the tight circle of power brokers who sit at the pinnacle of the new Republican hierarchy. Wherever one looks, the Republican Party has sped rightward.

The Base Moves to Right Field. The Republican "base," the most committed supporters of the GOP in the electorate and activist community, has come to play a starring role in contemporary American politics. It burst into popular consciousness in the lead-up to the 2004 campaign, when Bush's key adviser, Karl Rove, made it known that the president would not be tacking toward the center. Rove believed, as BBC News put it, that the key for Bush "lay not in reaching out to the middle ground, but in solidifying and energizing the base of the Republican party."[1] Rove's strategic calculation reflected two simple realities: the power of the Republican base has increased, and as it has, the base has grown much, much more conservative.

The figure below tells the story (fig. 1). The top line shows the trajectory of Republicans relative to independent voters on a liberal-conservative scale. (This figure draws on the highly respected National Election Studies [NES].) In the 1960s, Republican activists were about 20 percent more conservative than independent voters. By 2002, the last year for which we have poll results, they were almost 40 percent more conservative. Put another way, in the year that Barry Goldwater was crushed by Lyndon Johnson after declaring that "extremism in defense of liberty is no vice," Republican activists were *half as extreme*—relative to independent voters—as they are today.

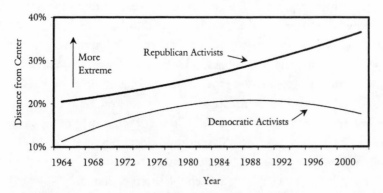

Figure 1. Republican activists are increasingly off center while Democratic activists are not. *Source:* National Election Studies Cumulative Data File, University of Michigan. "Activists" are respondents who identify with one of the two major parties *and* report three or more election-related activities. The figure shows smoothed trendlines.

What is most striking about these trends is that Democratic activists, who never gravitated as far from independents, have actually moved back to the center in recent years even as Republican activists have strayed sharply from it. Indeed, although the figure does not show this, Democratic activists in 2002 were actually only slightly more *liberal* than run-of-the-mill voters who identify with the Democratic Party. By contrast, Republican activists are not only far to the right of independents; they are also far to the right of ordinary voters within their own party. And they have been heading ever more sharply right since the 1980s.

GOP Politicians Abandon the Middle. The base has not been alone in its speedy rightward journey. The rightward march of rank-and-file Republican politicians has been every bit as striking. Thanks to the long labors of two respected political economists, Keith Poole and Howard Rosenthal, this statement can be documented with surprising precision. By tracing the recorded votes of every person who has ever served in Congress, Poole and Rosenthal have constructed a complex measure designed to answer a simple question: How far to the right (conservative) or left (liberal) is an individual member of Congress? And what they have found confirms what our Rip Van Winkle intuitively realized: The Republican Party in Congress is far more conservative than it was even a quarter century ago.[2]

Take the simplest measure of rightward movement: the median ideological position of Republican members of the House and Senate. (The median is simply the midpoint—in this case, the Republican exactly in the middle of the House or Senate GOP delegation.) Starting around 1970—when the two parties began to polarize sharply, according to expert observers of Congress—Republicans have moved almost uninterruptedly to the right. In the early 1970s, those in the middle of the House Republican delegation were approximately as conservative as current Republican Congressman Steven LaTourette of Ohio, whom the *Almanac of American Politics* notes has "the most moderate voting record of Ohio's Republican members." In 2003, the conservative anti-tax group the Club for Growth labeled LaTourette a "Republican in Name Only"—which may not be so surprising when one considers that the median House Republican in 2003 was about 73 percent more conservative than the median House Republican of the early 1970s. Rather than a moderate like LaTourette, the typical GOP "centrist" in 2003 was someone like Congressman Mark

Souder of Indiana—a one-time leader of the House Conservative Action Team, "an organization of fiscally and socially conservative House Republicans dedicated to protecting the traditional family, preserving mainstream American values, reducing the influence of the federal government, and respecting Congress' limited constitutional authority."[3]

The rightward shift of Senate Republicans is even more dramatic. The median stance for Senate Republicans in the early 1970s was significantly to the left of current GOP maverick John McCain of Arizona—around where conservative *Democrat* Zell Miller of Georgia stood before he retired in 2004. By the early 2000s, however, the median Senate Republican was essentially twice as conservative—just shy of the ultraconservative position of Senator Rick Santorum of Pennsylvania, a "strong conservative," according to the *Almanac,* who sparked controversy in 2003 when he compared consensual gay sex to polygamy, incest, and bestiality.[4]

Of course, the Democrats have moved left at the same time Republicans have moved right. This is almost entirely due, however, to the decimation of the Democratic Party's once-powerful coterie of Southern moderates at the hands of fiercely conservative Republicans. In contrast with the common view, partisan polarization in Congress has not been caused by Republicans moving right and Democrats moving left in equal proportion. To the contrary, the rightward shift of the GOP is the main cause of polarization.

The Poole and Rosenthal statistics make this clear. As the median score for Senate Republicans moved rightward from Miller past McCain and nearly to Santorum, the median for Democrats moved leftward by less than a seventh as much. Roughly speaking, this means that the median Senate Democrat has switched from a moderate-to-liberal Midwestern Democrat like Byron Dorgan of North Dakota (an upholder of the "Non-Partisan League" tradition, according to the *Almanac*) to, well, a moderate-to-liberal Midwestern Democrat like former Senate Leader Tom Daschle of South Dakota.[5] In the House, the Democrats' leftward shift has been larger, thanks in part to the steady depletion of the Southern Democrats who once dominated the House party. But the increase in the liberalism of House Democrats of roughly 28 percent still pales in comparison to the 73 percent increase in the conservatism of House Republicans.

The contrast implied by these numbers is striking in itself. But more important, it directly belies the common assumption that the Republican and Democratic Parties, like two similarly charged magnets, are simply repelling each other. What the Poole and Rosenthal statistics show is that the parties are indeed moving apart, but by no means at the same rate or from a fixed central point. Rather, Republicans are galloping right while Democrats are trotting left. There is indeed a widening gap in the political middle. But it is largely the result of the transformation of the Republican Party.

"The Right Man."[6] On 5 June 2004 conservative icon Ronald Reagan died peacefully at ninety-three. Reagan's passing occasioned an outpouring of remembrance from all points on the political spectrum—but especially from the American Right. For two decades, conservatives had claimed Reagan as their patron saint, the most consistently conservative president of the post–New Deal era. Now, they came to pay tribute. At the ceremony, the nation's Republican president, George W. Bush, eulogized Reagan before an audience that prominently featured most of the powerful GOP leaders currently running the Republican-controlled House and Senate.

The moment seemed fittingly symbolic of the enduring legacy of Reagan's conservative revolution. Bush, after all, has made Reagan's 1981 tax cuts the guiding light of his domestic agenda. He has called, like Reagan, for a fundamental transformation of the most enduring legacies of Democratic rule: the Social Security program of FDR and the Medicare program of LBJ. And yet, in many ways, Bush's conservative positions on these issues are even more ambitious than Reagan's. With the popular anti-tax tide of the late 1970s at his back, Reagan indeed cut taxes dramatically in 1981. But less than two years later, his party engineered a dramatic reversal of those cuts to reduce the deficit. And Reagan himself supported a major tax reform bill in 1986 that slashed taxes on the poor.

By contrast, Bush has led congressional Republicans in cutting taxes in every year since 2001, despite little public enthusiasm for the goal and a spiraling budget deficit. After his reelection in 2004, Bush explicitly invoked Reagan in calling for major tax reform. Yet it was clear that for Bush, the ideal proposal for tax reform was a plan that sheltered ever more business and investment income from taxation, lowering taxes on the rich even further. Of course, if he were to keep his promise of keeping the overall amount raised by taxes constant, this would imply raising taxes for ordinary workers and the poor.

The contrast on social policy is even more striking. Though Reagan attacked the public sector and conjured up images of "welfare queens," his achievements were considerably more modest than was his rhetoric. George W. Bush, by comparison, has adopted less vividly antigovernment language. Yet as president, he has sought policy reforms that Reagan never dared. On Social Security, for example, Reagan briefly broached benefit cuts, then ceded the initiative to a bipartisan commission headed by Alan Greenspan, which adopted changes that essentially preserved the government-centered system. In stark contrast, Bush has embraced a fundamental transformation of the system to divert a large share of workers' payroll taxes into private accounts, and he has deliberately ruled out a compromise that would preserve the existing framework.

Whether Bush is a more conservative president than Reagan is hard to say. Reagan's conservative goals were greatly tempered by the comparatively moderate Republican Party he led, as well as the reality that Democrats controlled the House throughout his presidency. But whatever their relative conservatism, Bush and Reagan are without question the leading contenders for the title of most conservative president since World War II. Certainly, the word "conservative" follows Bush in the news as it has not any president since Reagan.[7] And the main reason for this is that Bush consistently defines himself as a conservative through his words and deeds.

Back in his first (unsuccessful) run for Congress, for example, Bush ran very far to the right—as an "uncompromising hard conservative," in the words of Bill Minutaglio, whose book First Son offers a nonpartisan account of Bush's political rise.[8] Among the indicators of Bush's "uncompromising hard conservative" stance were his public spurning of proposed campaign visits by President Ford, his call for privatizing Social Security (when this was an extreme conservative view), and his opposition to both sanctions against South Africa and the Equal Rights Amendment.

Still, in judging Bush's ideology, his campaigns are less revealing than what he has done once in office. After the contested election of 2000, no one could credibly claim that he entered the White House with a mandate to enact a conservative agenda. And yet, as two political analysts from the right-leaning American Enterprise Institute wrote in 2003, "those predicting consistent bipartisanship or a cautious and incremental approach to policy making were wrong. . . . George W. Bush has chosen a tough-minded, sometimes confrontational, and strongly conservative approach to making policy—tossing aside conventional wisdom as to how to approach a narrowly divided Congress."[9]

The New Power Brokers. To sense the full scale of the GOP's ideological shift requires looking beyond the congressional rank and file, and even the president. The contours of the contemporary Republican Party cannot be understood without focusing attention on a group we term the "New Power Brokers"—a tight circle of political elites who oversee relations among the GOP's many factions and work to orchestrate the advancement of its political agenda. To say this is not to cry conspiracy. These individuals are far from all-powerful, and they often feud among themselves. But they are key players in an increasingly networked and coordinated conservative movement.

We will have much to say about the activities of the New Power Brokers in Part II. Here, however, we simply wish to emphasize a striking characteristic that makes them an important part of the Republican Party's great right turn. Like the GOP's activist base, its rank-and-file politicians, and its presidential standard-bearer, the New Power Brokers are tough-minded conservatives who hold views that lie significantly to the right of the mainstream of American public opinion.

Consider the quintessential New Power Brokers of the Republican Party: Karl Rove, Grover Norquist, and Tom DeLay. As anyone inside the Beltway knows, these are three of the most powerful dealmakers Washington has seen in many years. Unlike most dealmakers of the past, however, they are not anti-ideological or bipartisan in orientation. Quite the opposite: The New Power Brokers are fiercely committed to making the GOP the long-term party of government while remaking the country along conservative lines.

Karl Rove may be the best known of the three. His official title has changed as the years have passed, culminating, in early 2005, with the modest post of "deputy chief of staff in charge of coordinating domestic policy, economic policy, national security, and homeland security."[10] A campaign and policy adviser to President Bush since Bush's first run for the Texas governor's office, Rove is arguably the single most powerful force shaping Bush's stance on key issues. He is also probably the most pragmatic of the three power brokers under consideration. That does not, however, make him a moderate dealmaker. Rove has played a central role in building a new GOP coalition tilted heavily to the right. Rove's political strategy, battle-tested in two successful campaigns, rests on a core principle: rock-solid support from the conservative base. And Rove has encouraged Bush to take some of his most audaciously conservative policy steps, including his attempt to privatize Social Security.

Grover Norquist, by contrast, is an ideologue and not afraid to say so. The head of a fairly obscure conservative organization, Americans for Tax Reform (ATR), he has his fingers in nearly every important domestic policy venture conservatives hold dear. Norquist's ATR spends its time monitoring and shaping what goes on in Washington and who gets sent to Washington by the Republican Party. ATR's most prominent effort is an anti-tax pledge signed by nearly all Republicans, including President Bush. Norquist himself is almost a caricature of a right-winger. He has called Social Security, perhaps the most popular U.S. government policy of all time, "a lousy program."[11] He has compared arguments on behalf of preserving the estate tax to the line of thinking that produced the Holocaust. He has called bipartisanship "date rape." He has said he doesn't want to get rid of government; just reduce it to half its prior size, so he can "drown it in the bathtub."[12] But far from being shunned for such extreme views by fellow Republicans, Norquist is embraced. Indeed, he runs an informal coalition of conservative groups that meets weekly to strategize and to confer with the White House and congressional GOP.

And what about Tom DeLay? He is a paradoxical figure—a loyal Republican who seems to expend as much energy attacking members of his own party as he does going after Democrats, a man reputed to be at the center of everything that happens in Congress who rarely lets himself linger in the spotlight.[13] But if there is one characteristic that defines DeLay, it is his fierce conservatism. The most powerful majority leader in the modern history of the House of Representatives started on the hard right. In his first term (1985–86), he was one of only eight members of Congress to gain the American Conservative Union's perfect 100 rating (Dick Cheney was also a member of this select group). Nor did he moderate his stances in his rapid rise to power. After becoming majority whip (the number three position in the House Republican leadership), he confessed to a reporter that he could not think of a single federal regulation he would like to leave in place. DeLay is the conscience of the GOP's reliably conservative House majority. He is as committed to tearing down economic protections and health and environmental regulations as he is to building up the Christian conservative movement. He is frankly messianic, and to his mind, the reckoning has finally come for American liberalism.

From top to bottom, in short, today's Republican Party is far to the right of where the GOP stood twenty or thirty—or even ten—years ago. What was once the right wing of the party is now its moderate center. What was once its left flank is all but gone. And what remains is a new, hard-edged conservatism that almost completely defines the goals, operations, and identity of the contemporary Republican Party.

Is There a Problem?

Given that the GOP has become America's governing party, the natural conclusion many would take from the foregoing discussion is that the American people as a whole must be much more conservative than they were ten or fifteen years ago. At the very least, they must be much more supportive of Republican stances on a few key domestic issues. In this view, Republicans have not moved off center; they have simply followed the middle ground of public sentiment as it has shifted to the right. This view, however, is wrong. Even a cursory look at the evidence quickly dispels the notion that Republicans' "tough-minded, sometimes confrontational, and strongly conservative approach to making policy" reflects a massive right turn among the American people.

Most, we expect, will find this conclusion surprising. Some, we fear, may find it offensive. To those who experience the latter reaction, our suggestion that political elites are undermining democracy is likely to appear, well, undemocratic. From this point of view, our complaint isn't with American politics; it is with the American people, who've shown their true feelings by continuing to elect Republicans. As two journalists for the *Economist* wrote in 2004, America is "The Right Nation," and "a Democratic presidential victory in 2004 would barely change America's basically conservative stance."[14]

Of course, after November 2004, the case for claiming that Americans leaned hard right was even stronger. As Todd Purdum wrote in the

New York Times—scarcely a bastion of conservative thought—"President Bush's re-election, with larger Republican majorities in both houses of Congress, is the clearest confirmation yet that America is a center-right country."[15] What better evidence of this could there be than the simple fact that Republicans have remained on top? Politicians who get reelected must be doing what voters want.

This is a reassuring stance, and at first glance it may seem to settle the matter. But a moment's reflection reveals that it simply sweeps the most fundamental issues under the rug. Essentially, it boils down to a flat assertion that whoever wins elections must, by definition, be doing what the electorate wants. This, however, is precisely what is in question—whether elections are still playing their essential role of assuring responsiveness from those in power.

What's more, the proof-is-in-the-pudding view must ignore some uncomfortable electoral realities. Although seemingly forgotten, in 2000 Al Gore won half a million more votes than Bush. (This expression of popular sentiment prompted the following reaction from the new vice president, Dick Cheney: "The notion of sort of a restrained presidency because it was such a close election, that lasted maybe thirty seconds. It was not contemplated for any length of time. We had an agenda, we ran on that agenda, we won the election—full speed ahead.")[16] In 2004, running in wartime, Bush won one of the narrowest reelection victories in modern American history. The Republican "sweep" in Congress was also very narrow in historical terms, with strikingly few elections truly competitive. And these congressional results were profoundly shaped by a system of geographically separate elections that, thanks in part to partisan gerrymandering, now strongly favors the Republican Party.

For example, if Bush had received the exact same vote share in 2004 that he received in 2000 (that is, 48 percent), he still would have managed to win in 239 of the nation's 435 House districts—or almost 55 percent.[17] He actually won 255 districts in 2004, or almost 59 percent, while winning around 51 percent of the vote (slightly higher if the calculation excludes Ralph Nader's 1 percent). In other words, House districts are now drawn so that an evenly divided country can produce surprisingly lopsided GOP victories. Indeed, the Republicans gained seats in the

House in 2004 *only* because of Tom DeLay's redistricting scheme in Texas.

The mismatch between popular votes and electoral outcomes is even more striking in the Senate. Combining the last three Senate elections, Democrats have actually won two-and-a-half million *more* votes than Republicans. Yet they now hold only 44 seats in that 100-person chamber because Republicans dominate the less populous states that are so heavily over-represented in the Senate. As the journalist Hendrik Hertzberg notes, if one treats each senator as representing half that state's population, than the Senate's 55 Republicans currently represent fewer people than do the Senate's 44 Democrats.[18]

It simply will not suffice to brandish election results as the sole proof of Americans' views. We need to dig deeper into public opinion on the major issues of the day. And when we dig deeper, it becomes abundantly clear that ruling Republicans are pursuing policies whose key dimensions are well to the right of the center of public opinion.

What Polls Can (and Can't) Tell Us

Before diving into this evidence, however, it is important to emphasize that polls do not provide an undistorted window into the inner thoughts of the American voter. They are best treated like small keyholes that can illuminate a handful of important considerations that Americans use to judge competing options. A single poll is usually of limited value. Instead, we need to consider a number of surveys asked over time and in different ways. And this works only when Americans actually *have* opinions, which is not always the case. Even when Americans have strong views that potentially bear on specific debates, they may have such limited information that their opinions are largely ad hoc. Again, looking at questions asked several different ways and times helps weed out such "non-opinions" from more stable views.

A second limit of polling data is that the availability of polls ranges widely from issue to issue. On most high-profile issues, many surveys are done, and specific questions are usually repeated again and again. On many less prominent issues, by contrast, good polls are few and far between. This is a serious problem, because the low-profile issues on which polling is rare are precisely the issues on which we would expect politicians to have the most leeway to depart from public opinion. Indeed, politicians try to keep some issues low profile *because* they know that most Americans don't approve of what they are doing. This, of course, introduces a major bias into opinion research. Put simply, we will have the most polling evidence on the very matters where we expect the most congruence between what citizens say and what politicians do. And that, in turn, means that any examination of government responsiveness that uses opinion polls is "setting the bar low."

A third crucial reason why opinion polls can only take us so far is that even the best polls do not somehow isolate Americans' "unmediated" views—that is, the views citizens might have if no politicians or interest groups were trying to shape their perceptions and attitudes. Instead, opinion polls measure a mix of what Americans believe and what they are led to believe by those who want them to believe certain things. As a result, it is generally difficult to know the degree to which the views of the public are shaping the activities of elites, on one hand, or the activities of elites are shaping the views of public, on the other. This creates a bias toward thinking that political elites are responding to public opinion, because what we describe as politicians following the public may, in many cases, really be the public following politicians.

A final caution: This chapter and this book are concerned only with domestic policy. Besides the fact that this is a huge area in itself (and the one that we, as specialists on domestic policy, know best), we think that this, too, sets the bar realistically low. Whatever else political analysts believe, they generally agree that Americans have much firmer and better-informed views about domestic policy than about foreign policy.[19]

Fortunately, all these complex limitations and qualifiers yield a straightforward and unambiguous bottom line: Any disconnect that we find between the public and elites in opinion surveys probably *understates* the true extent of the divergence. By simply taking public opinion as given and focusing on those areas where the fit between polls and politicians should be closest, we are, again, setting the bar quite low. As we shall see in coming chapters, once we take into account elite manipulation of public opinion and the ability of political actors to pursue their unpopular goals through strategies of stealth, the gap between elite and public views looks more like a chasm.

The Public's Illusory Right Turn

Was the election of 2004 a sign of Americans' conservative mood? Like the mood of stock traders, the mood of voters is an amorphous entity habitually invoked to explain all sorts of disparate outcomes. But the notion is not without intellectual content. Public opinion does seem to swing through periods of conservatism and liberalism. And if it makes sense to think of politicians as ranging along a continuum from right to left, it also makes sense to think of public opinion in similar terms. Indeed, the often unspoken assumption is that the shift of politicians to the right or left reflects the shift of public opinion to the right or left—that the mood of citizens drives the mood of politicians.

Figuring out what the American mood is, however, is not an easy task. It requires combining large numbers of opinion surveys in a way that allows reliable comparisons of aggregate opinion from year to year. Thankfully, this is exactly what the political scientist James Stimson has done in calculating his respected measure of the "national mood."[20] Stimson uses nearly two hundred survey questions that have been asked every year for decades (about, for example, what people think the proper role of government should be). And what he finds belies the simple interpretation that Americans have been growing steadily more conservative. To the contrary, the index of the public mood that Stimson has developed suggests that Americans actually grew more *liberal* in the two decades after Reagan's election. When Reagan was elected in 1980, the public mood was more conservative than in any year since 1952. But by the time of George W. Bush's election in 2000, Americans had grown substantially more liberal, according to the measure. Indeed, their aggregate opinions were virtually identical to their aggregate opinions in *1972*.

Whatever else these numbers indicate, they make clear that American opinion as a whole did not move sharply to the right in the lead-up to the Republican takeover of American politics in 2000. Nor, it seems clear from Stimson's data, did Americans grow consistently more conservative

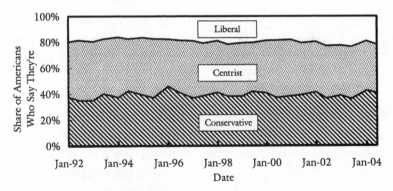

Figure 2. Americans' ideological self-identifications haven't changed much, if at all. *Source:* Gallup Poll, 1992-2004: "How would you describe your political views . . . very conservative, conservative, moderate, liberal, or very liberal?"

over the 1980s and 1990s—even as their elected leaders have, of course, become much more conservative.

We do not need to rely on Stimson's data alone. The political scientist Morris Fiorina has recently conducted his own careful study of public views of left-right issues. And he has reached the same clear conclusion: "Americans are about as liberal or conservative as they were a generation ago."[21]

Given these findings, it should come as little surprise that Americans' ideological self-identifications have not changed much in the past decade (fig. 2). Indeed, if these numbers are to be believed, Americans were more conservative when Bill Clinton was reelected in 1996 than when George W. Bush was reelected in 2004. But given the inevitable error and imprecision in any scale of this sort, we think the safest conclusion is that opinions have remained remarkably stable. They have certainly not shifted dramatically to the right.

The Public and Policy Issues

None of this, however, speaks to the opinions that Americans hold on specific high-profile policy issues. It could be that Americans are generally no more conservative than they were a generation ago but that on a few important items in the conservative playbook—say, tax cuts or environmental protection or Social Security—they are. But this is not the case. Chapter 2 looks at the politics of tax cuts and finds dismally low support for the central features of GOP proposals. And as Chapter 3 will show, the story is much the same in many other areas. Although Americans do sympathize with some aspects of Republican positions, the evidence in Chapters 2 and 3 carries a clear and consistent message: The public is sharply opposed to core GOP aims once one looks even slightly beneath the surface to examine the details of competing options.

But since we have not yet delved into this evidence, let us briefly examine the evolution of public opinion on a few major left-right issues. The National Election Studies is one of the most comprehensive catalogs of American public opinion in existence.[22] In particular, it has the great virtue of having been conducted every federal election year for decades, with most questions asked a number of times. And when the NES asked Americans if government was "too powerful," a healthy 49 percent of Americans agreed—in 1976. By 1992, the share had dropped to 40 percent, and the proportion was down to 39 percent in 2000.

Perhaps, however, this question is not specific enough to capture America's growing conservatism. What about Americans' views of government spending and services? On a seven-point scale, between providing fewer services and providing more services, "even if it means an increase in taxes," about the same share of Americans sided with spending as sided with cuts—in 1992. By 2000, more than twice as many Americans (39 percent) wanted to spend more than spend less (18 percent).

We would not argue that Americans are more liberal today than they were in the 1970s. That would strain the limited survey data as well as common sense. Still, it is striking that across all of the major left-right issues, one is hard pressed to find *any* evidence that Americans are markedly more conservative today than they were in the recent (and even relatively distant) past.

The partial privatization of Social Security—a conservative policy goal we take up in Chapter 3—provides a powerful case in point. After the election of 2004, Bush said he had a "mandate" from the voters to incorporate private investment accounts into Social Security—a goal he had talked about occasionally during the campaign. Nothing, however, could be further from the truth. According to polls, virtually no voters chose

Bush on the basis of his support for private accounts. (The *Los Angeles Times*'s exit poll found that only 5 percent of voters named Social Security as one of the two most decisive issues for their vote, and roughly twice as many of them voted for Kerry.) More important, the idea of incorporating private accounts into Social Security in the way that Bush wants to is *wildly unpopular*. This may come as a surprise: Don't a majority of Americans say they want private accounts? Actually, as of early 2005, the answer was no. But, certainly, in the years leading up to the election of 2004, one could find plenty of polls in which majorities say they liked the idea of "private accounts." In January 2004, for instance, 55 percent of Americans either "strongly approved" or "approved" of "changing the Social Security system to allow workers to invest some of their tax payments in the stock market."[23]

The rub is that support for the abstract idea of private accounts crumbles on the presentation of any of the details of privatization plans. When even the slightest hint is made of the inevitable consequences of private accounts—whether those consequences be cuts in the benefits of the guaranteed program, potential market risks, or new borrowing—support for such accounts plummets. For example, a poll by the respected Annenberg Public Policy Center found that when benefit cuts were simply hinted at, more Americans opposed private accounts than supported them. And when those who said they supported them were told that government would have to borrow large sums, more than half *of supporters* changed their minds and said they did not support them after all.[24] By more than a two-to-one margin, voters said in January 2005 that keeping Social Security as a program with a guaranteed monthly benefit is more important than letting younger workers decide for themselves how some of their payroll taxes are invested.[25] And according to a *Newsweek* poll done after the president's State of the Union Address in 2005, just 12 percent of the public would support cutting benefits to retirees to keep the program financially solvent.[26] These results are hardly aberrant: Poll after poll shows that Social Security as presently structured is more popular than almost any other government activity. And although concerns about its financial health are rife, there is overwhelming support for its mission and structure—support that has remained remarkably constant over the past twenty years.

But wait, the skeptic still might say: Have we forgotten about the other hot-button issues—namely, such powerful moral issues as abortion and gay marriage? If we had, we could be forgiven, for these issues have not been at the center of the Republicans' recent domestic agenda, which has focused much more on economic and social policy. But moral issues have certainly been a major part of Republicans' rhetoric, and a number of thoughtful commentators have argued that one way Republicans have managed to get so many to sign on to their economic and social policy agenda is by stoking Americans' moral outrage. In this view, off-center policies in the economic and social realm are fueled by growing voter conservatism in the moral realm.

Indeed, it has become fashionable to attribute the Republicans' entire electoral edge to the conservative moral agenda of the Right. This perception has been fueled by a badly phrased exit-poll question in 2004, which seemed to highlight the significance of "moral values" in voters' choices. Although this result was rapidly discredited, it nonetheless fed an instant consensus about why Republicans hold the upper ground: Voters were brought out by moral backlash against gay marriage and other affronts to conservative values, allowing Republicans to overcome their generally unpopular stances on "bread-and-butter" issues of economic and social policy.

Systematic research, however, does not support this view. True, Republicans receive the overwhelming support of voters who attend church frequently. Yet although such voters have become more important elements of the Republican base in recent elections, their share of the electorate has barely changed. Nor, according to careful analyses of exit-poll data, did such voters make the difference for Bush in the 2004 election. In fact, their proportion of the national vote and their split in favor of Bush were roughly the same in 2004 as they had been in 2000.[27] And as political scientists Stephen Ansolabehere and Charles Stewart III have shown, careful examination of county-level election returns does not support the notion that state-level efforts to ban gay marriage helped Bush. Quite the opposite: "In states where gay marriage was on the ballot, partisan voting patterns became more pronounced, with a net advantage for Kerry."[28]

In any event, there is a fatal flaw in the argument that the Right is gaining power because Americans are becoming more conservative on social issues: *Americans are not becoming more conservative on social issues.* Fiorina, whose judgment on public views we invoked earlier, has focused his attention on public opinion about two of the most divisive moral topics: abortion and homosexuality. His conclusion: "There is little indication that voters are polarized now or that they are becoming more polarized—even when we look specifically at issues such as abortion that supposedly are touchstone issues in the culture war. If anything, public opinion has grown more centrist on such issues, and more tolerant of the divergent views, values, and behavior of other Americans."[29]

The Public versus the GOP

In sum, Americans are not more polarized on left-right issues than they were a generation ago. And they have certainly not shifted sharply to the right. In stark contrast, Republican activists and political leaders *have* shifted sharply to the right. At every level of the Republican Party—the base of party activists, the congressional rank and file, the presidency, and the New Power Brokers—a hard-edged conservatism has come to dominate. It is as if a slumbering beast with a head but no body has awoken and, against all odds, is now roaming the political land.

Our disembodied monster is a living and breathing puzzle: How can growing GOP conservatism survive without having the body politic along for the ride? One possible answer is that it survives only because of increasing Democratic liberalism. Think about it for a moment: If the parties were running away from each other at equal speeds, then middle-of-the-road voters would be stuck between a rock and a hard place. The parties would be more disagreeable, yes, but they would be equally more disagreeable, and so moderate voters would have no viable option for expressing their dissatisfaction. This is a view common among commentators decrying "polarization"—again, a terminology that strongly suggests equal movement of two sides toward equally distant "poles." As Fiorina, who holds this view, colorfully explains, "The bulk of the American citizenry is somewhat in the position of the unfortunate citizens of some third-world countries who try to stay out of the cross fire while Maoist guerillas and right-wing death squads shoot at each other."[3-]

As we have seen, however, the evidence directly contradicts this view. Republicans have moved farther right than Democrats have moved left—not just within the halls of government but also within the ranks of party activists. The parties are not located, as Fiorina suggests, "at more or less equal distances from the mainstream."[31] One party is a few blocks from the mainstream, whereas the other is headed for another zip code.

Yet perhaps the puzzle has a simpler answer. Perhaps the GOP talks tough but doesn't get what it wants. To most analysts, polarization carries with it one big risk: gridlock. With the parties further apart, compromise become harder, and America's convoluted system of checks and balances grinds to a halt. Polarization is lamentable, in this view, not because it results in extreme policies but because it offends public sensibilities and gums up the political process. When two closely matched parties cannot agree, the worst that can happen is that nothing happens.

As the next two chapters will make clear, however, something *is* happening. The increasingly off-center Republican leadership is not simply banging its disembodied head against the checks and balances of our political system. Despite its clear and persistent departure from the political middle, it is achieving major policy changes that will shape the course of American government for decades to come. And perhaps the most fundamental of these changes is the next part of our story: an extraordinary series of tax cuts mostly for the well off that have turned the budget surpluses of the late 1990s into deficits as far as the eye can see.

2

PARTYING WITH THE "PEOPLE'S MONEY"

"The surplus is the people's money, and we ought to trust them with that money."
                                        —Republican presidential candidate George W. Bush, 2000

"The country has prospered mightily over the past twenty years. But a lot of people feel as though they have been looking through the window at somebody else's party. It is time to open those doors and windows and invite everybody in."
                                        —President George W. Bush, 2001

Republicans like tax cuts. The party that emphasized fiscal discipline in the face of the Great Depression now touts tax cuts no matter the budgetary consequence. Tax cuts are Republicans' all-purpose policy tonic, a solution perpetually in search of a problem. If the economy is doing poorly, taxes must be cut to promote growth. If the economy is roaring like a late-night party, the government needs to "open the doors and windows and invite everybody in." As the United States prepared to invade Iraq, Tom DeLay felt moved to declare that it was Congress's patriotic "duty" to cut taxes. "Nothing is more important in the face of a war," DeLay insisted, "than cutting taxes."[1]

The Republican Party has found lots of reasons to cut taxes lately. In every year since George W. Bush entered office, he and the GOP Congress have "opened the doors and windows" of the tax-cut festival. The biggest gala took place in 2001. But Republicans still felt festive enough to cut personal income taxes again in 2003 and 2004 and to give corporations a celebration of their own in 2002. And like any wild soiree, the bill has been high. All told, if the 2001–3 tax cuts are all extended as Republicans demand, they will cost the federal government more than $4 trillion by 2014, when the cost will be running in excess of 2 percent of the nation's economy a year. To put this staggering figure in perspective, the long-term cost of fixing the shortfall in Social Security—which the Bush administration now describes as catastrophically large—is less than 1 percent of the economy per year.[2]

Not everyone, however, has had as good a time at the tax-cut party as the Republican leadership clearly has. For those who worry about the federal deficit, the hangover is already painful. By 2004, the tax cuts had slashed income taxes (both corporate and personal) to their lowest level as a share of the economy since before the close of World War II and all federal taxes to their lowest level as a share of the economy since 1950. Running a twenty-first-century government on a mid-twentieth-century tax haul has had a predictable result: huge and growing deficits. In just four years, Republicans have overseen an unprecedented reversal from ten-year projected surpluses of more than $5 trillion to ten-year projected deficits of more than $4 trillion.

And although Bush vowed to "invite everybody in," the vast majority of Americans remain firmly parked beyond the reach of the roped-off open bar. Tens of millions of Americans who pay nothing in federal income taxes (but do pay federal payroll taxes for Social Security and Medicare) received no tax reductions at all, and most Americans received extremely modest benefits. The real party was reserved for the richest 1 percent of Americans, who reaped roughly 40 percent of the total tax rewards of the 2001 tax bill—a share almost identical to that received by the bottom 80 percent on the income ladder. These same wealthy Americans, of course, experienced extraordinary income rises in the 1980s and 1990s while most Americans experienced little or no improvement. The tax cuts of 2003 alone showered $184 billion over ten years on the 184,000 households with incomes above $1 million—a stunning $100,000 average tax cut. This $184 billion was the same total amount received by the 124 *million* households (90 percent of the population) with incomes below $95,000. While the average millionaire received $100,000, the average family in the middle of the income ladder received $217.[3]

Someday, moreover, all this largesse will have to be paid for—presumably, if tax-cut advocates are still calling the shots, without raising taxes. This means an inevitable clampdown on priorities that most Americans strongly support, from Medicare, Social Security, and education to reduction of the national debt. In fact, once the long-term financing of the tax cuts is taken into account, only the richest fifth of households will gain more than they lose from the cuts.[4] The rest of the country is footing the bill.

What's Going On?

It is quite a story. A political system perpetually prone to stalemate suddenly marshaled enough energy to upend the nation's basic fiscal priorities. Yet it is also a puzzling story. Most Americans received little from the tax cuts. Much that citizens clearly value was placed in jeopardy. How did this happen? In a representative democracy that enshrines the principle of one-person, one-vote, why would politicians champion legislation that promises relatively modest benefits and very large long-term risks to average voters? And perhaps more important, how could they ever get away with it?

These are the sorts of issues with which theorists of democracy have long grappled. The great political scientist Robert Dahl asked the fundamental question more than forty years ago: "In a political system where nearly every adult may vote but where knowledge, wealth, social position, access to officials, and other resources are unequally distributed, who actually governs?"[5] The tax cuts cast the question in especially sharp relief, for this was no dead-of-night legislative achievement, surreptitiously presented and covertly enacted. The tax cuts were the most prominent of Republicans' aims, of virtually unparalleled importance, and potentially far more transparent in their effects than are most changes in government activity. If any policy campaign should illustrate the reach of popular control in a democracy, the tax cuts should.

And what the tax cuts show is troubling. Far from representing public wishes, the major features of the tax cuts—their size, their structure, their distribution—were directly at odds with most Americans' views. When

Bush entered office in 2001, forecasts of large surpluses raised a fundamental issue of priorities: How should these considerable but finite resources be allocated among competing demands? Voters' opinions on this question were varied, but the basic sentiment of the vast majority can be summed up with confidence. When voters were prompted to consider the inevitable tradeoffs, tax cuts were assigned a very low priority. Even Americans who favored the general idea of tax cuts offered little support for the massive scale or skewed distribution of the 2001 bill. Insofar as it is possible to say what Americans wanted in 2001, most Americans did not get what they wanted.

This is not simply troubling; it is also surprising. The conventional wisdom about American politics is that elected leaders are sophisticated weather vanes, shifting at the slightest alteration in the winds of public opinion. As Lawrence Jacobs and Robert Shapiro write in their important book *Politicians Don't Pander,* there is a "nearly unquestioned assumption among observers of American politics that elected officials 'pander' to public opinion."[6] And who they are allegedly pandering to is not the extremes of the political spectrum. It is that great magnet of American political life: the center. In our political system—with its frequent elections, its myriad checks and balances, its dominant two-party system encouraged by winner-take-all elections—drifting too far from the moderate middle is a recipe for political disaster. In every election, political experts search for the all-powerful swing voter whose sometimes idiosyncratic wants and desires will dictate the terms of the next two to four years. Is the "undecided" voter a "NASCAR Dad," a "Soccer Mom", a "Security Mom," a "Reagan Democrat," or the ubiquitous, if less appealing-sounding, "Joe Six-Pack"?

Political scientists have refined this popular conception of an all-powerful center into a set of sophisticated models and propositions about the hold of moderate voters on political elites. (Others, however, strenuously dissent from this model.) These models and propositions are meant to be purely analytic, but they also provide a strong dose of reassurance. In American politics, these arguments suggest, voters elect politicians who do what they want, they punish politicians who don't do what they want, and, as a result, they get what they want. The center holds.

And yet, this conventional portrait of American politics completely fails to explain the tax-cut party. The tax cuts did not pass because ordinary voters wanted them. They passed because Republican political elites were eager to please their base—the partisans, activists, and moneyed interests that are their first line of support. And they passed because GOP leaders were able to manipulate the public face of the tax cuts through their language, their control over the governing agenda, and their crafting of the tax cuts themselves. What the tax cuts reveal is that Republicans now have the motive and the means to get into law major policies that few Americans support—and to shield themselves from the risk that the millions on the losing end of the bargain will realize they've been had.

Who Wants a Tax Cut?

Did Americans really want the tax cuts of 2001 and those that followed? Our guess is that most pundits would say they did. Indeed, the argument that citizens wanted the huge and skewed tax cuts that passed appears widely accepted even by those who find it bizarre that voters would support tax cuts from which they actually benefited so little.[7] Bizarre things do happen in American politics. But overwhelming public support for tax cuts that carry few tangible rewards and plenty of significant risks isn't one of them.

The main cause for thinking that Americans supported the recent round of tax cuts is the generally positive response found in polls that simply asked voters whether they favored "Bush's tax-cut proposal." On average, in these polls, between 50 and 60 percent of Americans said yes. This is not overwhelming support, to be sure, but it is support.[8]

Yet these results actually tell us little about Americans' views of tax cuts. This is because they say almost nothing about what kind of tax cuts the public wanted and how much priority they gave them. (They also ignore the efforts of politicians to shape public opinion, but we will take up this point later.) In fact, by isolating the issue of tax cuts from any mention or discussion of alternatives or tradeoffs, the polls fail to get at the basic issue: competing priorities. Scholars who study public opinion have long known that if respondents are asked, "Would you like to spend more on X, Y, and Z?" many spending programs will generate extremely high levels of support—typically 70 or 80 percent. It is easy to say,

"Spend more," after all, when you don't have to consider how to finance the spending or balance it against spending on other ends. For this reason, as the political scientist John Mark Hansen has argued, public views of spending and taxes cannot be understood without questions that tap into the "the essential aspect of the public budgeting problem: the tradeoffs inherent in establishing public priorities."[9]

Crucially, when we dig into public views of tradeoffs, it becomes clear that support for the tax cut's actual provisions was quite narrow. Contrary to what pundits often contend, Americans didn't think tax cuts were particularly important in 2000 and in 2001, and they don't think they are particularly important today. They also didn't want to spend massive sums on the tax cuts, nor did they want the tax cuts to benefit the rich disproportionately. Needless to say, what they wanted is not what the GOP gave them.

To begin with, there was little public clamor for tax cuts when Bush entered office. Before 2001 virtually never did more than a tenth of citizens say that taxes were the nation's "most important problem." As Bush's first term began, the figure was just 5 percent.[10] Not surprisingly, then, voters consistently put tax cuts behind other governing priorities. Recall that when Bush entered office, the debate was over what to do with the federal budget surplus: cut taxes, spend more on key programs, or pay down the national debt. Bush and the congressional GOP placed tax cuts at the top of their list of priorities. Voters did not. Indeed, voters consistently saw tax cuts as a lower priority than almost any plausible alternative use of the forecasted surpluses.

Lest doubt remain on this point, consider some of the poll findings from 2000 and 2001. Versus Social Security, tax cuts lost by a 74 to 21 percent margin. Versus Medicare, the margin is 65 to 25 percent. Even when Social Security is taken out of consideration, 69 percent of respondents preferred using extra monies on "education, the environment, health care, crime-fighting, and military defense" rather than a tax cut, which garnered just 22 percent support. These sentiments did not disappear when the tax cuts passed. Even after benefits began to flow to voters, large majorities said they would be willing to forgo their continuation in favor of alternative uses of the funds. Immediately after the election of 2004, for example, a *New York Times* poll found that reducing the deficit—hardly the sexiest political goal—trumped tax cuts as a public priority by a margin of more than two to one.[11]

But it was not just the size of the tax cuts that lacked public support. Another distinctive feature of the 2001 tax cuts was their distribution—namely, how tilted they were toward the rich. And here the evidence is no less striking. Public opinion was clearly and consistently hostile to the top-heavy skew of the Bush tax cuts. In fact, voters' leading concern about taxes in the years before the tax cuts passed was neither the tax code's staggering complexity nor the burdens they themselves faced. Rather, the top worry of Americans was that "the rich pay too little in taxes."[12] Given this, it is little wonder that large majorities of respondents consistently said that they wanted the legislation to distribute more of its benefits to middle- and lower-income Americans and less to the well off. Even in a poll conducted between House and Senate passage of the bill—the eleventh hour, so to speak—respondents by an extraordinary 53-point margin said they wanted the plan adjusted so more of the tax cuts went to lower-income taxpayers. Of course, these preferences were studiously ignored.[13]

Most Americans also rejected the Bush administration's assertion that the benefits of tax cuts should be distributed in rough accordance with current income-tax liabilities, with high-income voters receiving the largest share of benefits. A survey of March 2001, for example, asked respondents to compare two generic plans—the first of which "would reduce federal income taxes across the board" and give "the largest share of this tax cut . . . to wealthier Americans, who currently pay the most in taxes"; the second of which would "take full effect this year, and would be aimed more at middle income Americans . . . [and] involve either credits or reductions in the payroll taxes that are deducted from people's paychecks." Respondents preferred the second plan to the first by 73 to 20 percent. Similarly, when asked whether the "rich should get a bigger tax cut because they pay more in taxes" or whether "everyone should get the same level of tax cut," 70 percent of voters chose the latter option and just 24 percent the former.[14]

These polls strongly indicate that the Republicans' top domestic priority was far out of step with mainstream opinion. But we do not need to rely on polls alone. We can turn to the Bush administration itself.

Thanks to disillusioned former Treasury Secretary Paul O'Neill and journalist Ron Suskind, a number of important internal memos from the early Bush administration are now in the public domain. One that is particularly revealing dates from the unveiling of the Bush administration's first round of tax cuts in 2001 (fig. 3). It was written by Michele Davis, a top Treasury official and participant in daily meetings on the administration's communications strategy. Her prescriptions regarding "message" undoubtedly reflect strategies developed at the highest level. The memo begins innocently enough, asking O'Neill to plug tax cuts at a press event unveiling the president's budget. Then, however, Davis warns: "The public prefers spending on things like health care and education over

---

MEMO

To: Secretary O'Neill
From: Michele
Date: Tuesday 2/27/01
Re: Tomorrow's Press Conference Unveiling the Budget

You and Mitch Daniels are scheduled to unveil the President's budget at a press conference in the OEOB at 10:15 tomorrow morning. *This event, more than anything you've participated in to date, requires that you be monotonously on message.* In addition to the media attending, this event is simulcast to the White House press corp that is traveling with the President in Pennsylvania.

Key background information: The public prefers spending on things like health care and education over cutting taxes. It's crucial that your remarks make clear that there is no tradeoff here—that we will boost education spending and set aside Social Security and Medicare surpluses to address the future of those programs, and still we will have an enormous surplus. This isn't an "either/or" question.

Roll-out events like this are the clearest examples of when staying on message is absolutely crucial. Any deviation during the unveiling of the budget will change the way coverage plays out from tomorrow forward. For example, you do not want to discuss potential Social Security reform ideas. Your remarks should be very focussed and your answers during the Q and A should only repeat your remarks.

Figure 3. Memo from Michele Davis to Treasury Secretary Paul O'Neill, 2 February 2001. *Source:* Courtesy of Ron Suskind, "The Bush Files," http://thepriceofloyalty. ronsuskind.com/thebushfiles/archives/000058.html.

cutting taxes." This is a stunning admission. If the Bush administration had cared about responding to public opinion, it presumably would have counseled a much more modest plan. But to Davis, the views of the public on this profound question of governance offer only a motivation to spin. O'Neill is reminded to avoid talking about any possible trade-offs that tax cuts might entail. "It's crucial that you make clear that there is no tradeoff here," Davis writes. "Roll-out events like this are the clearest examples of when staying on message is absolutely crucial. Any deviation . . . will change the way coverage plays out from tomorrow forward."[15]

The Davis memo and the poll results just reviewed make clear that the tax cuts of 2001 diverged sharply from popular views about the cuts' appropriate scale and distribution. But they also raise a fundamental question: Why did Republicans so strongly wish to enact tax cuts designed in this way, and believe they could? The answer hinges on two sets of changes in American politics: those that have increased the benefits to politicians of departing from voters' opinions and those that have decreased the costs of such departures for politicians' fates.

The Republican Anti-Tax Crusade

In early 2003, Maine voters were greeted with the spectacle of television ads that compared their senior senator, Olympia Snowe, to French President Jacques Chirac. The ads announced that when "President Bush courageously led the forces of freedom" against Iraq, "some so-called allies like France stood in the way." Now that the president sought "bold job-creating tax cuts," the ads continued, "some so-called Republicans like Olympia Snowe stand in the way." Similar ads were run against Ohio Senator George Voinovich, a longtime Republican stalwart who had the temerity to suggest that the new round of tax cuts in 2003 was too expensive.

These ads were run by a once-obscure conservative group, the Club for Growth. By the standards of mass membership organizations, the club is Lilliputian, boasting just ten thousand members in 2003. Yet its affiliates are unusually well heeled: during the midterm elections of 2002, the organization's $10 million in contributions made it the leading source of campaign funds for Republicans outside of the GOP itself. Focusing on primaries and open-seat contests, the club bundles donations from its wealthy members to fund conservative anti-tax candidates. Perhaps the most distinctive feature of the Club for Growth is that it targets for defeat not only Democrats but also incumbent Republicans judged insufficiently fierce in their tax-cutting commitment. Former club president Stephen Moore (who recently handed the reins of power to Pat Toomey, the far-right Republican challenger who nearly knocked off moderate GOP stalwart Arlen Specter in 2004) calls these Republicans RINOs, or Republicans in Name Only. He jokes that when he threatens a primary challenge against wayward Republicans, "they start wetting their pants."[16] Club-supported House Republican Jeff Flake of Arizona is equally blunt: "When you have 100 percent of Republicans voting for the Bush tax cut, you know that they are looking over their shoulder and not wanting to have Steve Moore recruiting candidates in their district."[17]

The strategy of the Club for Growth has dovetailed with the activities of another relatively recent anti-tax group: Grover Norquist's Americans for Tax Reform. Like the Club for Growth, ATR has focused its energies on Republican members of Congress. Its central strategy has been to demand a written anti-tax pledge—currently signed by 216 representatives, 42 senators, and President Bush—to "oppose any and all efforts to increase the marginal income tax rates for individuals and/or businesses."[18] Some Republicans, mostly moderate incumbents, resisted the ATR pledge for a time. But the logic of contemporary GOP primaries is clear. For nonincumbents, agreement to this pledge has become a necessary component of any Republican run for Congress.

In their commitments and aims, the Club for Growth and ATR symbolize the tax-cutting fervor of a major activist wing of the GOP. And in their operation and influence, the club and ATR are emblematic of many of key forces at work in American politics today, from increasing polarization to growing economic inequality to the enhanced role of ideological and partisan forces in determining politicians' agendas and fates. As will become clear, the tax cuts of the first Bush term represented the culmination of decades-long trends in American politics that have increased the incentives for politicians to appeal to the ideologically extreme, particularly when the ideologically extreme are affluent, attentive, and organized. These trends have encouraged Republican politicians to abandon the middle on crucial policy issues and race to the base represented by their most vocal and partisan supporters.

Although the tax cuts were consistent with the views of the small minority of well-off and zealously anti-tax Americans that make up a crucial component of the Republicans' fundraising and electoral base, they were at odds with what most voters wanted. Usually—we are told—when the public and the base conflict, the public wins. In this case, however, tax-cut advocates chose not to moderate their ambitions but to doctor the plan's marketing and design in an attempt to sidestep public views and short-circuit political accountability.

Marketing the Tax Cuts

It will come as no shock that politicians twist the facts. Still, in the run-up to the tax cuts of 2001, many analysts expressed surprise at the sheer volume of misleading—and, at times, patently dishonest—information released by the White House and congressional GOP. The biggest splash was made by the 21 May cover of the *New Republic,* which featured a photo of Bush and the headline "He's Lying." Less colorful was a nonpartisan indictment written by veteran tax analyst Martin Sullivan in the highly respected journal *Tax Notes.* Observing that Congress and the Treasury Department had ceased to produce analyses of the distributional effects of tax cuts, Sullivan complained that the Treasury's analysis had by early 2001 become "so embarrassingly poor and so biased, we thought we had seen the last of its kind." "If this continues," Sullivan wryly complained, "the Treasury's Office of Tax Policy (OTP) may have to change its name to the Office of Tax Propaganda."[19]

The propaganda efforts to which Sullivan objected were not isolated examples. Throughout the debate over tax cuts, Republicans carefully calibrated their presentation of the tax cuts to circumvent hostile public opinion. Three strategies were central—each attuned to the tax cuts' principal liabilities. First, unrealistic projections of federal surpluses and of the costs of the tax changes were used to justify the tax cuts and obscure their effects on competing priorities. Second, Republican leaders managed the legislative agenda to prevent consideration of the tax cuts' specific effects on valued programs. And third, tax-cut advocates worked assiduously to make the cuts look far less tilted in favor of the rich and well connected than they really were.

Tradeoffs? What Tradeoffs? The administration and its allies came into office determined to overstate the size of the surplus and understate the size of the tax cuts. Their determination reflected a simple fact: Hiding the true fiscal realities would minimize the prospect that the massive budgetary tradeoffs that were inherent in the tax cuts would become apparent to voters.

In their efforts, Republicans were helped by hopelessly optimistic budget estimates of the Congressional Budget Office (CBO). The CBO was required by law, for example, to assume that Congress would abide by all the dictates of previous tax and spending legislation, even dictates that had been habitually overridden or had no chance of being observed in the future. The White House exploited this and other assumptions to the fullest extent. For instance, whenever the CBO was legally compelled to assume that popular credits and spending initiatives would expire, the administration pocketed those (highly unlikely) savings.

Perhaps the most unrealistic of the White House's assertions was the conceit that Congress would not fix the alternative minimum tax (AMT). The AMT may seem arcane and peripheral, but it looms large in the tax-cut saga. Moreover, it provides one of the clearest examples of how Republicans have hidden their radicalism in a thicket of policy detail. The AMT is a feature of the tax code originally inserted in 1969 to ensure that higher-income taxpayers do not use deductions, exemptions, and credits to avoid paying income taxes entirely. Because the AMT is not adjusted for inflation, the share of Americans who must pay it will rise dramatically in the decade ahead—from less than 2 percent of taxpayers in 2002 to roughly one-third in 2010.[20] In 2001 no one believed that politicians would let this rise occur—certainly not key members of the administration, who began to muse about the need for cutting the AMT down to size before the ink had dried on the 2001 tax legislation. Yet for the purposes of making budgetary estimates, the administration assumed that all revenues projected from a rapidly expanding AMT would flow into government coffers.

What is more, as we will discuss shortly, the legislation of 2001 included two sleights of hand that served to dramatically understate its true costs: "phase-ins," or delays in the implementation of legislated tax cuts; and "sunsets," or tax provisions that expire on a given date. Most tax cuts for higher-income earners, for example, were phased in slowly, mushrooming only in the later years. The entire package was then unrealistically scheduled to expire at the end of 2010, with all taxes affected by the cuts reverting to their pre-2001 levels. The White House also failed to include in its budget new funds for major initiatives that the president had already declared he would support, such as a Medicare prescription drug benefit and additional defense spending. And all these higher costs carried with them the interest payments on the additional debt they required. All told, these distortions reduced the apparent cost of the tax cuts by at least 40 percent.[21]

Benefits for the Rich? What Benefits for the Rich? Tax-cutters also worked assiduously to create the impression that the tax cuts would shower huge benefits on middle-class taxpayers. Few efforts were as transparently false as Bush's statement during the 2000 campaign (repeated, in slightly altered form, during the 2004 race) that "by far the vast majority of my tax cuts go to the bottom end of the spectrum."[22] Instead, advocates crafted their appeals to imply—without quite saying so outright—that middle-income Americans would reap huge rewards from the tax cuts.

Tax-cut advocates insisted, for instance, that the cuts would help "all taxpayers," ignoring the one-third or so of families that pay only payroll taxes. They consistently conflated the *average* tax cut with the *average family's* tax cut. So, for example, the bill of 2003 that aided millionaires so dramatically resulted in an "average tax cut" of more than $1,100, according to the White House—when, in fact, middle-income families would receive less than a fifth of that amount. (Apparently the administration had taken to heart the familiar joke about the conservative who screams, "We're rich!" when Bill Gates walks into a bar, because the average wealth in the room is now in the billions.) They argued that eliminating the $20 income-tax burden of a family of four making $26,000 was a "100 percent cut in taxes," even though that $20 represented less than 1 percent of the family's overall tax burden. Bush repeatedly invoked the example of a waitress with two kids, earning $22,000 a year, whose federal income tax would be eliminated—a waitress who likely had no income tax liability in any case. This language was backed up by a range of colorful media events at which, for example, business lobbyists donned hard hats—to appear as what one leaked congressional leadership memo called "*REAL WORKER* types."[23] At one event, a reporter, impressed by the large number of "average families" the White House had presented, asked who was there to represent the wealthy. With a smile, President Bush assured the reporter that he was.[24]

Designing the Tax Cuts

If the presentation of the tax cuts was blatantly distorted, their design made the marketing look like a model of candor and clarity. Consider the following thumbnail sketch of the tax treatment of estates— an expensive, potentially controversial, and hardly atypical feature of the law. The legislation of 2001 dictated incremental reductions in the estate tax between 2002 and 2009, culminating in total repeal in 2010. In 2011, however, the entire tax schedule that was in force *before* Bush came to office is set to be restored as the law "sunsets." To say the least, this is a peculiar policy structure—especially in an area where the need for proper financial planning makes long-term stability so imperative. And the incentives the policy design creates are a little perverse. The columnist cum economist Paul Krugman has dubbed this the "throw momma from the train" design: If mom dies on 30 December 2010, her heirs will pay nothing. If she dies two days later, they will pay 50 percent.[25] What were lawmakers thinking?

They were thinking that tax-cut designs that make little or no sense as public policy can make a great deal of sense as political strategy. It is well known that politicians spin the facts. But political warfare goes well beyond spin; it also includes the design of policies themselves. In the case of the tax cuts, two types of design choices stand out: first, features of the tax cuts that were meant to distort the public's initial view of what politicians were up to, and, second, features that were tailored to shape the politics of tax cuts down the line in ways that favored tax-cutters' long-term goals.

To be sure, the lasting effects of the tax cuts are not yet fully known. But even now, it's clear that the tax cuts will have a huge long-term impact on the financial standing of American government. It is also clear that Republicans believe these features load the political dice heavily in their favor. A quick glance at three manipulative features of the tax cuts—phase-ins, sunsets, and what we call "time bombs"—strongly suggests that they are right.

Phase-ins. Let us start with the phase-in features of the 2001 tax cuts, which delay implementation of many of the cuts for almost a decade. The normal expectation is that politicians load the goodies up front—and this indeed was what politicians did when it came to most Americans' benefits. Yet some of the tax cuts show exactly the opposite tendency. To take the most prominent examples, the top four income tax rates were only gradually reduced, with the largest cuts coming *after* 2004. The contribution limits for individual retirement accounts (IRAs) were increased from $2,000 to $5,000, but again mostly after 2004, and indexed to inflation in 2008. The estate tax was reduced by a percentage point a year starting in 2003, with all but the biggest estates exempted in 2009, and then eliminated entirely in 2010—but only for a year, as we've seen.

This odd pattern makes little sense in economic or policy terms. But it has some big political benefits. Most obvious, it reduces the official price tag of the tax cuts, because the big payouts come later and (officially) stop quickly. Even more important, however, it plays up the benefits to the middle class while playing down the (much bigger) benefits to the rich. The phase-ins are not applied willy-nilly; they consistently affect tax cuts that go to the well off. As a result, the share of the total tax cuts received by top 1 percent of Americans balloons between 2001 and 2010, while the share received by the bottom 80 percent plummets (fig. 4).

Another way to get a sense of the skew in the timing of the legislation's benefits is to look at who get their cuts when. The lowest fifth of Americans received 85 percent of their total ten-year tax savings immediately, while the second fifth received 72 percent and the middle fifth, 68 percent in the first year of the bill. By contrast, for the fortunate top fifth of Americans, about two-thirds of the total tax cuts were set to be distributed after 2001—a figure that rises to 95 percent for the richest 1 percent of Americans.[26]

An editorial cartoon humorously makes the same point (fig. 5). Homer Simpson—an archetypal working stiff—does not recognize he is being

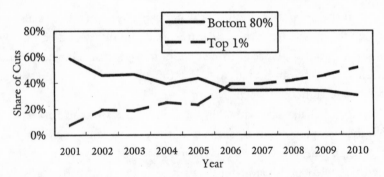

Figure 4. The growing tilt of the Bush tax cuts toward the well off. *Source:* Citizens for Tax Justice, "Year-by-Year Analysis of the Bush Tax Cuts Growing Tilt to the Very Rich," 2002, available at http://www.ctj.org/html/gwb0602.htm.

robbed. Happily celebrating his visible, immediate, but meager benefits, he fails to see the much less visible, much less immediate, but vastly more generous rewards reaped by Mr. Burns. The very peculiar over-time features of the tax cuts—which Mr. Burns recognizes but Homer doesn't— make sense only if we take seriously differences in perception and power, and politicians' attempts to exploit them.

The Sun Never Sets on a Sunset. Until 2001, sunsets (again, rules that curtail provisions of legislation on a specified date) were a relatively minor feature of the tax code, and their usually routine extension posed a quite minor cost. After 2001 that changed. If, for example, 2002 is used as the base year, extending all the expiring provisions placed in the code by the 2001 tax bill would cost nearly 2 percent of gross domestic product over ten years. Once the tax cut of 2003 is taken into account, the figure rises to nearly 2.5 percent.

As already noted, this policy design reduced the estimated cost of the tax cuts. Yet, just as important, it means that future politicians will face a fundamental political quandary: Should they allow enacted provisions of the tax code to expire, explicitly taking from (for the most part, wealthy) taxpayers benefits that they already enjoy? Or should they extend these provisions, incurring the $4 trillion in lost revenue and additional debt service that the sunset provisions of the tax cuts represent? The sunsets, in short, create an unprecedented new political environment—one that is highly favorable to tax-cutters' core goals.

Figure 5. *Source:* Cartoonist Group.

None of this is accidental. Republicans reasonably predict that the pressure to extend the tax cuts will be intense, not least because well-off folks who receive the big tax provisions that take effect just before the sunsets kick in will be unusually well poised to make their voices heard. They also expect, no doubt, that the need to protect these provisions will provide a powerful motivation for the wealthy to bankroll Republican reelection efforts in the future. As Tod Lindberg put the point in the *Washington Times*, "The lesson of the Bush tax-cutting record is that what matters is structural change and political leverage down the line."[27]

Bombs Away. Another design feature also reveals Republicans' intention to set the political agenda for years to come: time bombs primed to detonate in a politically favorable way. The key example of this is the law's treatment of the alternative minimum tax. We have already noted that the administration's projections of the future surplus failed to include the large cost of fixing the AMT. Yet policy designers did not simply ignore the AMT in 2001; they systematically made the problem much worse (fig. 6). Thanks to the tax cuts of 2001, the share of taxpayers facing the AMT after 2004 will explode. And although many families caught in the AMT net

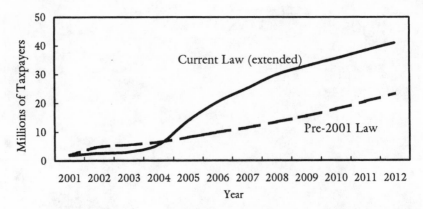

Figure 6. More Americans face the AMT "time bomb" because of the tax cuts. *Source:* Leonard Burman, William G. Gale, and Jeff Rohaly, "The AMT: Problems and Projections," *Tax Notes,* 7 July 2003, 105–17. Available at http://www. taxpolicycenter.org/TaxFacts/TFDB/TFTemplate.cfm? Docid=187

will be quite well off, more than half will have family incomes of less than $100,000 (compared with just 9 percent of AMT-payers in 2002).[28]

Republicans could have fixed the AMT problem in 2001. They did not do so because they figured that eventually Congress would feel compelled to act anyway, giving them yet another big round of tax cuts. And by making the problem so much worse, they could use the projected revenues that would come in when tens of millions fell victim to the AMT to "finance" still more tax cuts. One has to admire the beauty of the deception: more tax cuts now and more tax cuts later when the "time bomb" goes off. The cost of extending the AMT provisions of 2004 just through 2013 is now estimated to be almost $800 billion.[29]

Rounding Up the Vote

The story is stark. To respond to their base, Republicans misled most Americans. On an unprecedented scale, phase-ins, sunsets, and time bombs were used to give the tax cuts of 2001 the most attractive public face possible while systematically stacking the deck in favor of Republicans' long-term aims. From top to bottom, Republicans larded the tax cuts with features that made sense only for the purposes of political manipulation.

Still, for all these efforts, the passage of the tax cuts in 2001 was not assured. It is difficult to recall in the wake of 9/11, but Bush's standing in early 2001 was hardly secure. The election of 2000 had not delivered a clear verdict—even beyond the contested presidential race. In the Senate, Republicans emerged holding the slimmest of margins. Only Vice President Cheney's role as tiebreaker delivered control of the 50–50 chamber to Republicans (a control the GOP temporarily lost after the tax cuts passed due to the defection of Vermont Republican James Jeffords). On its face, this was not an auspicious moment for a legislative adventure as large and controversial as Bush's plan.

We have already seen how Republicans sold and designed the tax cuts to overcome public concerns. Still, the question remains: Where did Republicans get the votes in a closely divided Congress to pass them? The GOP strategies we have examined were designed to keep Americans from responding with hostility to their ambitions. But to deploy these strategies, Republicans needed absolute control over the political agenda. In 2001, with Republicans in charge of the House, Senate, and the White House, they got it.

One thing they did not need, however, was 60 votes in the Senate—the magical three-fifths threshold that must be crossed to overcome the oft-exercised tradition of unlimited debate known as the filibuster. Unlike most major policy reforms, tax cuts could be pursued through the "budget reconciliation" process, which is not subject to filibuster. There was, however, a catch. To use the reconciliation process, the tax cut was limited to the amount Republicans were willing to finance within their ten-year budget resolution outlining spending and revenue changes. Essentially, then, the cost of lowering the necessary Senate margin by ten votes was a tax cut small enough to ensure the fiscal integrity of the agreed-upon ten-year budget—or, rather, the semblance of such integrity. But the price was paid, and the closeness of many of the key Senate votes in 2001 shows that the tax cut would not have been passed otherwise.

When President Bush signed the tax cut, he credited "bipartisan leadership" and thanked "the members of Congress in both parties who made today possible."[30] Yet Democrats were almost nonplayers in the development of the tax cut. Instead of striking a bipartisan deal, Republicans used the powers of their congressional and White House leadership to control the language of the debate and the policy alternatives considered. In the House, where the majority party reigns supreme, Republicans played their advantages to the hilt, sending specific tax cuts to the floor without public testimony, without having yet passed a budget resolution, and at times without even specifying the details of cuts. In the Senate, thanks to the unity of Republicans, the administration and its allies needed only two Democratic votes. Conservative Democrat Zell Miller of Georgia had signaled his strong support for the initiative from the outset, so the bill's supporters had to peel off just one additional Democratic vote. This gave Republicans enormous leverage, especially since many of the most moderate Senate Democrats came from the sparsely populated states that Bush had dominated in 2000.

In achieving all this, Republicans benefited from all the same techniques that had quelled potential public discontent. Control of the congressional agenda pushed the issue of trade-offs effectively off the table. Techniques to lower the perceived size of the tax cuts and mask its true effects on middle-class Americans made it hard to offer a competing account of what was being done. For example, in the Senate, several centrist Democrats and Republicans insisted that the cost of the tax cut over ten years be reduced by $300 billion. The GOP leadership and the Bush White House eventually gave in. But the victory was symbolic. Rather than reducing the number or size of individual cuts, the new target was met by delaying the tax cuts' implementation and moving up the date of the sunset. Despite the much-publicized "concessions," the estimated cost of the tax cut over the long term was *unchanged* from the original Bush proposal.

The Democratic Party, by contrast, was greatly disadvantaged. It lacked the considerable advantages that come with control of Congress. It also lacked a prominent, well-liked, and credible spokesperson to counter President Bush and the congressional leadership. And, in the Senate, it faced the problem that Republicans could offer the handful of moderate Democrats who might sign on to the tax cuts unbeatable deals for their support—including, potentially, the promise that Bush would not campaign against pliant Democrats in the Republican friendly, low-population states so overrepresented in the Senate chamber.

To be sure, once legislation became inevitable, and the final vote was framed as "tax cuts: yeah or nay," a small but nontrivial fraction of

Democratic members of Congress (28 of 212 in the House, 11 of 50 in the Senate) voted in favor. More important, however, was the behavior of Republican moderates. Virtually without exception, they proved willing to endorse profoundly important legislation with contents remarkably distant from the views of most voters. These legislators, of course, faced strong incentives to swing right. Challenging the president on tax cuts would have meant risking the wrath of the leadership and the base. Most ominously, it would mean risking a primary challenge. But, crucially, GOP moderates could only race toward the Republican base if they believed Bush and congressional leaders had lessened the chance that voters would sour on tax cuts. It was success on this critical score—the ability of Republican leaders and the Bush administration to give the tax cut as moderate a face as possible—that was at the heart of the tax-cut victory.

Lessons Learned? The 2003 and 2004 Tax Cuts

The tax cuts of 2001 were just one piece of legislation, albeit an extremely important one. Maybe, just maybe, they were an aberration. Politicians occasionally depart from the political center. But in the conventional view of American politics, the reaction of the public brings them back in line. Politicians are forced to learn, painfully, from their mistakes, and the ironic result of such episodes of "overreach" is the reassertion of the hegemony of the center.

This is a plausible, and reassuring, line of reasoning. It is also mistaken. For although Republicans did indeed learn from the experience of the 2001 tax cuts, the lessons were not painful. If the tax cuts enacted in later years are any indication, the main lesson was that the instruments of backlash insurance work. By 2003, Republicans had become even more confident about their capacity to enact tax legislation that most Americans view skeptically.

In 2003, after all, there was no big surplus to obscure the tradeoffs. Indeed, the government was heading deeper into the red, in part because of the cuts of 2001. And if there had been little popular demand for tax reductions in 2001, there was even less in 2003.

Yet all of the machinations on display in 2001 came back with a vengeance in 2003. As in 2001, the benefits of the tax reductions were greatly skewed toward the well off. As in 2001, benefits for those with average incomes were front-loaded. As in 2001, middle-class Americans received checks within weeks, while the much larger savings for the wealthy came in the later years of the bill. There was one big change from 2001: Less affluent Americans received no new benefits in 2003—their checks reflected the acceleration of cuts already slated to take place. The *new* tax cuts in 2003 were aimed exclusively at the well-to-do.

And all the strategies used to mask the true size of the tax cut in 2001 reappeared in even starker form in 2003. As Congress took up the president's proposals, moderate Republicans in the Senate staged a show of independence. They ostentatiously insisted that their concern with fiscal propriety would not allow them to vote for the president's $700 billion proposal, committing themselves to a "ceiling" of $350 billion. The leadership responded to this challenge with a legislative design that employed sunsets even more aggressively than in 2001. The result was a tax cut advertised at $350 billion that would cost an additional $736 billion if its provisions were extended through 2013. During the debate over the tax cut, Tom DeLay openly belittled the official, lower estimates of the total costs: "The number . . . is meaningless."[31] After the 2003 legislation passed, Senate Republican leaders gathered at a press conference to celebrate passage of a cut that was formally far smaller than the one they had originally sought but which was anticipated to cost far more. When a reporter skeptically inquired as to whether the bill just passed was "smoke and mirrors" designed to make a large tax cut appear smaller, Senator George Allen of Virginia said, "I hope so." All the senators laughed.[32]

The success of this strategy is already apparent. In 2004, despite a deficit of almost half a trillion dollars, provisions of the 2001 bill scheduled to expire were instead extended, by votes of 339–65 in the House and 92–3 in the Senate. It is not coincidental that these provisions—the least skewed toward the rich of the 2001 and 2003 cuts—were set to expire right before the hotly contested election. Nor, given what we have shown, is it surprising that Republicans used the opportunity to introduce *new* tax breaks for higher-income groups. Despite razor-thin majorities, Republicans have created a self-reinforcing political cycle that is remarkably effective at producing tax policies at odds with voters' basic priorities and opinions.

The Real Lessons

The tax cut debates shine a bright light our political system. Big issues were at stake. Big money was on the line. And Americans, and the American media, were paying attention. But on the major issues in the debate, the opinions of ordinary voters were systematically ignored. Far from dictating what Congress did, voters proved vulnerable to extensive manipulation, while a small minority of privileged citizens reaped the rewards.

A wag once paraphrased Abraham Lincoln by saying, "You can fool some of the people all of the time, and all of the people some of the time—and if you think about it, those are pretty good odds." In the new world of American politics, ordinary citizens face formidable obstacles to harnessing government to their purposes. Control of language and alternatives can be used to frame discussions in ways that exploit voters' lack of knowledge. Policy designs can be used to direct distinct signals to different target populations. The political scientist V. O. Key was right: "Voters are not fools."[33] But in certain settings, on certain issues, many of them can be fooled.

Not all citizens are equally vulnerable to such efforts. Surveys on tax issues reveal that F. Scott Fitzgerald was right: The very rich *are* different—not just in their opinions but in their level of knowledge. In a poll conducted in 2003, for example, a majority of the richest 5 percent of Americans answered the knowledge questions correctly. Only a fifth of other Americans did, with knowledge lowest among the least affluent. Strikingly, only half of Americans even knew there had been a tax cut in 2001.[34]

Conservative elites have developed sophisticated strategies to prey on such limitations in ordinary citizens' knowledge. And as the tax cuts show, these strategies can have profound effects. In making policy choices whose effects were, in principle, quite knowable, politicians repeatedly chose to shower their largesse on the attentive and well off. Rather than respond to public sentiments, they exploited gaps in knowledge and used policy design to create political pressures in favor of the ends they supported—ends that abandoned the middle and raced to the base.

To be sure, not all matters lend themselves to the same depressing dynamic. Not all issues make voters' eyes glaze over as the details of tax policy do. On matters such as abortion or the environment, extreme initiatives tend to run up against opposition that is knowledge-rich, organized, and poised to make appeals to elements of the public that are at least moderately attentive to politics.

But with respect to economic and class issues, the situation is different. On these matters, as the tax cuts reveal, it is now possible for policymakers to venture far from the average voter. Sadly, there is nothing random about the kinds of forays that are possible, the types of voters most likely to benefit, or the citizens most likely to pay the price.

3

NEW RULES FOR RADICALS

The Republican tax-cut crusade makes clear that our vaunted system of representation has shifted off center and that the normal guardians of democratic accountability have not been up to the task of bringing it back. For more than a decade, conservatives have wanted to slash taxes on the well off and shove American government back into the painful vise of fiscal scarcity. With the arrival of George W. Bush and the perfection of sophisticated techniques for circumventing hostile public opinion, the anti-tax movement finally got up and running. Now some of our most fundamental policies are careening off the centrist track of American politics.

A skeptic might ask: "But aren't the tax cuts small bore in the big scheme of things?" The answer is a resounding no. The Bush tax cuts outstrip even the Reagan cuts in total magnitude. And unlike the Reagan tax cuts, they show few signs of being reversed by moderates worried about the skyrocketing deficits they have produced. The tax cuts arrive, moreover, on the eve of the retirement of the baby boom generation, which will put major strains on federal finances. In fiscal terms, the Reagan tax cuts were a lavish party by an immature thirty-something, who spent the next fifteen years working overtime to pay off the debt. The Bush tax cuts, in contrast, are the equivalent of a fifty-five-year-old blowing his nest egg on lottery tickets and then loading up his credit card to keep the fun going. And just as the true consequences of our near-retirees' gambling spree won't become transparent until the repo man arrives and his retirement check doesn't, the big effects of the tax cuts won't become clear until America's recent debt binge becomes too expensive to sustain. But when the day of reckoning comes, the tax cuts will affect almost everything government does. The biggest domestic policy change of the past quarter-century, they are as powerful an example of off-center governance as one could imagine.

Still, the tax cuts *could* be an isolated example—a worrisome moment when the system went awry rather than an indication of broader trends. Unfortunately, they are not. In this chapter, we show that off-center policymaking did not begin or end with budget-busting tax cuts. From environmental and workplace protections to health care and Social Security, America's political leadership has been busy rewriting laws, upending established administrative rules, and developing new plans to push American government off center. And when this coordinated political elite cannot get exactly what it wants, it has proved equally adept at making sure that Americans do not get what *they* want by blocking efforts to update policies to respond to public concerns.

The New GOP Playbook

Republicans have developed what we will call, with apologies to left-wing organizer Saul Alinsky, the "new rules for radicals."[1] Alinsky's original rules for radicals were designed to mobilize public opposition to corporate and elite power. The Republicans' new rules are designed to minimize popular concern about policies and actions that frequently cater to these same corporations and elites. If we are to understand how Republicans have successfully pursued policies inconsistent with popular wishes, we need to understand each of the six strategies they live by.

Rule 1: Control the Agenda. Political elites know well that they are advantaged on certain issues, and they try to stay on the terrain that serves them best. Even when elites don't control which exact issues come up, they may be able to dictate which proposals receive attention—a formidable political weapon.

Rule 2: Don't Focus on the Label; Worry about What You Can Put in the Box. Political analysts too often judge victories by looking only at the label slapped onto whatever has passed. But politicians know well that an enormous range of government activities can fall under the heading of any broad label. To see off-center policymaking in all its dark glory requires looking past labels and examining what legislation actually does.

Rule 3: Run from Daylight. Passing laws is generally a high-profile venture and therefore potentially risky. But there are powerful ways to change policy without changing laws. And these alternative routes typically throw up fewer roadblocks and attract less attention, which makes them especially attractive for moving public policy off center.

Rule 4: Don't Just Do Something; Stand There. In American politics, power often means the ability to block things you don't like. And sometimes, to block new policies is to change existing policies. When policies have to be updated to achieve their goals or deal with pressing social problems, successful obstruction means government does less.

Rule 5: Starve the Beast—Later. Most of what our government does requires money. As a result, conservatives have long argued that the way to downsize government is to "starve the beast" by slashing taxes. But much of what government does is also very popular. So conservatives have learned to delay the starvation diet for later. Chip away at the financial foundations of government today, so that, down the road, it finds itself—like Wile E. Coyote in the old Road Runner cartoons—running in thin air, with nowhere to go but down.

Rule 6: Tilt the Playing Field. The powers of a coordinated, aggressive political majority can be used to change policy. They can also be used to change the rules of the game, so that the room to pursue off-center initiatives will be greater in the future.

These six rules provide the roadmap for this chapter. In the pages to follow, we show how each rule has greased the wheels for some remarkable excursions from the moderate center. As we shall see, the new rules for radicals offer no guarantee of success. Our goal is to explain why Republicans often do win even when their aims are vastly to the right of the center. But we want to make clear that Republicans don't always win and explain why they sometimes falter. For it turns out that some of the factors that explain why they occasionally fail—they venture too far to the right, they face a well-organized group of highly attentive citizens, they confront established sources of accurate information, they need to overcome specific roadblocks in the legislative process—are important clues about why, in contemporary politics, they so often win instead.

Rule 1: "Control the Agenda"

One of the greatest powers enjoyed by the Republican majority is the power to set the policy agenda. And on a range of important issues, Republicans have done just that, choosing where to wage their most relentless campaigns. We have already looked at tax cuts, the Republicans' most effective frontal assault. Yet other recent examples of Republicans on the offense are not hard to find. We begin with the impeachment saga of the late Clinton years, where many of the strategies used in later struggles were road tested and honed.

"Impeach the Bastard." The story of the GOP's concerted effort to impeach Bill Clinton is well known. But the verdict often taken from this saga ("The system worked!") is not the one that GOP leaders took from it. Rather, the impeachment process was a testing ground for strategies of agenda control and arm-twisting that would become regular weapons in their arsenal. Most important, it was proof positive that they could get away with far more than they had once thought in the court of American opinion.

We will not repeat the sometimes sordid details of the impeachment saga here.[2] Suffice it to say that Republican House and Senate leaders found themselves in 1998 prepared to launch only the second serious attempt at presidential impeachment in more than a century. What they consistently lacked, however, was the support of the American people. At every point in the drama that played out on Capitol Hill, overwhelming majorities of Americans said that Clinton should not be impeached. Instead, the public endorsed a congressional resolution of censure. A president who had just been reelected without an absolute majority of the popular vote (thanks to the third-party candidacy of the political gadfly Ross Perot) consistently enjoyed the support of at least two-thirds of Americans on the question of impeachment.[3] Indeed, it is absolutely clear that a majority of *members of Congress* would have endorsed censure if they had been given the opportunity to vote on it.[4]

On the day the House voted to move forward with impeachment hearings, 68 percent of Americans opposed impeachment. A strong majority of Americans endorsed censure instead, and an equally strong majority was opposed to Congress's holding hearings on impeachment. Strikingly, in the month preceding the House vote to move forward, the approval rating of Congress dropped by more than ten points, and public support for the congressional GOP's handling of impeachment fell by more than twenty points.[5] These are exactly the signals that are supposed to pull the majority party back to the center. But, of course, that is not what happened. Instead, Republican leaders pursued impeachment in spite of the strong, stable, and seemingly well-informed views of the public, using a range of techniques that would solidify their power in Congress and set the tone and content of their leadership in the years to come.

At the center of these actions and strategies was an obscure congressional leader: Tom DeLay. It was DeLay who orchestrated the impeachment drive. It was DeLay who buttonholed, buttered up, and sometimes brutalized House members reluctant to join him on his quest. Perhaps most important, it was DeLay who blocked efforts to allow the House to vote on censure, which would certainly have passed. Stoking the outrage of an increasingly organized, coordinated and intense Republican base, DeLay called his all-out struggle to force the ouster of Clinton "The Campaign." And, according to *Washington Post* reporter Peter Baker, it was truly that:

> In addition to constantly distributing anti-Clinton information to House Republicans and keeping up a steady drumbeat of public criticism of the president, DeLay was using a network of conservative talk shows and party fund-raisers to generate pressure within the GOP. He would go on as many as ten radio talk shows a day, and his staff would blast-fax talking points and tip sheets to perhaps two hundred such programs at a time, revving up the conservative audiences that would then turn up the heat on their local congressmen. Similarly, major campaign contributors and local party officials were encouraged to talk with members about

impeachment. . . . [DeLay] recognized better than most the various pathways of modern American politics that do not emanate from the nation's capital.[6]

In the House, this is what off-center leadership is all about—not winning over Democrats but pressuring wavering Republicans to follow the party's lead despite public opposition. DeLay was helped by the fact that, as Baker reports, "the most serious threat to many moderate Republicans appeared to be not the possibility of losing in a general election, but the prospect of facing a conservative challenger in a party primary."[7] But, of course, one of the main reasons that moderates feared a conservative primary challenge was that Tom DeLay was stoking the Republican base into ever greater outrage.

Perhaps the most revealing moment in the drama came not when the House voted on impeachment but two months earlier, in the weeks after the midterm election of 1998. Republicans did not do well in the midterm. In the sixth year of a presidency, losses for the party in power are almost a historical guarantee—one had to go back to 1822 to find a counterexample. But Republicans lost five seats, and Speaker of the House Newt Gingrich ended the election year on the verge of losing his leadership role.

The midterm elections were a reality check: Impeachment was killing the Republicans. And if House Republicans had acted in accordance with the conventional wisdom, they should have retreated reluctantly to the center. But if the message of the election was clear to most Americans, it was not clear to DeLay and his allies. Republicans on the House Judiciary Committee, most from safe conservative districts, voted to move full speed ahead. When Gingrich's presumptive successor, Bob Livingston (soon to be derailed by his own marital infidelities), had reservations and decided that censure was the best course, his aide was aghast and instructed him to look at the reams of material regarding allegations of Clinton's sexual predation that DeLay had assembled. "So what you are saying," Livingston asked, according to Baker's account, "is we have to impeach the bastard."[8] The answer, of course, was yes.

DeLay also took matters into his own hands. He drafted letters from Judiciary Committee Chairman Henry Hyde to key members of the leadership and pressured Hyde to sign them. He also had Gingrich's signature forged on a letter he sent to the news media indicating that no censure vote would be held. The move was interpreted as a sign of the Republicans' unity when in fact it was a signal of DeLay's savvy and brazenness.[9] It was also the strongest indication yet of the impressive power DeLay would soon wield as a New Power Broker in George W. Bush's GOP.

The Social Security Salvo. The impeachment saga showcased Republicans on the offense, and it was an offensive posture they carried over to tax-cutting once George W. Bush arrived on the scene. Bush's second term began with a similarly audacious goal: his proposal to partially privatize Social Security. Despite strong evidence that Bush's campaign will not succeed in the first two years of his second term (and perhaps ever), the GOP-supported idea of injecting private accounts into Social Security is still the ultimate showcase for Republicans' off-center strategies—a remarkable sign of how far from the middle America's political leaders have veered.

We called the president's plan "partial privatization."* But this does not truly give a picture of how much it is at odds with existing policy. Social Security is a social insurance program. It offers a guaranteed benefit in retirement that is more generous to families who fall on bad financial luck. This insurance role would be substantially undercut by the president's proposal. Workers would see their guaranteed benefits largely replaced by the returns on their private accounts, which could vary greatly from person to person. Workers who become disabled, who end up living long after retirement, who earn low incomes, who retire when

---

* Advocates of overhauling Social Security to incorporate IRA-style investment accounts have objected to the use of the term "privatization"—which they, in fact, introduced into the lexicon. (Until recently, for instance, the conservative Cato Institute hosted the "Project on Social Security Privatization.") The substance of the objection—rather than the motive, which is that "privatization" polls badly—is that "privatization" implies that government will cease providing retirement income, as opposed to regulating and mandating investment in private accounts. But the term "privatization" has long been used to describe both public withdrawal from an area of government action and policy steps to increase public reliance on the private sector as a substitute for government benefits. Throughout this book, we use "partial privatization" and "private accounts" interchangeably to denote the latter sort of change.

the stock market drops—all might end up with much less than the guaranteed Social Security benefit, as could the families of workers who die before retirement. In short, much greater risk would suddenly be placed on the shoulders of individual workers and their families.[10]

This shift would do nothing to improve Social Security's financial standing. Quite the opposite: Most Social Security taxes—now and in the future—pay for benefits for current retirees. The only way to establish new accounts and reap the higher potential rewards (and risk) of the stock market is to come up with new funds to fill the accounts, by raising taxes, cutting benefits, or running up the national debt. In fact, supporters of private accounts envision trillions of dollars in (hopefully hidden) borrowing to pay for their establishment. Even so, the president and his allies recognize that major cuts in benefits would have to be made as well. Social Security as it has been known for sixty years would cease to exist.

In sum, President Bush's plans have no modern precedent. They are far more radical than anything President Reagan contemplated, much less tried. In the early 1980s, with the Social Security system about to run out of money, the Reagan administration floated the idea of significant benefit cuts in Social Security. But these were never endorsed by the president and unanimously repudiated by the Senate. Ultimately, President Reagan and Congress handed the issue over to a bipartisan commission that came up with a classic compromise approach: a mix of higher taxes and cuts in benefits that paved the way for the building up of significant surpluses in the Social Security trust fund.[11]

Today, however, the story is almost perfectly the reverse. Social Security's current fiscal position is sound. Even under cautious assumptions, the program will be able to pay promised benefits for at least another forty years and roughly three-quarters of promised benefits thereafter.[12] Nonetheless, Bush and his allies have so far proved unwilling to consider a bipartisan compromise of the sort that emerged in the early 1980s. Instead, they are committed to transforming Social Security into an entirely different program—one that is less about social protection and more about individual asset accumulation. This goal was once on the fringes of Republican thought. But in recent years it has become a central goal of the antigovernment conservatives who make up the intellectual firmament of the Republican base.[13]

Speaker of the House Dennis Hastert was perhaps too candid when, in early 2005, he called Social Security a "Ponzi Scheme," after the infamous pyramid swindle of Charles Ponzi. (He quickly added that he didn't mean the accusation in a "derogatory way.") But Hastert's view of the program—and the comparably candid assertion by the head of the Republican National Committee that the Social Security fight would bring out Republicans' "core constituents" in the midterm elections of 2006—is indicative of the Republican commitment to upending Social Security.[14] For key GOP operatives, replacing Social Security with a system of individual accounts would be an unprecedented policy achievement. As a well-connected Republican lobbyist told the veteran Washington reporter Elizabeth Drew, "What [Republicans] want to do is break the hold of the Democrats on Social Security."[15] An aide to Karl Rove put it more strongly in a memo in 2004: "This will be one of the most important conservative undertakings of modern times. If we succeed in reforming Social Security, it will rank as one of the most significant conservative governing achievements ever. The scope and scale of this endeavor are hard to overestimate. . . . For the first time in six decades, the Social Security battle is one we can win—and in doing so, we can help transform the political and philosophical landscape of the country."[16]

Much as we saw with impeachment, however, there is one group conspicuously unwilling to enlist for the Republican "battle": a clear majority of the American people. Public support for Social Security is overwhelming. Public opposition to changing Social Security in ways that would require new government borrowing or exposing citizens to stock market risk is nearly as high. And, despite repeated administration insistence that current retirees will be exempted from the changes, opposition is highest among the group of ordinary voters most consistently mobilized, informed, and attentive—the elderly. With watchdogs like the AARP blasting its highly attentive and active members with ads and facts, it will be harder to obscure the distributional effects of Social Security privatization than the real effects of the tax cuts.

That does not mean Republicans won't try. The refining of poll-tested language to put the most positive face possible on Bush's aims has been a major part of the White House's effort. First, "privatization"—once a conservative catchphrase—was banished, replaced with "private accounts." Then, the phrase "private accounts" was disabled, with "personal accounts" taking over. The search for a compelling line on Social Security is a measure of how much Republicans believe that they can sell the public on off-center policies. As a memo to Republicans from GOP pollster Frank Luntz put it, "A compelling story, even if factually inaccurate, can be more emotionally compelling than a dry recitation of the truth."[18]

The rhetorical lengths to which Republicans have gone to sell Social Security reform are impressive even in the age of political spin. The Social Security Administration, whose one clear mission is to carry out the laws that established Social Security, was strenuously pressed by the White House to assume a leadership role in advocating privatization of the very program it runs. Talking points distributed to agency staff argued that "modernization must include individually controlled, voluntary personal retirement accounts to augment Social Security." And the agency's own Web site and customer service telephone lines stressed the need to "modernize and reform" the system, emphasizing that the future shortfall is "massive and growing."[19]

Still, the Social Security fight is not one that will be won with rhetoric alone. It will require ramrod discipline in the House, which seems likely to materialize so long as there is some prospect of Senate action. It now goes almost without notice that the House debates huge and highly conservative pieces of legislation in a matter of hours, without any formal input from Democrats, without serious consideration of competing issues, and without any real prospect of defeat or amendment on the House floor.

The barriers faced by Republicans in the Senate, however, are vastly higher—mainly due to the filibuster, the Senate tradition of unlimited debate that takes a three-fifths majority to overcome. Initially, Republicans hoped that they could overcome the filibuster by putting Social Security reform, as they had put tax cuts, into the budget that the president submitted to Congress.[20] As we noted in the last chapter, budget-related legislation is protected from the risk of a Senate filibuster. What counts as "budget-related legislation," however, is governed by arcane rules that must be interpreted by the Senate parliamentarian. And the rules in this case are clear: Social Security reform cannot be legitimately included. Thus, President Bush and his allies will have to reach the magical sixty-vote margin in the Senate—which will strain their powers of persuasion and coercion like no off-center project they have yet attempted.

One aspect of this persuasion and coercion that has by now become a familiar feature of big GOP policy drives is the concerted mobilization of supportive interest groups even before the details of legislation have come into view. Our image of Washington lobbying is of big interests controlling politicians. But in recent years, deep-pocketed interests have been asked repeatedly to sign on to GOP legislation before it comes down the pike (with the promise, of course, that their interests will be safe) and then told to mobilize "grassroots" pressure on wavering politicians, particularly Republicans who might be insufficiently committed to the party cause.

In 2005, for instance, the Coalition for the Modernization and Protection of America's Social Security (known as "Compass") launched a $20-million campaign on behalf of the president's still-undefined privatization proposal. Although Compass is a collection of major business and trade associations, the effort had all the trappings of a grassroots campaign. Similar efforts were launched by the anti-tax Club for Growth and by Progress for America, an ultraconservative activist network—both of which targeted the Republican base in key GOP districts. All told, at least $100 million was on tap for the lobbying blitz, most of it coordinated by the White House. "With the president's leadership and the White House leadership, they have really put together a campaign-style effort to enact Social Security reform," said a leader in the Compass coalition. "They've got all their assets involved in this thing."[21]

Even with outside support, however, Bush's overhaul of Social Security will require fiscal chicanery and manipulative policy design at least rivaling that of the tax cuts. There is simply no way to divert so much of younger workers' payroll taxes out of the traditional Social Security system otherwise. In light of strategies chosen in the tax-cut debate, we can expect highly creative attempts to borrow the trillions needed to fund private accounts and even more creative measures to obscure the benefit cuts that privatization will require. The new accounts will be offered up front as manna from heaven that, once granted, can never be taken away. The benefit cuts will be delayed, hidden in the obscure language of cost-of-living increases, or ultimately left to future Congresses to deal with. But the basic strategy will be clear. Get private accounts into law in any way possible. Assure their recipients that these accounts are theirs, never to be altered or touched. Hide the huge costs and risks. And hope that, when the day of reckoning comes, voters won't recognize how and when America's most popular program was hijacked.

None of this will be easy. Indeed, we doubt that it will take place. But the very fact that changes so substantially at odds with public opinion are on the table speaks volumes about the transformation of American politics. President Bush and congressional Republicans now see themselves in the terms that FDR and his New Deal Congress did—as vanguards of an overhaul of America's basic social contract. But FDR had won landslides, and worked with huge congressional majorities. Today, President Bush and the congressional GOP want to take American public policy off center without having public opinion remotely on their side. Social Security privatization would be the ultimate triumph of off-center policy-making.

Moderation Goes Bankrupt. Social Security represents the biggest and most high-profile initiative of Bush's second term. Yet it entered the agenda accompanied by a number of aggressive efforts to move other legislation of special interest to business. Perhaps the most revealing was legislation dramatically tightening the nation's bankruptcy laws. As Harvard law professor Elizabeth Warren, who has studied the growing risk of bankruptcy, summarized the legislation, it would "make debtors pay more to creditors," "make it more expensive to file for bankruptcy . . . so that the people in the most trouble can't afford to file," create "more hurdles and traps, with deadlines that a judge cannot waive," and "make it harder to repay debts . . . so that more people will be pushed out of bankruptcy without ever getting a discharge of debt."[22]

The stated rationale for the legislation was that bankruptcy filers were spending lavishly and then asking to be bailed out. So Senate opponents of the bill introduced a series of amendments designed to prevent such shiftless behavior while carving out protections for those who found themselves in dire economic conditions because of job loss, health problems, or divorce—the catastrophic events that are overwhelmingly the catalysts of bankruptcy. Amendments were also offered to protect service members and veterans and those caring for ill or disabled family members. Every amendment was beaten back by a solid wall of Republicans and a much smaller, shifting group of Democrats.

Tellingly, the same players also rejected amendments designed to tighten bankruptcy rules for millionaires. In recent years five states—Alaska, Delaware, Nevada, Rhode Island, and Utah—have introduced laws to permit people living anywhere in the country to set up "asset protection trusts." These trusts can be used by the wealthy to shelter their portfolios from creditors. Reform of this "millionaire's loophole" was rejected with the explanation that the matter needed "further study."

The victory capped an eight-year campaign by credit-card companies and banks, which spent tens of millions on campaign contributions and lobbying efforts to encourage passage. Legislation had been blocked in the previous Congress, when Democrats succeeded in adding a "poison pill" amendment limiting bankruptcy protection for anti-abortion protesters facing government fines. But with four new Republican senators joining the chamber in 2004, a similar gambit failed. Fourteen Democrats joined all 55 Republicans in voting to end debate, and the bill went on to pass the Senate 74–25, with 18 Democrats (including 3 of the 4 from states where "asset protection trusts" have become a nice legal industry) voting in favor.

Even David Broder, the sober and unfailingly moderate dean of Washington pundits, had trouble finding language harsh enough for the bill. An act of "blatant hypocrisy" was his description: "A perfect illustration of how the political money system tilts the law against average Americans. . . . It's all too typical of what takes place now in Washington with most issues. Few policy battles . . . draw enough public and press interest for the legislators to feel real scrutiny. Most are in a netherworld where media coverage is cursory and interest groups' pressure determines the outcome."[23] The bankruptcy bill was a classic contest pitting concentrated and powerful interests against diffuse interests with limited

resources and little ability to attract the attention of the millions of potentially affected citizens (few of whom would even know their interests were
at stake until they experienced a calamity, at which point they would have
more pressing concerns than writing their representatives).[24] In the new
world of off-center politics, this turned out to be no contest at all.

Energetic Extremism. Alongside the 2001 tax cuts, Bush's energy plan
was the centerpiece of the president's first-term agenda. The battle to
restructure U.S. energy policy has played out much more slowly than the
tax cuts or bankruptcy revisions did, and to date the result has been less
happy for the conservative coalition. But it is hardly a reassuring story for
those confident about the solidity of the obstacles to off-center policy.

The acrimony over the Bush energy plan is understandable. The
administration adopted a highly pro-industry stance that emphasized
production over conservation and called for such controversial moves as
oil drilling in protected Alaskan wilderness. Environmental groups—an
attentive constituency if ever there was one—leapt into action to fight
against key elements of the GOP plan. But the bitterness of the conflict
is not the best measure of how off center the energy plan was. Instead,
we have to look at what Republicans actually proposed.

Like the Social Security overhaul, the energy plan was a presidential
initiative. Indeed, its design clearly reflected the personal commitments
of Bush and Vice President Cheney, both of whom had strong and long-
standing ties to the energy industry. (In 2000, the Bush-Cheney ticket
received nine times as much in campaign contributions from energy companies as did the Gore-Lieberman ticket.)[25] The plan itself was formulated in a secret White House task force—which became less secret after
a lawsuit tried to force the White House to divulge its records. The task
force's "industry representatives" read like a who's who of GOP contributors: Edison Electric Institute (fourteen visits to the task force and
more than $500,000 in campaign contributions in 2000), the energy
conglomerates Southern Company and Exelon Corporation (seven and
six visits and roughly $1.6 and $1 million in contributions, respectively),
and, of course, the ill-fated Enron Corporation (nine visits, including
three with Cheney himself, and $1.4 million in donations).[26]

The industry romp was almost a parody of fat-cat self-dealing. One
e-mail sent out by the secretary of energy's top assistant asked a lobbyist

what he would do if he were "King, or Il Duce." (It was done.) Critics of the affair joked that for Bush, "diversity" meant having two different energy companies in the White House.

But the energy plan was a serious matter. It roughly doubled the $33 billion in subsidies that the energy industry was already slated to receive for exploration and the development of nuclear and coal technologies. More telling, if less transparently costly, it threw open public lands and waters to additional oil drilling and granted the federal government new powers to seize property for energy-related construction. The basic philosophy of the plan was summed up by a lobbyist for the world's largest coal-mining company: "We're all on the supply side—the electric utilities, the coal companies—and the energy plan is basically a supply-side plan."

The energy industry and White House may be "on the supply side." But Americans are not. Environmental protection is highly popular with Americans: In early 2004, three-quarters of Americans said they wanted "stronger environmental regulations," the highest support recorded for any law or regulation mentioned in the survey.[27] And the public thinks that conservation is an extremely important part of that protection. The Gallup Poll has asked for years whether "conservation of existing energy supplies" or "production of more gas, oil, and coal supplies" should be a higher priority. Consistently, Americans side with conservation by a two-to-one margin or greater.[28]

Vice President Cheney was thus leaning heavily against the winds of public opinion when, in a major speech detailing the plan, he mocked conservation as a "personal virtue," not the basis for a "sound, comprehensive energy policy." When the comments received bad press, the White House shifted within hours to trumpeting how much the plan encouraged conservation. On CBS's *Face the Nation,* Cheney made the preposterous claim that "there are no new financial subsidies of any kind for the oil and gas industry." At one point, he even argued that the plan was consistent with eleven of the twelve planks of the Sierra Club's energy proposal. The Sierra Club joked that Cheney's math was the kind of accounting that brought Enron down.

Nonetheless, the energy plan sailed through the House with few changes on essentially party-line votes. Introduced on 27 July 2001, the massive bill passed the House just after midnight on *1 August*—before most members of Congress had even had a chance to read it. Debate was perfunctory, the outcome foreordained. As is increasingly the case, the bill was considered under Republican-engineered rules that limited general debate to ninety minutes and allowed only a specified list of amendments. Conspicuously missing from those allowed amendments was a Democratic proposal that would have required that Republicans explain how they would pay for the bill's new subsidies.

The bill faced tougher sledding in the Senate, where it confronted the threat of a Democratic filibuster. But exploiting territorial divisions that are often pronounced on energy and environmental issues, Republicans were able to attract a handful of rural Democrats who supported some aims of the legislation. Especially helpful was the bill's promotion of the corn-based fuel additive Ethanol, which won over such unlikely allies as South Dakotan Tom Daschle. After failing in 2001, the Republican leadership was finally able to peel off enough Democrats to get a bill through the Senate in 2003, but only after some of the most controversial provisions (such as plans to open the Arctic National Wildlife Refuge to drilling) were stripped.

Several years of hard legislative work thus left Republicans at the brink of victory—until, that is, they were abruptly tripped up by a most unlikely figure: Tom DeLay. Not content with the bill's major shift toward production and against environmental protection, DeLay insisted that the bill also include a so-called reach back provision that barred lawsuits over MTBE, a gasoline additive that has been at the center of major lawsuits due to its risks to health and the environment. The provision barred MTBE lawsuits filed since the previous October, not just future lawsuits. This was a nonstarter in the Senate. But DeLay would not budge. "Tom DeLay killed the bill," explained an energy lobbyist in December 2003. "It would have been signed into law now if he would have agreed to compromise on one issue." A public interest lobbyist who came from a very different vantage point agreed: "It was a lousy bill. It was an industry bill. And DeLay did the country a great favor, regardless of his intentions."[29]

DeLay's intention, of course, was to get a bill more to his liking, and there is reason to believe he miscalculated in this instance. As we explore later in this chapter, the fiscal vise that Republican-backed tax cuts have increasingly tightened started to pinch the Republicans' own legislative agenda after Bush's reelection, catching the still-unpassed energy bill in its squeeze. But the reasons why the Republicans' energy plan found itself stuck in neutral in 2003 should not provide much consolation. In the end, its travails had little to do with how far from the center it was and everything to do with DeLay's frustration that it was not off center enough.

Rule 2: "Don't Focus on the Label: Worry about What You Can Put in the Box"

Republicans cannot always control the policy agenda. At times, issues arise because of overwhelming public demand. At others, crises elevate issues that had lain dormant. And sometimes—though infrequently—Democrats manage to keep an issue high on the agenda on their own. As a rule, Republicans are more likely to get what they want when they set the agenda. But the powers of ruling elites do not evaporate when they face issues they would rather ignore. Indeed, perhaps the most notable measure of the impressive power, savvy, and coordination of current GOP leaders is their remarkable ability to turn defense into offense.[30] And perhaps the most skillful of these jujitsu moves culminated in Medicare drug coverage—a long-standing Democratic goal that Republicans adroitly seized and used for their own ends.

Medicare Deform. The passage of a prescription drug plan for elderly and disabled Americans who depend on Medicare would not have been predicted at the start of George W. Bush's first term. After all, in prior years Republicans had posed the greatest barrier to action on the issue.[31] But after the midterm elections in 2002, Bush and Republican leaders came to believe that action on the issue was vital. For one, public and Democratic pressure for action was so powerful that Republicans—and especially President Bush—might suffer politically if they did not allow something to pass. For another, with strengthened control of Congress and the White House, Republicans were in a position to design and pass a bill almost solely of their making. Thus it happened that in late 2003 Republicans enacted a Medicare drug bill that headed off many of their previous objections to a drug benefit, protected the turf of key medical industry interests while showering key Republican allies with huge new benefits, and became a vehicle for achieving some of the conservatives' long-standing aims for restructuring Medicare to make it more market-oriented and reliant on private health plans.

The ostensible centerpiece of the Republican plan is new voluntary drug coverage for Medicare beneficiaries. Yet the coverage that the Republican plan creates has the dubious distinction of being at once stingy and costly. It is stingy in two senses: it will cover a relatively small share of drug expenses, and it has a major gap in coverage (often called the "donut hole," because it leaves a large void between $2,250 and $5,100 in drug spending). Moreover, the bill explicitly forbids Medicare beneficiaries from purchasing private coverage that fills in the gap. The advocacy group Consumers Union has estimated that because of the relatively limited coverage of the bill, most seniors will end up paying more for prescription drugs after the bill takes effect than they did in the years before its passage.[32]

The stinginess of the coverage would be more understandable if the drug plan was a modest initiative costing relatively little. It is not. The bill is projected to cost between $500 billion and $1 trillion in its first ten years, despite the Republican leadership's deployment of the same technique of slow phase-ins that worked so effectively in the battle over tax cuts.[33] Indeed, even with the phase-ins, the cost is so high that the Bush administration had to hide the true expense to get the bill passed. In Bush's 2003 budget, $400 billion was set aside for prescription drug coverage. But the chief actuary of Medicare calculated that the coverage would actually cost roughly $535 billion. This huge discrepancy did not feature in congressional debate only because the head of Medicare (who was, at the time, negotiating for a lucrative private sector job lobbying for health care interests) threatened to fire the Medicare actuary if he released the actual numbers.[34] The story eventually came to light, but not before the prescription drug plan squeaked through the House over ultraconservatives' objections that even at $400 billion, it cost too much.

The seeming paradox of a drug plan that is at once so crabbed and so costly is easily resolved. Inside the package labeled "new drug benefit for the elderly" were contents carefully designed to fill the rather particular prescriptions of the Republican base. The most important of these concessions is the bill's failure to do anything to reduce the meteoric rate of increase in prescription drug prices. Medicaid for the poor and the Veterans Administration (VA) restrain drug prices by using their bargaining power to hold down costs. According to a detailed study by the National Academy of Sciences, the VA has reduced the amount spent on drugs by 15 percent, without any adverse effects on the health status of patients.[35] The idea of having Medicare use its bulk purchasing power to buy lower-cost drugs for senior citizens is overwhelmingly popular.[36] But the Medicare drug plan explicitly prohibits the federal government from bargaining for lower drug prices. Instead, it requires that the private sector provide drug insurance. Even when there are no private insurers willing to offer coverage in a particular region, Medicare still cannot provide drug coverage directly. It has to contract with a private insurer that does all the administration. Medicare simply gets to cover the tab.

If this sounds like a dream plan for the pharmaceutical and insurance industries, it is. And not surprisingly, these sectors were on the forefront of the push to get into law the GOP plan. The drug industry contributed nearly $30 million in the 2002 election cycle—up from less than $10 million a decade earlier—three-quarters of which went to Republicans. In 2003, according to one estimate, the drug industry (including related advocacy groups and drug benefit managers) spent more than $100 million on federal lobbying.[37] When the debate over prescription drug coverage picked up in the late Clinton years, the pharmaceutical lobbying group PhRMA (Pharmaceutical Research and Manufacturers Association, pronounced "Farma") went so far as to establish a faux grassroots organization that putatively represented the elderly: "Citizens for a Better Medicare." Despite the lofty title, Citizens for a Better Medicare had few, if any, actual citizens on its rolls. Its main activity was to spend millions of PhRMA dollars on slick ad campaigns supporting an industry-friendly drug plan. When Citizens for a Better Medicare came under fire, PhRMA switched its "grassroots" effort over to the United Seniors Association, a conservative direct-mail organization that had cut its teeth with frightening scare letters to senior citizens. The United Seniors Association board included, among other GOP political operatives, Jack Abramoff—a well-connected lobbyist with close ties to congressional Republicans who, in 2004, would become the subject of a criminal probe by the Federal Bureau of Investigation, Internal Revenue Service, Justice Department, Interior Department, and even the National Indian Gaming Commission for transforming his close connection with the congressional GOP into tens of millions in lobbying fees.

PhRMA was not, however, the only group that signed on to the Medicare legislation. As the political scientist Michael Heaney has found using detailed interviews with lobbyists, the Bush White House and Republicans in Congress undertook a disciplined, aggressive, and highly successful effort to get interest groups on board their drug plan before its details were even unveiled.[38] This was a coalition not just of the willing but also of the worried. Key groups, such as PhRMA and the major insurance industry groups, signed on purely because they trusted Republicans to expand their market and protect their interests. But many more were convinced by Republicans' vigorous "reverse-lobbying" effort that if they did not sign up with the Republicans' plan—sight unseen— they would be shut out of the process entirely. As one industry lobbyist told Heaney, "On the Medicare bill, we took internal member pressure for supporting it. If we had opposed it, we would have taken heat from the Republican leadership on the hill."[39]

The plum in the Republicans' interest-group effort was the eventual support of the AARP. The motives of the AARP have been endlessly dissected, but one seems to have been paramount: a fear of being left out of the reform process entirely.[40] Moreover, the AARP, like many other interests involved in the struggle, seems ultimately to have failed to recognize how far the bill would tilt in the direction of protecting pharmaceutical manufacturers and providing new subsidies to other industry groups—concessions that would significantly undercut the bill's ability to provide broad drug coverage to the AARP's members.

How extensive were these concessions? Consider some of the major features of the legislation. As already mentioned, the bill prohibits any effort by Medicare to use its bargaining power to hold down drug costs, despite overwhelming public support for this approach.[41] This "noninterference" provision alone means that the federal government will pay drug manufacturers a great deal more for pharmaceuticals than they otherwise would. The bill also includes extensive new subsidies for private health plans to encourage them to cover senior citizens. These direct subsidies are on top of the billions in implicit subsidies that private plans receive because, as study after study has shown, Medicare overpays them for the generally healthy seniors they enroll. And on top of these subsidies is $72 billion over ten years for new tax-free Health Savings Accounts (HSAs) for the nonelderly, a proposal that conservatives insisted be in any bill (and which, besides doing nothing for current Medicare beneficiaries, experts believe could destabilize private health insurance by encouraging healthier and wealthier Americans to opt out of group health plans). Finally, the plan includes another $72 billion in subsidies for employers with retiree drug coverage to encourage them not to drop insurance for seniors newly covered by the law.[42]

If the Medicare bill proved to be highly popular with the drug and insurance industries, the same was not true of the public.[43] While Americans were strongly supportive of adding prescription drug coverage to Medicare (just before the bill passed, three-quarters of American supported Medicare drug coverage and nearly 80 percent of supporters said they would be *personally* willing to pay more in taxes to foot the bill), the specific proposal that Congress passed enjoyed anemic levels of support.[44] Asked just after the Republican-backed bill passed whether they approved of "the Medicare changes voted on by Congress last month," fifty-six percent of those who said they were closely following the debate were against the changes, while 39 percent approved.[45]

The disconnect between public support for action in general and public opposition to what the president and Congress actually did is readily understandable once one looks past the label "Medicare drug plan" and glances at what Americans actually expected a drug plan to do. For example, polls revealed that by large margins Americans wanted the plan to be much more generous and were willing to pay for it.[46] Not only did Americans want the plan to be much more generous, they were also lukewarm, at best, toward the GOP's insistence that private health insurers handle the new benefit.[47] Above all, Americans believed that Medicare should be allowed to negotiate lower prices for prescription drugs and even import them from Canada if that would lower prices.[48] In other words, on each of the three major design issues raised by the bill—how much it should cover, whether it should be run by Medicare or the private sector, and how it would control costs—a majority (in most cases, an overwhelming majority) of Americans were against the specific choices made by Republican political leaders.

Not surprisingly, this remarkable legislation had to survive an equally remarkable odyssey that carried it through dangers in both legislative chambers and at destinations in between. And every step of the journey revealed additional elements of off-center politics in action. In the Senate, a bipartisan group led by Democratic Senator Ted Kennedy of Massachusetts coalesced behind a relatively moderate bill that Kennedy touted as a down payment toward a more generous benefit. However, this bill was viewed with deep skepticism by House GOP leaders—and downright hostility by the most conservative wing of the Republican Party.

Passage of the bill in the Senate led to a conference committee between delegates of the two chambers. Conference committees are a long-standing device for reaching a compromise between differing House and Senate bills that address the same subject. Their recent evolution, however, reveals some unflattering features of the new political order. In this case, the Senate's relatively moderate plan had to be reconciled with a hard-edged conservative plan that had been pushed through the House by Tom DeLay and other GOP leaders. This was another of those moments in American politics when the center is supposed to take control. It did not turn out that way. Instead, as is more and more often the case in the GOP-controlled Congress, the Republican leadership stacked the committee majority with Republicans willing to play along.[49] They then proceeded to shut out all but the most compliant Democrats, refusing even to talk to the House Democrats who had been appointed to the committee. Little surprise, then, that the massive bill that emerged from the conference committee, less than two days before the House voted on it, leaned heavily in the direction of the House bill. It included expensive new HSAs, extensive subsidies for private health plans, and a demonstration project in which Medicare would be made to compete with private plans in six regions. It even included a new standard for Medicare "insolvency" (contained in *neither* the House bill nor the Senate version) that was certain to create new pressures to cut Medicare spending down the road.

The new insolvency standard may seem esoteric, but it is a crucial and revealing development. The new measure all but guarantees that Medicare will be declared "insolvent" sometime in the next few years. It also requires that when this inevitable declaration is made for two years in a row, the sitting president has to propose measures to cut Medicare's spending or raise its revenues, and the House must consider the president's legislation under expedited procedures. Like the GOP's obscure but hugely important maneuver on the alternative minimum tax, the insolvency provision plants a time bomb within the popular Medicare program. While not restraining Medicare spending directly, this provision ensures that, within a short time, Medicare cuts will move to the top of the political agenda.

The aggressive (mis)use of conference committees by the GOP majority has become commonplace. And in this instance, it served its purpose perfectly. When the transformed bill came back to the Senate, a betrayed Kennedy tried to rally fellow Democrats to invoke a filibuster. But it was too late. Many Americans, and even many Democratic Senators, seemed unaware of how much the bill had changed. More important, because bills emerging from conference committees cannot be amended, Democrats now faced a single moment in the spotlight, standing to say "Yeah" or "Nay" on a "prescription drug bill," something many had advocated for years. Enough said "Yeah" to pass the bill.

The machinations on the House floor were even more dramatic, because conflicts usually hidden behind a wall of Republican unity spilled over into public view. The problems in the House came not from disgruntled Democrats but from a handful of Republicans who objected to the expensive new entitlement that emerged from the conference committee, despite the bill's many conservative features. In response to the hard-right rebellion, the Republican leadership (including Billy Tauzin, who would shortly retire and accept a lucrative position as the head of PhRMA) pulled out all the stops. Indeed, no sooner had the bill passed into law than allegations began to swirl that the Republican leadership had engaged in bribery on the House floor. The story—which prompted a wave of calls for House ethics actions and eventually an FBI probe— swirled around Congressman Nick Smith, Republican of Michigan, whose son happened to be running to replace him in Congress (his son ended up losing). After the vote, Smith alleged that he had been repeatedly pressured to change his vote by House leaders, who said that his son's campaign would receive $100,000 from "business interests" if he supported the bill. When Smith refused the bribe, it turned into a threat. Smith refused to budge—and soon after telling of the bribery attempt, he was pressured to recant his story.[50]

Eventually House leaders were able to convince enough Republicans to sign on to the legislation to pass the bill by a five-vote margin. They did so only by holding the longest recorded vote in modern House history, lasting three hours. Votes are supposed to take fifteen minutes. When Democratic Leader Jim Wright left voting open for an extra ten minutes in 1987, then-Republican Whip Dick Cheney called it "the most arrogant, heavy-handed abuse of power in the ten years I've been here."[51]

After the bill passed, some rueful Democrats predicted the bill would hurt Bush. But Republicans had thought of that, too: The full legislation did not go into effect until after the election in 2004, a move that also lowered its official cost. Even that may not have been deemed sufficient political cover, for no sooner had the bill passed than a new controversy erupted over the use of federal money to fund aggressive "public information" efforts.[52] During the 2004 election season, roughly $20 million was set aside by the Bush administration to fund TV spots lauding the Medicare drug plan.[53] Late in 2004, an investigation by Congress's nonpartisan General Accounting Office (GAO) found that the Bush administration had broken antipropaganda law when it distributed videos to news stations in which actors playing reporters explained the new drug law in sunny terms.[54] (This was not the only time the administration's public relations crossed the line into propaganda. In early 2005, the media world was rocked with the revelation that three prominent conservative commentators—Armstrong Williams, Maggie Gallagher, and Michael McManus—had been paid by the administration to promote its education and marriage proposals, with Williams receiving $240,000. All told, the Bush administration spent $250 million on PR contracts in its first term, twice what was spent during Clinton's last four years in office.)[55]

By itself, the controversy over the faux news pieces seemed small, perhaps even humorous. But against the backdrop of what had come before, it cast a darker shadow. A bill that contained complex yet calculated provisions, that was rammed through Congress by subverting normal congressional procedure, that showered money on deep-pocketed interests, and that threatened to undermine the popular Medicare program arrived on the public scene wrapped in a ribbon paid for by the very citizens whose key demands had been ignored.

Rule 3: "Run from Daylight"

The legislative process is the most visible and best-recognized means of changing policy. It is the stuff of popular drama and historical legend—from Jimmy Stewart's filibuster in *Mr. Smith Goes to Washington* to Preston Brooks caning Charles Sumner on the eve of the Civil War. The legislative process is also, however, fiendishly difficult to navigate even for the most disciplined political movement. The system of checks and balances that James Madison and his fellow Founders devised was not meant to be neat, tidy, or efficient. It was meant to elicit compromise and moderation—and without them, stalemate—in a framework of "separated institutions *sharing* powers."[56]

Yet the legislative process is not the only means of changing national policy, as president after president has learned. The nation's chief executive has a range of unilateral powers vested in him by the constitution, by convention, and by legislative statute. Most notably, presidents can issue executive orders—in essence, rulings that direct the executive branch to do certain things.[57] But the ability of presidents to shape policy does not end with their unilateral powers. Through their influence over the executive branch atop which they sit they can have a pervasive effect on how the laws that Congress passes are enforced and implemented.

The attractions of these routes are obvious. The president acts; Congress either acquiesces or responds. And when the president's party controls Congress, such responses are relatively unlikely—indeed, congressional leaders may be quietly egging the president on. No less important, the actions of the executive branch are subject to much more limited scrutiny than is the legislative process. Simply put, presidents often choose executive action because they want to keep what they are doing beneath the radar screen. As will become clear in our consideration of two important areas where Bush has acted unilaterally—workplace protections and environmental policy—that often means that what's going on would be unlikely to win the approval of the American people.

Workplace Antiregulation. Workplace protections are the responsibility of many parts of the federal government, but one stands above the others: the Occupational Safety and Health Administration. Established under President Richard Nixon, OSHA (pronounced "Oh-Sha") has the dubious distinction of being the federal agency that business groups and conservative Republicans probably most detest. The *National Journal*— a nonpartisan source—has dubbed OSHA "the most reviled federal agency in Washington."[58]

OSHA is not, however, reviled by the public. Indeed, most Americans probably know little about it—which is precisely why it has proved such a good place for Republicans to direct their antiregulatory ire. But when asked, Americans do seem to like what it does. In 1997, the Council for Excellence in Government asked Americans how much they supported "enforcing workplace safety and health regulations."[59] Almost nine out of ten Americans said a "great deal" or a "fair amount"; only 3 percent said they did not support such enforcement at all. To give a sense of comparison, this was exactly the same level of support received by Medicare— one of America's most popular programs. By contrast, only a slim majority of Americans supported "welfare programs," and over 10 percent did not support them at all.

What is most notable about OSHA and its mandate, however, is how little knowledge there is of what it does. A humorous example is a poll conducted in 1999 about "ergonomics."[60] Even when given multiple choices, roughly a fifth of Americans thought the word was a polite way of describing corporate downsizing, another 20 percent or so thought it described a form of computer-assisted accounting, about 10 percent saw fit to volunteer a wrong answer of their own, and more than a fifth had no idea what it meant. Less than a third correctly answered that ergonomics described the tailoring of the work environment to prevent injury—and given the overall results, one has to conclude that many of these folks were just guessing. What makes the poll not simply humorous but revealing is that it was conducted when OSHA was designing new ergonomics standards to protect workers from repetitive stress injuries.

The important point about workplace safety, in short, is that it is the kind of low-profile area where public knowledge (but not necessarily public support) is low and where opinion polls are infrequent. As we noted in Chapter 1, we need to look at these areas alongside high-profile policy fights, because they are precisely where we should expect politicians to be least constrained by public opinion.

And in fact ergonomics was the first battleground in the assault on workplace regulation that Republicans launched after 2000.[61] Quickly and without comment, Congress and President Bush acted to block the implementation of new rules designed to address the alarming incidence of repetitive stress injuries. The rules had originated in the first Bush administration—more than a decade earlier—and two studies conducted by the National Academy of Sciences (with money appropriated by a Republican Congress) had underscored their need. But key corporations, such as UPS, FedEx, and Anheuser-Busch—all top GOP campaign donors—strenuously objected. The repeal passed narrowly, and almost completely along partisan lines, just a few days before the House's scheduled "bipartisan retreat" in early 2001. Exactly one hour was allocated for House debate.

The OSHA end-run required action on Congress's part, and in that respect it was more visible than many other recent workplace changes. (It was not visible enough, however, to warrant a single national poll.) Another controversy, no less significant for workers, has remained surprisingly low profile despite its huge potential implications: changes in the rules governing overtime pay. Roughly 80 percent of Americans are subject to overtime rules, and many of these workers depend on overtime pay for their livelihood. Bush's Labor Department, however, wanted to make overtime apply to a smaller share of workers. Although dispute over the exact effect of the proposed changes was fierce, employers and business groups—including the U.S. Chamber of Commerce and National Association of Manufacturers—strongly supported them on the grounds that they would reduce employer costs. Hewitt Associates, a leading human resources consultant, wrote in a memo to clients: "These proposed changes likely will open the door for employers to reclassify a large number of previously nonexempt employees as exempt. . . . [E]mployees previously accustomed to earning, in some cases, significant amounts of overtime pay would suddenly lose that opportunity."[62]

The stealth strategy of changing the overtime rules seemed to be humming along when cries of foul play by organized labor helped build momentum in the Senate for language that would block the changes. Bush quickly vowed to veto any spending bill that contained such a provision. But Democrats in the Senate managed to win sufficient Republican support to include it in a 2003 spending bill. GOP leaders, however, quickly mobilized to overturn this momentary setback. Once again the House-Senate conference committee provided the opening they needed. By threatening to strip more than $5 billion in health and education spending from the bill unless the provision was removed, they ensured that the new overtime rules would go into effect.

Thus, thanks to tight Republican coordination and control in Congress, Bush was spared of the need to go on the record vetoing legislation that would have saved existing overtime protections. Indeed, it is a measure of how disciplined, savvy, and firmly in command congressional Republicans are that President Bush has yet to veto a single bill. In January 2005, he became the first president to finish a full term without doing so since John Quincy Adams, our sixth president.

Although the overtime dispute never received much attention, it was high profile compared with the quiet changes to workplace regulations that the Bush administration has pursued.[63] In its first two years, the administration eliminated fifty-seven OSHA positions, and in 2004, it proposed cutting OSHA's budget and eliminating seventy-seven new positions, including sixty-four enforcement workers. The time spent on workplace inspections by OSHA's already-strapped personnel has declined. Average penalties for violations dropped by a quarter in Bush's first two years in office, while total penalties fell by more than 10 percent. This decline occurs, moreover, against the backdrop of weakening enforcement over the past two decades. A *New York Times* series on workplace deaths, for instance, concluded: "OSHA has increasingly helped employers, particularly large corporations, avoid the threat of prosecution altogether."[64]

Environmental Deregulation. In the Introduction, we described Christine Todd Whitman's *It's My Party, Too: The Battle for the Heart of the GOP and the Future of America*—the latest in a string of tell-alls by disgruntled moderates in the Bush administration.[65] Besides lamenting her party's right turn, Whitman also offers a rare inside glimpse of the making of environmental policy within the Bush White House. And what that glimpse shows is that much of the attack on existing environmental laws under Bush was done not through legislation but through stealth executive actions against which Whitman frequently fought.

Although Americans do not have simple or monolithic views about the environment, they are generally supportive of environmental causes and broadly sympathetic to the environmental movement. And on the question of whether government should regulate business to ensure that it does not pollute the air, water, or land, they are singularly aggressive. A 2002 CBS News/*New York Times* poll, for example, asked, "When it comes to regulating the environmental and safety practices of business, do you think the federal government is doing enough, should it do more, or should it do less?"[66] Strikingly, 67 percent of Americans felt that current regulation was insufficient; only 7 percent felt it was too aggressive. The poll then asked for respondents' views on the following statement: "Protecting the environment is so important that requirements and standards cannot be too high and continuing environmental improvements must be made regardless of the cost." The results: 57 percent of Americans agreed with this "costs-be-damned" perspective; only 36 percent disagreed. Public views on the environment have also remained quite stable, according to the General Social Survey.[67]

After 2000, however, the EPA's actions on the environment changed dramatically. The most rapid and obvious changes came in the form of "rollbacks" of tightened environmental standards adopted in previous years. On Bush's first day in office, his chief of staff issued a memorandum (of doubtful legality) that forbade all federal agencies from issuing new regulatory standards and placed a sixty-day stay on any standards promulgated at the end of the Clinton administration.[68] The Bush administration pulled out of the Kyoto Protocol, an international agreement to regulate carbon dioxide emissions to control global warming that Clinton had signed (but which still needed Senate approval). In March, Bush undercut his EPA administrator by reversing a campaign pledge to begin regulating carbon dioxide emissions—after the idea came under heavy fire from the energy industry.[69] The administration also indicated it would loosen a Clinton administration regulation that, when it took effect, would have lowered permissible amounts of arsenic in drinking water—then, revealingly, backtracked when the issue became public. And it all but abandoned ongoing litigation against power plants for violating the terms of the Clean Air Act, which required that older plants install modern pollution controls when they significantly upgraded their plants (a rule known as "New Source Review").

Bush's EPA administrator was not a fan of many of these changes. From her perch within the agency, Whitman wrote to Cheney (in a memo later leaked to environmentalists), "As we discussed, the real issue for industry is the enforcement cases. We will pay a terrible political price if we undercut or walk away from the enforcement cases; it will be hard to refute the charge that we are deciding not to enforce the Clean Air Act."[70] But the change was ordered ahead, and federal lawyers found themselves in the awkward position of denying the legal basis of claims they had previously made against energy producers.

The New Source Review program was one of the first major casualties of the White House attack on existing regulations. The energy industry representatives on Cheney's energy task force viewed the program as onerous. They wanted new pollution control measures to be required only if a plant made very large upgrades, and that is what they got. In 2002 and 2003, the EPA finalized new rules that allowed plants to make major upgrades even if doing so increased pollution. Under the new rules, antipollution technology had to be installed only if the value of the upgrades exceeded one fifth of the cost of all the equipment that the plant used to produce electricity, a very high level. "This appears to be the biggest rollback of the Clean Air Act in history," inveighed Senator James Jeffords, the former Republican from Vermont who became an Independent in 2001. "It is clear . . . that this administration is intent on undoing more than 25 years of progress on clean air."[71] In her account of her time at EPA, Whitman writes: "The major reforms were proposed after I had left the agency. I must say I'm glad that they weren't able to finish the work until after I was home in New Jersey."[72]

The New Source Review controversy was, however, only the most visible tip of an iceberg of changes in the EPA's basic stance. Indeed, most of the reversal and relaxation of environmental protections occurred through changes of the lowest possible profile.[73] The least visible of these low-profile shifts fall into a category that will be discussed in more depth shortly: failure to update existing regulations over time. For example, the EPA developed only three new regulatory standards during Bush's first three years. In contrast, the initial three years of his father's administration featured twenty-one new standards, and the initial three years of the Clinton administration, thirty. Plus, more than sixty new standards were under development when Clinton left office. All were abandoned.

Another low-profile change of perhaps even greater long-term significance is the decision to drastically curtail enforcement of existing laws. We have already mentioned the decision to undercut existing litigation against power-plant producers. But this about-face was a much more prominent gambit than the more common practice, which was simply to prevent the litigation in the first place. In Bush's first term, enforcement personnel within the EPA were cut by 12 percent, EPA inspections dropped by roughly three thousand a year, and civil environmental penalties fell by 50 percent. A careful investigation found a major shift in the enforcement of clean air laws against oil refineries, one of the nation's largest sources of pollution. In Bush's first term, "comprehensive clean-air inspections, a crucial step in identifying violations, are down 52 percent. . . . Notices of violations have plummeted 68 percent for refineries. . . . And formal enforcement actions are down 31 percent."[74] EPA's staff attorneys were required to clear all prosecution with the agency's top political appointees—a departure from past practice.

What connects all these changes is not just their consistent direction but also the difficulty of recognizing and mobilizing against them. Getting new legislation passed is a dramatic, high-conflict process. Getting new regulations in place is far less visible. Even less visible is moving to undercut existing regulations by failing to enforce them. And least visible of all, in many cases, is simply to do nothing. The most telling indication of the EPA's new stance—a stance at odds with Americans' support of environmental enforcement—is not what the agency has done; it is what it has not done, even as gaps and weaknesses in existing regulation have become apparent.

This is not an isolated story. In area after area, "Don't just do something, stand there," has become the new motto of America's political leadership.

Rule 4: "Don't Just Do Something, Stand There"

There is an old adage that lawyers like to quote: "If the facts are against you, argue the law. If the law is against you, argue the facts. If both the facts and the law are against you, change the subject." It is a useful bit of advice, and not just for lawyers. Savvy politicians know well that the deck is often stacked against direct policy change. That is why they have perfected a range of indirect, low-profile means of achieving what they want. But what if that, too, is impossible? What if both the facts and the law are against politicians? Well, then, changing the subject can be an extremely effective way for them to get what they want. Sometimes decisions *not* to act can be a powerful means of reshaping the role of government in the lives of Americans.[75]

Of course, given the near-infinite range of issues that government could address, not any old failure to act counts as an off-center strategy. What we are talking about here is deliberate obstruction in the face of significant popular support for government action. Obstruction of this sort does not, however, have to be highly visible. With control over the legislative agenda, the Republican leadership can generally keep matters quiet on issues it would rather not discuss.

As we have shown, Republican elites have pushed through some major legislative changes and overseen an important shift in the regulatory climate. But the GOP's power has not just stemmed from the ability to change policy directly (an ability that, as we have also shown, is certainly not unlimited). Engaging in the kind of behavior that psychiatrists would diagnose as "passive-aggressive," Republicans have also achieved important policy goals simply by doing nothing when doing something was widely demanded. We look at three examples of how active inaction works—from explicit decisions to allow laws that require reauthorization to die (the assault weapons ban) to successful blockage of modifications to laws that require periodic updating to be effective (the minimum wage) to keeping issues off the agenda that have life and death consequences for millions of Americans (health insurance).

Assaulting the Assault Weapons Ban. The assault weapons ban was passed in 1994 over the opposition of most congressional Republicans. It attempts to prevent the production or importation of a narrow range of weapons that have no use other than to kill large numbers of people quickly. Every major law enforcement organization supported the ban in 1994, and it was overwhelmingly popular.[77] To get the bill passed, however, President Clinton agreed to let the bill expire in 2004. Since its passage, the National Rifle Association, an organizational foundation of the Republican base, has waged a relentless campaign to repeal the ban. Support for repeal was one of the leading criteria the NRA used in deciding whether to endorse and work for congressional candidates.

In 1996, the GOP leadership managed to get a repeal through the House, but not the Senate. Success finally came, however, when the Republicans could achieve their goal by doing nothing. With the ban set to expire, Republicans were able to block Democratic efforts to renew it. In a purely theatrical moderate gesture of a kind that we will see repeatedly throughout this book, President Bush earnestly announced that he would sign a renewal. Unsurprisingly, he made no effort to pressure Congress to act. The ban therefore lapsed in September 2004. Gun manufacturers are now free to make AK-47s and other semi-automatic assault weapons again.

Minimizing the Minimum Wage. The minimum wage—the lowest amount that employers are allowed to pay most workers, now $5.15 an hour—is not adjusted for inflation. Its value therefore declines over time unless Congress and the President agree to raise it, and for many years they routinely did. The minimum wage, however, has not been raised since 1996. Today, a full-time minimum wage worker makes $10,712 per year, well below the poverty line for a family. Indeed, the minimum wage would have had to have been raised to $8.49 in 2004 to equal the purchasing power it had in 1964. David Lee, an economist at the University of California at Berkeley, has concluded that failure to increase the minimum wage accounts for about half the increase in the disparity between average wages and the wages of workers in the bottom tenth of the wage distribution.[78]

By 2004, 94 percent of Americans favored an increase in the minimum wage.[79] But Republicans have resisted. As a *New York Times* article noted in 2004, "The Republicans are the obstacle; they say so themselves, although they are less outspoken in an election year. Their constituents include tens of thousands of small-business owners who pay their employees the minimum wage and don't want it to rise."[80] During the campaign of 2004, Bush said he would support a Senate bill sponsored by Republican Mitch McConnell of Kentucky. It raised the minimum wage less than Democrats wanted and included still more new tax breaks for small businesses. McConnell never introduced his bill.

Halting Health Reform. The number of Americans with workplace health coverage—long in decline—has fallen steadily since Bush entered office, mainly because of skyrocketing insurance costs. State-run programs for lower-income Americans have covered some of the loss. But the number of Americans who lack insurance nonetheless rose to an all-time high of forty-five million in 2003—five million higher than in 2000.[81] Americans see growing medical costs and the rising number of uninsured as two of the most important issues facing the nation.[82] And, overwhelmingly, they support the expansion of public programs to reach low-income families disadvantaged by these trends.

Yet Bush and congressional Republicans have failed to pass a single bill substantially expanding the reach of health coverage. To the extent that they have talked about health care at all, they have focused on medical liability reform and Health Savings Accounts, neither of which will make a real dent in the number of uninsured. (In fact, as already noted, HSAs could increase the number of uninsured by encouraging affluent and healthy Americans to drop out of group health insurance, increasing the cost for those left behind.) Indeed, Bush's budgets for 2004, 2005, and 2006 included measures that would cut back public programs for the poor and disabled.[83] Democrats and some moderate Republicans have resisted such changes, and they may successfully do so again. But while the battle rages, the ranks of the uninsured grow.

As the conflicts over assault weapons, the minimum wage, and health care suggest, inaction is often especially valuable for conservatives. It is an important element of the conservative credo, after all, that government should be restrained—at least when it comes to providing retirement and health security, regulating corporations, controlling firearms, and the like. Frequently what conservatives want government to do is nothing, especially when standing still actually means that government will, over time, be doing less and less. This is yet another reason why increasing partisan polarization does not affect Republicans and Democrats equally. To the extent that polarization makes it less likely that our convoluted system of checks and balances will act, it often—though, of course, not always—plays into the hands of the antigovernment party.

Rule 5: "Starve the Beast—Later"

One area where Republicans have been eager to act, of course, has been tax cuts. But here, too, there is a broader strategy for advancing a long-run antigovernment agenda: stepping firmly on the hose that funnels tax revenues to Washington. Tax cuts deliver benefits to key Republican constituencies, which makes them valuable to the GOP cause. They also abet deficits, which makes them even more valuable. For deficits are perhaps the most powerful weapon that Republicans have for restricting and reshaping American government. Like a sinking ship, fiscal scarcity creates the need for unpleasant choices; somebody must go overboard. And just as a ship may sink long after the decisions that caused it to run aground were made, the unpleasant choices that rising deficits will force on American government will be on the agenda long after the tax cuts were enacted—which is exactly how Republicans want it.

The first big foray of the post-Reagan Republican Revolution faltered in the mid-1990s, when President Clinton was able to outmaneuver Newt Gingrich by successfully linking proposed tax cuts to unpopular spending cuts.[84] But Republicans appear to have learned their lesson. The current GOP strategy is to separate these two sides of the budgetary coin as much as possible. Tax cuts come first; spending cuts only later, when their link to tax cuts will be much less clear.

A facetious law of economics attributed to Herbert Stein holds that "things that can't go on forever, won't." And, indeed, tax cuts without spending cuts cannot go on. But the day of reckoning so feared by many will be joyously (if privately) welcomed by conservatives who hope to "starve the beast" of the federal government. With tax cuts locked in, they believe the only piggybank left to raid will be the huge middle-class programs that make up the vast bulk of federal spending. As conservative GOP consultant Chuck Muth explained in August 2001, "If we want smaller, less-intrusive government, we have to 'starve the beast.' Cutting their allowance is the only way to put politicians on a spending leash. And that means tax cuts, tax cuts and more tax cuts."[85] To be sure, deficits will mean tougher scrutiny of even Republican priorities. Yet as the rhetoric of tax-cut crusaders suggests, there is good reason to believe that the fiscal crunch will hurt Democratic aims much more. After all, it is Republican majorities that decide which programs to slash. Equally important, deep deficits will make "Don't just do something, stand there," the new official motto of the government, preventing Democrats from achieving such goals as broadened health coverage and increased education spending. "Starve the beast—later" is a high-stakes gamble, but it is one Republicans expect to win.

Rule 6: "Tilt the Playing Field"

In shifting policy off center, Republicans have used all the weapons of political warfare that the rules of American government give them (and arguably a few the rules don't). But they have also worked energetically to tilt the political playing field ever further in their favor. This last set of changes—changes in the rules themselves—is the GOP's new punch line to the old lawyer's joke: "If both the facts and the law are against you, change the rules." But the goal, in the Republicans' case, is not to win a court battle; it is to move the United States closer toward a true one-party state in which the only compromises that have to be made are made among Republicans.

The battle over rules is an element of political conflict that goes on all the time, often below the radar screen. Occasionally, however, it rises into public view, as two recent high-profile examples indicate. In Texas in the lead-up to the election of 2004, Republicans and Democrats sparred dramatically over reapportionment—the seemingly arcane matter of drawing boundaries for congressional districts. What made the Texas battle so visible was that it occurred outside the normal postcensus schedule of redistricting and that Tom DeLay helped orchestrate it to augment the

Republicans' majority in Congress. As we discuss in more depth in the next chapter, partisan redistricting has been an increasingly important tool for creating safe seats and allowing a legislative majority to get the biggest political advantage possible. As the Republicans' off-cycle redistricting of Texas soon showed, the impact can be enormous. Were it not for DeLay's successful maneuver, Democrats would have gained seats in the House in 2004 rather than losing ground. Pleased with the results of 2004, Republicans have started to discuss further off-cycle redistricting efforts to add Republican seats in the future.

In the spring of 2005, the Republican leadership in the Senate also inched toward "the nuclear option"—a parliamentary maneuver requiring just fifty Senate votes that would allow the Senate's presiding officer (who just happens to be Vice President Cheney) to issue a ruling that would prevent filibusters of judicial nominations. This would shift the number of votes needed to approve court nominees from sixty to fifty. If Republicans succeed in this audacious move—and even after a hastily devised deal among Senate moderates in May that kept the "nuclear option" temporarily at bay, it remains a key goal of Republican leaders—they will have greatly increased their capacity to remake the court along conservative lines.

The stakes could scarcely be higher. Although the battle is ostensibly over nominations for the Circuit Courts of Appeals, everyone knows that the big battle will be over the Supreme Court. The Court currently lacks a working majority of extreme conservatives who consistently see eye-to-eye with their counterparts in Congress and the White House. Outside observers agree that it would take no more than two additions to the Court's conservative wing to change that. In short, Senate Republicans are eager to change the rules within their chamber so that they can appoint like-minded people to serve as the ultimate referees in the American polity.

The composition of the Court will effect the determination not only of high-profile issues like abortion. It will shape all major areas of public policy. And it will shape future conflicts over such basic rules of political contestation as apportionment and campaign finance. As the political scientist Thomas Keck demonstrates in his aptly titled *The Most Activist Supreme Court in History,* despite the rhetoric of "judicial restraint," the

Rehnquist Court has shown little reticence about imposing its will on elected officials.[86] Indeed, since 1994, the Court has been striking down federal laws at an unprecedented rate. Doctrines have been developed, especially related to federalism, that would constrain or prohibit federal action in a wide range of areas. In the vision of the Court's most conservative members, these doctrines lay a foundation for much more far-reaching efforts to reimpose a pre–New Deal vision of the appropriate role of the federal government—irrespective of public views on this fundamental question.[87]

One feature unites the battles in Texas and the Senate. Each reflects the Republican Party's ambition to translate the same number of votes (both popular votes and votes in Congress) into much greater political power. Wherever they can, Republicans are using their majority powers to change the rules to their political advantage—and further decrease the hold of the ordinary voter and the political center. The success of these efforts strengthens the Party's hand as it moves to the next round of policy struggles. Yet the ultimate destination sought by strategists like Karl Rove and Tom DeLay is more ambitious: a permanent party of government.

Republicans are not there—yet. But, as this chapter has made clear, the playing field of American politics already exhibits a marked tilt in favor of the conservative agenda. On a range of issues of great importance to the American people, Republicans have been able to work with very thin majorities to produce off-center shifts in policy. They are not always successful. When opposition is well organized, when the sixty-vote hurdle in the Senate cannot be avoided, and when issues are both high profile and present themselves in clear terms, their capacity to move off center remains circumscribed. But with their new rules for radicals, Republicans have frequently found it possible to stray far from the moderate center of the electorate and win.

In sum, Republicans are running the show in American politics. They are doing so in opposition to the moderate center of public opinion. And they are getting away with it. How can this be? What changes in American politics have made this unlikely vision a reality? Why have Republicans sought to do so much at odds with public opinion, and why haven't they paid a price for doing so? These are the questions we take up in Part II.

PART

BROKEN CHECKS AND BALANCES

4

THE RACE TO THE BASE

When Republican Marge Roukema of New Jersey was swept into Congress on the wave of Ronald Reagan's victory in 1980, she became one of only nine Republican women in the House of Representatives. In most other ways, however, she was emblematic of the moderate Northeastern "gypsy moths" who formed a decisive voting bloc within the congressional GOP—a fiscal conservative who was broadly supportive of tax cuts yet favorable toward social programs and generally moderate on social issues. Roukema made waves in the late 1980s when she spearheaded efforts to pass a family leave bill, which Congress eventually enacted under President Clinton in 1993. But she was no Democrat in Republican clothing. Roukema backed Reagan's tax cuts in 1981, supported a balanced budget amendment, and defended the death penalty. She also was committed to climbing the internal ladder of the House to power, declaring in 1981 that the committee system was where she would make her biggest mark.[1]

When Roukema retired from Congress in 2002, there were eighteen Republican women in the House—a modest twenty-year gain. But everything else had changed dramatically. Roukema was no longer one of many moderates in the Republican caucus. She was one of only a handful. And far from holding a position of prominence, Roukema had seen the prize committee chair for which she was in line yanked out from under her by Tom DeLay, who privately accused her of insufficient fundraising on behalf of the Republican cause. Dispirited by two tough primary challenges from her right—the second financed lavishly by the anti-tax Club for Growth—and facing yet another primary fight without the support of DeLay or his political action committee (PAC), Roukema announced her retirement. "That's the way it's done these days," Roukema later said of DeLay's strong-arm tactics.[2] What she didn't have to say is that it was not the way it had been done when she entered Congress. Back then, Roukema had said that being in Congress was "everything I had hoped it to be, and more."[3] Twenty-two years later, she left Congress with less power than she started with, spurned by her own party's leadership.

Marge Roukema experienced firsthand the iron-fisted control of the tough GOP operatives we have called the New Power Brokers. But as Roukema's experience shows, the influence of these brokers reflects a much bigger shift in the American political universe—the growing pull of the Republican base. It used to be said, as Reagan-era House Speaker Tip O'Neill put it, that "all politics is local"—that national forces mattered much less than local concerns.[4] But the old-style Democrat was speaking at the end of an era. Republican Dick Armey, the ultraconservative House majority leader of the Gingrich years, much better captured contemporary reality when he replaced O'Neill's maxim with another: "The first rule of politics is: Never offend your base."[5]

The "base" is a party's most committed and intense supporters: the first line of support, the leading source of money, the wellspring of ideological purity. Pleasing the base has always been part of a politician's job. Yet in the years that trace the arc of Roukema's increasingly frustrating congressional career, it has become a much more important part, especially on the Republican side of the aisle. In the process, the Republican Party has changed fundamentally. Marge Roukema was hardly the only Northeastern "gypsy moth" when she came to Congress, and she often found herself allied with another now-near-extinct political insect, the "boll weevil"—centrist to conservative Democrats from the South. Like the bug exterminator he once was, Tom DeLay has been on a crusade to kill off these pesky remnants of the ancient regime. Boll weevils still hang on, but they no longer form a large moderate bloc. Instead, conservative Republicans have come to dominate the once safely Democratic South and, with it, the GOP and its leadership. Meanwhile, Republican moderates from the Northeast have gradually retired, lost office—or reluctantly tacked right. Marge Roukema's unceremonious exit from Congress captures, in miniature, the more than twenty-year decline of the moderate wing of her party.

These trends have made the GOP a consistently and fiercely conservative party. Perhaps more important, they have also made it a party that is much more willing and capable of deploying its growing powers to achieve its goals. The base provides energy and intensity, but it is a powerful force without precise focus. The task of providing that focus has fallen to the New Power Brokers, who have pursued a partisan grand strategy of breathtaking ambition and scope.

The relationship between the brokers and the base is symbiotic. On issue after issue, party leaders have responded not to the center of congressional opinion (much less of American opinion) but to the interests and demands of their base, aggressively structuring agendas and alternatives to please the hard Right. Yet party leaders have done more than work with the party material they have—they have sought to tame or weed out politicians deemed feckless and to elect or elevate those deemed loyal. The base plays a crucial role in this process of recruitment and discipline. They certify and work for conservative candidates, they keep conservative issues and ideas in the spotlight, and they threaten the politically wayward with excommunication. And so, election by election, the pull of the base grows and the sway of the center declines.

This chapter tours the new political landscape over which the Republican base towers, tracing the roots of the ultra-Right's growing sway. It begins at the ground level, so to speak: the increased inequality of resources and organization between the rich, the radical, and the rest. It then moves up from the ground to examine the intertwined transformations of the Republican Party, exploring how the increasingly conservative (and increasingly Southern) leadership of the GOP has reflected and refracted the growing power of the base in its successful quest to reshape the party it heads. The next two chapters show how, in responding to and cultivating this base, the New Power Brokers have audaciously pursued their conservative aims, steamrollering their opponents and the political center in their headlong race to the base.

America Unequal

As we will see, the race to the base has been fueled by many forces—from the growing role of the parties in campaign finance to the proliferation of districts safe for one party or the other. Yet perhaps the most basic source of the base's increasing influence is the growing political leverage of the well off and well organized. Over the past thirty years, American politics has become more money-centered at exactly the same time that American society has grown more unequal.[6] The resources and organizational heft of the well off and hyperconservative have exploded. But the organizational resources of middle-income Americans—from labor unions to mass-membership groups—have atrophied. The resulting inequality of resources and organization has not been neutral in its effects. It has greatly benefited the Republican Party while drawing it closer to its most affluent and extreme supporters.

"What else is new?" a skeptic might ask. Republicans have always been the party of business and the rich, and Democrats the party of the "little man." Yet the gap between the "big man" and the "little man" is much greater than it was two decades ago. Between 1979 and 2002, the average after-tax income of the richest 1 percent of Americans more than doubled, increasing from around $300,000 (in 2002 dollars) to more than $630,000.[7] By contrast, the average income of Americans on the middle of the economic ladder rose by a comparatively modest 15 percent, while the poorest fifth of Americans saw only a 5 percent increase.[8] Wealth is even more concentrated at the top, with the wealthiest 1 percent controlling nearly two-fifths of the nation's household wealth—higher than at any point in American history since 1929.[9]

It would be comforting to conclude that this dramatic increase in economic inequality has had no effect on *political* equality in the United States. Yet both common sense and a growing body of evidence suggest otherwise. Let us start with the most basic resource—not bills but ballots. As is widely known, turnout of the voting-age population in presidential elections has declined since the 1960s, a striking fact given that

Americans are increasingly well educated and the best educated are most likely to vote.* In 2000, for instance, barely more than half of the voting-age population cast a ballot. Turnout rose in the exceptionally combative election of 2004. Yet despite much celebration of the "highest turnout in history," the proportion (rather than the raw number) of people that went to the polls was essentially the same as in 1992—and lower than every presidential election between 1948 and 1972.

Less well known is how skewed voting is by income. In 2000, more than 40 percent of those in the bottom third of the income spectrum reported that they did not vote, compared with just 13 percent of those in the top third.[10] And the gap is probably growing. One recent study found that voter turnout rose by 5 percent among the richest fifth of the population between 1964 and 1988 *yet* fell by 14 percent among the poorest fifth.[11] A perfectly middle-class voter would be richer than half of Americans and poorer than half. In 2000, a voter in the middle of voters' income distribution was richer than three-fifths of Americans.

And turnout is by far the most *equally* distributed of political resources. On the other side of the spectrum is money, and money has become far more important in American politics than it was a generation ago. In 1974, the average candidate successfully challenging a sitting member of the House of Representatives spent around $100,000 in real terms (that is, adjusted for inflation). In 2002, the average winning challenger spent more than $1.5 million.[12] Between 1980 and 2000, the average expenditure of Senate campaigns more than doubled in real dollars and the cost or running for an open Senate seat increased more than sixfold.[13] Indeed, the midterm election of 2002 was by far the most expensive off-year election in history, exceeding the 1998 midterm by an astonishing 50 percent. Whatever other effects political money has, the dramatic rise in the cost of campaigns means that candidates are reaching out to donors much more often and aggressively than in the past.

---

* The decline is less striking, however, when the rising numbers of U.S. residents *ineligible* to vote, such as ex-felons, are taken into account. Still, in only two presidential elections since 1972 has the share of those eligible to vote who go to the polls exceeded 60 percent—a standard exceeded in every postwar presidential election but one up to that point.

And who they are reaching out to is not ordinary Americans. If the typical voter is slightly richer than average, the typical individual contributor is vastly richer. In 2000, an eighth of American households enjoyed annual incomes greater than $100,000. Yet these fortunate households made up 95 percent of those who gave a thousand dollars or more to political campaigns that year.[14] According to research by Harvard political scientist Andrea Campbell, the parties each directly contacted about a quarter (the Democratic Party) to a third (the Republican Party) of the wealthiest Americans in 2000, up from less than 15 percent in the 1950s.[15] This should come as no surprise. Almost every adult has the vote. Many have at least a little time to commit to politics. But scant few have the resources to become big campaign givers. Across all forms of political participation—voting, campaign work, community activism, membership in a political group—contributing is the political activity most marked by economic bias. And it is precisely the political activity that today's costly media-centered campaigns devour. As money has come to dominate, politics has become more like the parable in Matthew 13: "For whosoever hath, to him shall be given, and he shall have more abundance."

A glimpse at the effects of this growing skew can be found in a recent study by Princeton political scientist Larry Bartels. Comparing senators' voting patterns with the opinions of constituents in their states, Bartels found that senators (and especially Republican senators) appeared most attentive to constituents at the top of the income ladder while ignoring almost entirely those at or near the bottom. Even moderately well-off voters were much more likely—about three times as likely, in fact—to see their views on public policy reflected in their senators' votes than were Americans of more modest means.[16]

Political inequality of this sort is a cause for concern whichever party it favors. But make no mistake: A system biased in favor of well-off voters is also a system biased in favor of the Republican Party. *New York Times* columnist David Brooks and others have had much fun casting the battle between Republicans and Democrats as a clash of civilizations between decadent, highbrow coastal regions and the patriotic, lowbrow heartland.[17] Yet traditional economic divisions have not been supplanted by a culture war between tolerant, latte-sipping progressives and patriotic, NASCAR-loving traditionalists. To the contrary: Class is actually an increasingly important dividing line between the parties. Since the 1950s, the relation between income and party allegiance—with poor and working-class voters favoring the Democrats—has become *stronger*, not weaker.[18]

The obvious problem for Democrats is that the appeals that they might use to reach downscale voters are less naturally resonant with the affluent than are the Republicans' anti-tax, antigovernment themes. So while both parties have felt compelled to mobilize higher-income citizens, the Republicans have found the goal much more consistent with their aims. For them, the money chase reinforces their core antigovernment message. For Democrats, it blunts the traditional populist rhetoric of the party (and potentially reinforces negative stereotypes about the party's penchant for the permissive social liberalism of Brooks's latte-sipping left).

The deeper problem for the Democrats, however, is organizational. At the height of the post–New Deal party system of the 1950s and 1960s, a powerful network of organizations, integrated with a locally rooted Democratic Party structure, represented middle-income Americans on pocketbook matters. These organizations have dramatically weakened, leaving many who once depended on them unmoored from the kinds of intermediate groups that are necessary for true influence. Little surprise, then, that lower-income Americans are only about a third as likely as the affluent to belong to an organization that takes a stand on public issues.[19]

Consider trade unions, which once represented more than one in three workers in the United States (and, indirectly, those workers' families). Since the 1970s, the proportion of workers that is unionized has plummeted, and today less than a tenth of private-sector workers belong to a union.[20] Amid the ongoing debate over whether unions are good for the economy, we often forget that they have always been crucial *political* actors, helping workers identify common issues, informing them about political and policy considerations, and shaping political debates. No organization representing working families today has anything remotely like the same reach, influence, or cohesion as American unions did during their halcyon years.

The decline of unions stands out as the biggest change in the political representation of lower-income and middle-class voters. Yet, as political scientist Theda Skocpol has shown, organized labor is certainly not the only "voluntary membership-based association" that has been in a tailspin. As recently as a few decades ago, so-called fraternal organizations—

for example, the Elks and Shriners—and other nation-spanning voluntary federations provided important forms of civic education and political leverage to large swaths of the population. "For millions of citizens," Skocpol explains, "federations offered ways to work together—to 'combine' nationally as well as locally—and thereby had an impact on public opinion and the actions of government."[21] They were also true "cross-class" associations, bringing together both the upper and lower rungs of the economic ladder to discuss common issues and pursue shared goals.

Since the 1970s, however, such large-scale membership organizations have been in steep decline. Meanwhile, the number of business and professional groups has exploded. Business associations have always had a prominent place on the political landscape. But today, they lobby and contribute as never before. And although corporate America faces organized challengers on consumer and environmental issues, it is now almost the only loud voice on most economic and business issues. A report issued by the American Political Science Association in 2004, *American Democracy in an Age of Rising Inequality*, noted that less-advantaged Americans "are so absent from discussions in Washington that government officials are likely to hear about their concerns, if at all, from more privileged advocates who speak for the disadvantaged. Politicians hear most regularly about the concerns of business and the most affluent."[22]

Rising economic inequality, in short, has abetted political inequality, hardened the class divisions between the parties, and bolstered the GOP in particular. For well-off Americans, the political world is increasingly their oyster: They vote in high numbers, contribute with abandon, and happily watch as politicians compete for their favor. For less well-off Americans, the political world looks ever more forbidding. Largely neglected by the parties, reliant on the media and candidates for basic information, they have to work ever harder just to have their voices heard. And as the political influence of business and the well off has grown, the political influence of the Republican Party has grown, too.

Southern Comfort

If Republicans have benefited from the growing clout of their most affluent and ideologically committed supporters, they have also benefited from a great *geographic* shift in the electoral roots of the parties. Although the New Deal coalition that ruled Congress with only brief interruptions through the 1970s was popularly identified with the Northern working class, its geographic backbone was the solidly Democratic South. One-party rule in the South not only ensured large congressional majorities for the Democratic Party; it also placed Southern Democrats at the pinnacles of congressional power by virtue of a seniority system that favored long-serving members of Congress who haled from safe, one-party districts.

Today, however, the solid Democratic South is dead and buried, replaced with a less solid but even more influential Republican South. Between 1974 and 2004, the party breakdown of House members from the eleven former states of the confederacy reversed—from two-thirds Democrat to almost two-thirds Republican.[23] As everyone who follows politics knows, this massive transformation is the key to understanding the Republican Party's capture of Congress in the 1990s. It is less well recognized as one of the chief reasons why American politics has shifted so significantly to the right. Southern Democrats of yore were certainly conservative compared with their Democratic brethren. Yet on every issue but race relations, they were usually more liberal than are today's Southern Republicans. The increasing Republicanism of the South is the most immediate cause of the increasing conservatism of the Republican Party.

To be sure, while the South was heading into the Republican fold, the rest of the nation was not standing still. In the Northeast—to cite the major countervailing trend—moderate Republicans have faced increasingly tough sledding. And of course, the Democratic Party has also been transformed by the decimation of its conservative Southern wing.

Yet the big story is the right turn of the GOP. Sean Theriault of the University of Texas has examined, seat by seat, the ideological shift of Congress over the past thirty years.[24] And what he has found offers a striking window into the Southern-led transformation of the GOP. The single leading cause of the rightward shift of the Republican Party, Theriault finds, is the replacement of moderate Southern Democrats by conservative Republicans. Indeed, virtually all of the divergence of the parties caused by cross-party replacement (Democrats replacing Republicans, and vice versa) is accounted for by the replacement of

Southern Democrats by Republicans. Moderate Republicans have indeed lost to Democrats in the Northeast, but this has had only a marginal effect on the average position of the two parties.

The cross-party replacement of Democrats by Republicans in the South, moreover, is not the only cause of increased Republican conservatism. Almost as important, Theriault's research shows, is the replacement of Republicans by *Republicans.* When Republicans defeat or succeed other Republicans, they are generally much more ideologically extreme than their predecessors. This is considerably less true, it turns out, among Democrats.

Perhaps the biggest finding, however, is that Republican members of Congress generally head right once in office. Such "adaptation" (as Theriault calls it) has been a major cause of the increasing ideological extremism of the Republican Party, nearly equaling the replacement of existing members of Congress in its aggregate effect. Again, the same is not true of the Democratic Party. The bulk of congressional adaptation, notes Theriault, "occurs within Republican Party members" as they march steadily rightward over their careers.

In short, Democrats and Republicans have polarized, but at profoundly different paces and for profoundly different reasons. Democrats as a whole have clearly grown more liberal. But this is almost entirely because of the loss of their most conservative Southern members. Outside the South, Democrats are roughly as liberal, on average, as they were thirty years ago. The typical Republican politician, however, is much more fiercely and consistently conservative than the GOP stalwarts of thirty years ago—both in the South and outside it. The Republican Party has been transformed across the board. It has not simply added a new conservative Southern wing. It has undergone a top-to-bottom makeover that has exerted a strong rightward pull on Republican districts and Republican politicians throughout the country.

And if the typical Republican politician is different, the typical Republican leader is an entirely new creature. Republicans in Congress used to be split down the middle between their moderate wing and their more conservative members. As a result, their leadership was usually drawn from the center and, often, the Northeast and Midwest. Senate Minority Leader Hugh Scott of Pennsylvania and House Minority

Leader Gerald Ford of Michigan—bland, careful legislators with middle-of-the-road views—were quintessential Republican leaders of the 1970s.

The current leadership of the House and Senate is, of course, scarcely bland or middle-of-the-road. It is superconservative and mostly Southern. Texan Tom DeLay is second in command behind Speaker of the House Dennis Hastert. A Midwesterner, Hastert succeeds the great Southern firebrand of the modern GOP, former Speaker of the House Newt Gingrich of Georgia. DeLay, for his part, succeeds another Texan, the previously mentioned Dick Armey.

The Senate has been slower to succumb to the Southern juggernaut. But in 1994, Trent Lott of Mississippi—who in 2002 gained infamy for his praise of Strom Thurmond's 1948 presidential run on the arch-segregationist "Dixiecrat" ticket—took the number-two GOP position by just one vote from moderate Alan Simpson of Wyoming, the chosen candidate of Republican chieftain Bob Dole. He then rose to the top spot, before the furor over his comments about Thurmond derailed his bid to maintain his leadership post. His successor, however, is another Southerner: Bill Frist of Tennessee. Frist is backed up by Mitch McConnell of Kentucky. And, of course, there is Texan George W. Bush in the White House. It is nearly a Southern clean sweep. On most maps, the South doesn't sit atop the nation. But for a decade now, it has sat atop our nation's political hierarchy.

Does this make a real difference? The leadership, after all, can't lead without the support of its followers. Among professional students of Congress, sharp disputes center on the role of party leaders. Do they simply do the bidding of party members, or do they push party members to adopt positions different from those they would have embraced otherwise?[25] Without delving too far into the debate—which we take up in the next chapter—we can say that it *does* matter immensely what party leaders want and do. Little noticed by most Americans, a major shift has taken place in Congress over the past two decades. Power is much more centralized, and that centralized power is used much more aggressively. The Southern right-wingers are not simply titular heads of their party; they are increasingly running the show.

What is more, it is a profound mistake to assume that party leaders have power only to the extent that they press members of Congress to depart from their own personal ideologies. Perhaps the most important ways in which the GOP elite shapes what Republican members do have nothing to do with changing members' minds. They have to do with selecting the issues on which members take a stand ("agenda setting") and selecting the politicians who are taking the stand ("recruitment"). Indeed, perhaps the most important reason why rank-and-file Republicans are so much more favorable toward conservative projects is the GOP's increasing ability to recruit and certify politicians *before* they enter office. If today's Republican leaders rarely have to twist the arms of the unfaithful, that's in crucial part because they have worked so hard to ensure that only the faithful are there in the first place.

But, of course, these elites do not act alone. Their influence rests on the powerful organizational supports that they can marshal to their causes. The foundations of this Republican base include the true grassroots—the Christian Right, the small business lobby, the NRA, and other widely federated conservative organizations with strong local ties. Above the grassroots lies the elite interest groups and political action committees that do so much of the day-to-day lobbying and fundraising in Washington and the hinterlands. Inside the Beltway, they are flanked by the growing assemblage of conservative think tanks that have become a fixture on the Washington political landscape since the 1970s, such as the Cato Institute, Heritage Foundation, and American Enterprise Institute. These organizations and groups do not always see eye to eye, much less speak in perfect unison. But for more than a decade, the New Power Brokers have worked—and, against the backdrop of America's fragmented constitutional structure, have proved remarkably able—to tie together this loosely knit network of conservative activists and institutions and direct it toward nationally determined and carefully delimited ends. (For those who want to know more about how they actually do this, we can only urge patience: Much of Chapter 5 is devoted to explaining the brokers' surprising success.)

The goal of these complex activities is ultimately simple: to encourage the right turn of the GOP through electoral replacement and ideological adaptation. But the story of how the base and the brokers have replaced moderates with loyalists, and frightened many of the moderates who remain into submission, is a rich tale filled with tur-

moil, tragedy, and triumph. To start the story, we need to head
north—to the comfortable New Jersey suburbs where the conservative
base and GOP elite waged what seemed a long-odds campaign for
Republican purity, and won.

Roukema's Last Stand

If you want to understand the power of today's right-wing network, you need go no farther than Marge Roukema's old congressional
district, the New Jersey Fifth. It is an unlikely destination for those interested in understanding the pull of the Republican base. Stretching from
well-off Bergen County into northernmost New Jersey, it has "the well-
settled look of so many northeastern suburbs, with touches both of afflu-
ence and small-town hominess, criss-crossed at its edges with limited
access highways lined with shopping centers."[26] Although it was one of
only two New Jersey districts won by George W. Bush in 2000, its constituency is scarcely a model of hard-right conservatism, as moderate
Roukema's long tenure suggests. Indeed, many believed Roukema's departure would put the district in the Democratic column, which makes
what actually happened all the more revealing of the base's sway.[27]

Scott Garrett, the Republican who now represents the Fifth District,
could not be more different from Marge Roukema. A former trial lawyer,
he began his political career in the New Jersey statehouse in the late 1980s
and quickly became known as its most conservative legislator. Whereas
Roukema was a pragmatic supporter of tax hikes to rein in the deficit,
Garrett loudly proclaimed to have never voted for a tax increase of any
kind. (In 2003 he received the "Hero of the Taxpayer" Award from
Americans for Tax Reform. The award is given to members that side with
ATR's anti-tax agenda on at least 85 percent of key votes; Garrett voted
with the organization 100 percent of the time.) Whereas Roukema was a
social moderate who supported abortion rights and gun control, Garrett
was a social conservative who opposed both. He was also fiercely antigovernment in outlook, going so far as to vote against radon testing in
daycare centers and minimum hospital stays for women who had just
had mastectomies because government should not regulate private
enterprise.[28]

It hardly takes a political scientist to spot the differences between Garrett and Roukema. The up-and-coming conservative made them crystal clear by running against the veteran congresswoman not once but twice, savaging her for her social liberalism and her less-than-religious commitment to tax-cutting. Garrett's runs were lavishly financed by the Club for Growth, another anti-tax organization, which often targets moderate Republicans for defeat. When Roukema—twice nearly beaten by Garrett, lacking the support of Tom DeLay and the rest of the Republican leadership, tired of the political grind and, it turned out, sick with cancer—finally stepped aside, the Club for Growth was there to help out Garrett again, spending heavily in the Republican primary to tar his two major opponents (one was "backed by liberal groups like the Sierra Club," according to a slick club ad; the other was "a 23-year Trenton insider who voted to raise taxes 23 times").[29] The National Rifle Association pulled out all the stops on Garrett's behalf as well, and perhaps most crucial, so did the Republican Party. Issue ads financed by the Republican National Campaign Committee flooded the airwaves in the final days of the campaign. Perhaps the most devastating suggested that Garrett's Democratic opponent was anti-American for warning against "jingoistic patriotism" in the wake of 9/11.[30]

For all the idiosyncrasies of New Jersey politics, Scott Garrett's road to a congressional seat that is now considered safe for the foreseeable future is not unusual. Indeed, occurring in a relatively moderate Republican district, Garrett's journey *understates* the power of the Republican base in the growing number of districts that are locked up for the party. Tracing the circuitous path by which a modern ideologue came to replace an old-style centrist reveals three great lessons about how the Republican base has come to dominate the selection of GOP foot soldiers in Congress.

Primary Colors

The first lesson is that primaries matter. Garrett softened up Roukema before her retirement with two near misses that forced the sitting congresswomen to spend all her campaign funds (thus angering the Republican House leadership, which criticized her for failing to give money to other GOP candidates). Even though Roukema managed to hold him at bay, his challenges pushed her to the right during her time in office, and they were the key reason for her exit from Congress. Garrett then outflanked two moderate primary opponents (who split the centrist Republican vote) by appealing directly to the most conservative members of his primary constituency in a typically low-turnout primary in which the most ideologically enthused disproportionately came out. What Garrett knew, and his opponents underestimated, is that in primaries, the base rules.

Primary contests have become more important than they once were not because they are more common—they aren't—but because more and more congressional districts are safe for one party or the other. Mark Gersh, the Washington director of the National Committee for an Effective Congress, puts the point bluntly: "No matter how the voters feel, about 90 percent of the districts are now preordained to go to a certain party."[31] In 2004, fewer than 30 House races (out of 435) were won by 55 percent of the vote or less, compared with 96 races a decade earlier. The issue is not just that incumbents cannot be beat. Even so-called open races, in which no incumbent is on the ballot, have become strikingly uncompetitive—and they have become most uncompetitive when they favor Republicans. Only four of twenty open seats won by Republicans in 2004 were won with 55 percent or less of the vote, a modern low. And in those races, Democrats were outspent almost fifteen to one, strongly indicating that they knew they would lose.[32] Increasingly, the greatest electoral challenge facing most congressional officeholders and aspirants—especially Republican officeholders and aspirants—comes not from the other side of the party aisle but from within their own party.

Why are districts becoming so much safer for the party holding them, particularly on the Republican side? One reason is that the regional bases of the parties have sorted out, as the durable electoral map forged in conflicts over Reconstruction—Democrats in the South, Republicans in the North—has finally yielded to contemporary political realities. Another is the development of "majority-minority districts" that allow black and Hispanic voters to elect black and Hispanic politicians but which, by cramming Democratic voters into majority-minority districts, usually make adjoining districts more Republican.[33] But a third crucial reason is explicit partisan gerrymandering, which Republicans have aggressively engaged in over the past decade.

Partisan gerrymandering has always been a weapon of the parties. But it has become a much more lethal weapon. Due to the hardening of partisan allegiances, voters' leanings are more easily predicted than they once were. At the same time, the technology for drawing partisan districts has become vastly more sophisticated. These enabling factors have intersected with the growing influence of the GOP in statehouses and the federal capital to produce a series of concerted and mostly successful attempts by Republicans to redraw districts in their favor.[34]

The most brazen of these efforts was spearheaded by none other than Tom DeLay in his home state of Texas. Before the election of 2002, DeLay created a political action committee, Texans for a Republican Majority (TRMPAC), to promote the election of a Republican state legislature. (TRMPAC has since become embroiled in scandal, with three of its top fundraisers under indictment for illegally funneling corporate funds to Republican candidates.) Once Republicans won the statehouse, it became clear that the PAC's name referred not just to state Republicans but to the congressional GOP as well. Urged on by DeLay and Karl Rove (who frequently conferred with Texas's GOP lieutenant governor), Texas Republicans managed to squeeze through a controversial, off-year redistricting plan. The new district map was a Republican fantasy come to life. As long as the Republicans captured at least 45.9 percent of the statewide vote, they held the statehouse and won a majority of congressional districts. If they carried 51.9 percent of the statewide vote, they would win nearly 70 percent of statehouse seats, and twenty-two of thirty-two congressional districts.[35] Not surprisingly, Republicans cleaned up in 2004: Four congressional Democrats, all placed in new districts, were defeated for reelection while every Republican incumbent and almost every Republican open-seat candidate won handily. These four seats, plus two others picked up in the state, turned out to be a boon to the congressional GOP. Without them, Republicans would actually have lost seats in Congress. With them, they strengthened their conservative majority.

Partisan gerrymandering has become an increasingly useful way of protecting incumbents and encouraging ideological conformity in the

House. And although Democrats have shown little reluctance to engage in the practice when they have had the power to do so, they have not had the power to do so often. As noted in Chapter 1, the effects are displayed in the contemporary congressional map. In the razor-close election of 2000, Bush narrowly lost the popular vote to Al Gore. In the process, he carried 227 of the nation's 435 congressional districts—well more than a majority. But the 227 total is nothing when compared to what Republicans soon engineered. The 2002 district map would have given Bush 237 districts with the same vote he received in 2000. The 2004 map would have given him 239 districts, or almost 55 percent.[36] As it was, Bush actually won 255 congressional districts in the election of 2004—almost 59 percent, compared with his popular vote share of less than 52 percent of the two-party (Democratic-Republican) vote.[37] Nationwide, huge numbers of reliable Democrats are squeezed into a handful of districts (what gerrymandering specialists call "packing"), while Republican-leaning districts are more likely to feature small (but comfortable) GOP majorities. In the lead-up to the election of 2004, the political scientist Michael P. McDonald estimated that Democrats would need to pick up a stunning 57 percent of the congressional vote to control Congress.[38]

The story is different in the Senate. Here, because state boundaries are fixed, gerrymandering is not an option, perennial tongue-in-cheek proposals for dividing California into multiple states notwithstanding.[39] Nor do incumbents in the Senate enjoy the same overwhelming advantages as incumbents in the House do. But Senate elections still feature many of the same distortions that plague House ones.

To begin with, Senate elections are closely following the House trajectory in one crucial respect: They are becoming less competitive, making primaries—and the party base—more important. Though still more contested than House races, the reelection rate of Senate incumbents has risen substantially—from an average of 72 percent in the 1970s to over 90 percent in the 1990s. In 2004, only one incumbent, Senate Minority Leader Tom Daschle of South Dakota, went down to defeat.[40]

Furthermore, because senatorial aspirants need to raise such large sums of money, the party base is crucial for candidates without independent wealth. In Senate elections, money flows freely from outside state lines, emanating from top ideological and interest-group supporters and the parties themselves. Consider Tom Daschle's victorious opponent, conservative Republican John Thune. His top two contributors were Senator Majority Leader Bill Frist's "Volunteer PAC," which gave over $132,000; and the anti-tax watchdog group, the Club for Growth, which gave over $131,000. (In 2004, Volunteer PAC raised more than $4.3 million to fund Republican candidates.)[41]

In short, congressional seats are increasingly safe for one party or the other—more often, the Republican Party. No longer do the parties truly compete to capture the broad battleground of American politics. Instead, skirmishes are fought over small stretches of still-contested territory, which the winning side immediately tries to take out of contention for the future. This development has had many effects. But the most obvious impact is to make the processes that precede general elections more important—not just the selection and recruitment of candidates but also the all-important primary stage in which parties select their standard-bearers.

The impact of primary-centered elections is felt in ways big and small, visible and hidden. The biggest impact is ideological extremism. When candidates worry less about reaching out to swing voters in the general election and more about pleasing mobilized partisan voters in low-turnout primaries, they have a very clear directive: *please the base*. The political scientist Barry Burden estimates that a credible primary challenge pulls a typical congressional candidate ten points toward the ideological poles on a scale of zero to one hundred.[42] The greater the threat posed by primaries, the greater the pull of the poles, and the more incentive candidates have to tack toward the extremes. Indeed, they may end up winning only because they move sharply from the center. For this reason, it is a mistake to dismiss the threat of well-financed primary challenges simply by noting that incumbents rarely lose to primary opponents. Even when serious primary challenges fail, their targets are usually driven closer to the base.

Indeed, even when a primary challenge does not materialize, the fact that one might occur can effectively pull candidates toward their base. Like a tax audit, a primary challenge is a rare but potentially devastating event that conditions behavior even when it doesn't take place. The effect of primaries, therefore, can be almost invisible. Yet that does not make the effect any less real. The crucial issue is where candidates see the greatest electoral threat arising: in their own party or outside it. The moderate Republicans who looked over their shoulders when considering Clinton's impeachment knew what Congressman Jim Leach told *Washington Post* columnist E. J. Dionne, Jr., in 2004: "Because congressional districts are increasingly drawn to guarantee victory for one party or the other, incumbents worry mostly about primary challenges from ideological hard-liners."[43] When the greatest risk comes from within the party, the call of the swing voter is drowned out by the cries of the base.

Base Brawl

This brings us to the second lesson of Scott Garrett's seemingly improbable journey to victory: Activist groups within the GOP now play a distinctively important role in certifying conservative candidates and bringing out voters on Election Day. Garrett is a darling of conservative advocacy groups. Endorsed by the National Rifle Association, he received an "A" grade for his pro-gun voting record (the Coalition to Stop Gun Violence gave him a score of zero). The conservative Christian organizations the Christian Coalition and Family Research Council each gave him scores of 100 percent (Planned Parenthood gave him a score of zero).[44] While Garrett's more moderate opponents in the New Jersey primary warred with each over for the allegiance of centrist Republicans, many of whom stayed home on primary day, Garrett swept past them with the support of local conservatives, who turned out enthusiastically.

Democrats have long been viewed as the party of single-issue organizations demanding fealty to particular causes: environmentalism, the right to choose, civil rights, support for organized labor. Yet as the grassroots on the Left has wilted, the grassroots on the Right has flourished. And as the conservative grassroots has grown, its role in Republican politics has dramatically expanded. The Christian Coalition, the National Rifle Association, the National Federation of Independent Business, and other widespread, locally rooted organizations that back Republican candidates do not just say which candidates deserve the label "conservative." They are also unrivaled organizers of get-out-the-vote campaigns and local political drives. Woody Allen's quip that 90 percent of success in life is showing up rings true in the low-turnout world of American elections. The activist base of the GOP shows up.

The Christian Right is a case in point. Momentarily noticed by the punditocracy after the Republican sweep in 1994, its main organization—the Christian Coalition—has since lost ground. Denied tax-exempt status, the group's donations have plummeted. Its membership, which is often claimed to be as large as two million, is probably less than half that. Antidiscrimination lawsuits have recently plagued the organization. And yet, a study conducted in 2002 by the nonpartisan magazine *Campaigns and Elections* concluded that, if anything, Christian conservatives are now *stronger* politically than they were in 1994.[45]

In 1994, for example, *Campaigns and Elections* classified (based on hundreds of interviews with politicos) eighteen state Republican Party organizations as strongly under the control of Christian conservatives and thirteen as moderately so—for a total of thirty-one state Republican Parties significantly shaped by the Christian Right. By 2002, the first number (that is, strong states) had not changed, but the second (that is, moderate states) had doubled—for forty-four state parties in the Christian conservative fold. Christian groups looked weaker in part because they were stronger; insinuated deeply into party organizations, they no longer needed to mobilize as often or as widely as they once had. As *Campaigns and Elections* concluded, "The influence of Christian conservatives within the GOP has made them less visible, distinctive and independent, but it has also made them a critical component of the Republican coalition."[46]

The story of the Christian Right is the story of many conservative activist groups. The strength of today's conservative activists is based in part on local roots—in their ability to influence internal party organization and low-turnout elections at the state and local levels. Yet, increasingly, the power of conservative activists is nationally oriented, avowedly focused on putting conservative Republicans into federal office, and, indeed, explicitly coordinated by Republican leaders. Initially, many conservative groups entered the political fray quietly and almost exclusively at the local level, organizing in churches to shape school boards and local party organizations. Ralph Reed, the baby-faced executive director of the Christian Coalition, once said that the "first strategy, and in many ways the most important strategy, for evangelicals is secrecy."[47] Conservative groups were reluctant to flex their muscles nationally for a number of reasons—not least their distrust of government and politics. But as conservative groups have become more deeply integrated into the national GOP, that reluctance has all but vanished.

As conservative activism has shifted toward national politics, it has also focused increasingly on the recruitment and certification of aspirants to elected office and the monitoring and punishment of politicians once they are elected. Ideological "box scores" are a revealing indicator of the trend. A few decades ago, only a handful of prominent conservative groups (notably, the American Conservative Union, or ACU) assembled ideological issue scores based on members of Congress's recorded votes on hot-button topics. Today, the ACU's scores compete with those of such conservative watchdogs as the National Tax Limitation Committee, Americans for Tax Reform, the National Taxpayers Union, Citizens against Government Waste, the Republican Liberty Caucus, the Christian Coalition, the Eagle Forum, the Campaign for Working Families, the Family Research Council, and the subtly named Center for Reclaiming America. These groups range in size and clout. But even the smallest can often exert considerable power when it can credibly claim to be the arbiter of whether a candidate or elected official is a true believer in a central conservative cause.

Perhaps no two groups better illustrate the rise of recruitment and certification on the right than the two anti-tax organizations we met in Part I: Grover Norquist's Americans for Tax Reform and Stephen Moore's Club for Growth (CfG). Each, it bears emphasis, is a recent creation. ATR began as a Reagan White House operation headed by Norquist in the mid-1980s. Founded with backing from conservative think tanks, media figures, and financial interests, the Club for Growth started only in 1999—an astonishing fact, given its current significance.

These two groups share three key characteristics that increasingly define the organizational base of the GOP: they are radical; they focus on guiding and disciplining Republicans in Congress, not mobilizing large numbers of citizens; and they are effective. Norquist, whom we have already met, is about as pure an example of a conservative ideologue as one could imagine. Meanwhile, Moore (who gave way to Pat Toomey after Toomey's narrow primary loss in 2004 to moderate Senator Arlen Specter of Pennsylvania) is an ardent devotee of supply-side economics and a libertarian. Before founding CfG, he trained on the policy circuit of the hard Right, working at the Heritage Foundation, on Republican Dick Armey's staff, and at the ultraconservative Cato Institute.

As their founding stories attest, both ATR and CfG are elite rather than mass operations. They have small memberships, and they have been heavily reliant on large donations (including, in ATR's case, sizable contributions from the Republican Party). The "mass" element of these influential organizations, such as it is, largely consists of electioneering, rather than grassroots mobilization. But that electioneering can be powerful. During the midterm elections of 2002, as noted in Chapter 2, the CfG doled out $10 million in contributions, making it the leading source of campaign funds for Republicans outside the GOP itself.[48] In 2004, the club's even more aggressive spending included a staggering $2.3 million contribution to a single *primary* campaign, in which it backed Toomey in his unsuccessful primary challenge from the right against Arlen Specter in Pennsylvania.[49]

Each of these organizations, finally, has developed strategies that are well tailored to the new world of congressional elections. In particular, each has focused its energies on ensuring that turnover within the Republican Party will promote increasing conservatism. For ATR, a central tool has been the introduction of tax pledges, in which elected officials and candidates for office pledge to "oppose any and all efforts to increase the marginal income tax rates for individuals and/or businesses."[50] Some incumbents initially resisted these pledges. But the logic of contemporary Republican primaries is clear: Signing the ATR's anti-tax contract has become a necessary component of most Republican runs for Congress (and in many places, state office as well). Incumbents wishing to shore up their position have also generally signed; if not, their successors do. By the end of 2003, ATR had signed pledges from 216 House members (just two short of a majority), 42 senators, and President Bush.

Like ATR, the Club for Growth has focused its energies on increasing the ranks of committed conservatives in Congress. Its preferred technique is candidate recruitment for open seats, combined with efforts to challenge moderate Republican incumbents. The CfG's actual record is more mixed than Moore's bragging about moderate Republicans "wetting their pants" (which we cited in Chapter 2) suggests. While the club has had success in getting its candidates elected to open seats, it has never won a primary challenge, though it has come close several times. Still, as far as conservatives are concerned, its efforts have had salutary effects. They set moderates on notice, reinforce conservative economic dogma, and can provide a launching pad for later campaigns—such as the successful bid of Scott Garrett, a Club for Growth darling.

Party Favors

The third lesson of Garrett's win in New Jersey is that in the electoral arena, parties matter in a way they did not in the recent past. One big reason is money, or more precisely, the need for candidates to raise huge sums of it. Garrett won not because he personally outspent his general election opponent—in fact, he was outpaced in the general election after focusing his spending on the primary—but because the Republican Party pulled out all the stops on his behalf. And if money is the measure, the parties are pulling out the stops as they never have before. In 2000, the two major parties raised more than $400 million (in 2004 dollars) to fund campaigns and voter outreach efforts. In 2004, the figure was almost $1.6 *billion,* and the rise shows little signs of slowing. The parties are fast becoming the one indispensable source of campaign funds and advertising. In 2000, for example, six challengers managed to defeat sitting incumbents in the House. In nearly every one of these races, according to the political scientists Michael Malbin and Anne Bedlington, funds provided by the parties or by members of Congress working on behalf of the parties were instrumental to the incumbents' defeat.[51]

To be sure, parties are not the only—or even the largest—source of funds in congressional races. PACs and individual donors have stepped up their giving at the same time that the parties have. But neither is wholly independent from the parties or partisan causes. Most PACs and big donors lean heavily toward one party or the other—and with the Republican congressional ascendance in the mid-1990s, they now lean much more often to the Republicans than the Democrats.[52] The largest source of campaign funds—between 70 and 80 percent—is groups and individuals affiliated with the corporate sector, which generally favors Republican candidates. (The labor movement, in contrast, heavily favors Democrats but accounts for less than 10 percent of campaign funds.) When Democrats controlled Congress, business-oriented interest groups gave grudgingly to the party of FDR to preserve their access to the halls of power. But over the past decade, with this impediment removed, corporate money has headed toward its natural home, bolstering the Republican Party's fundraising advantage.

Campaign finance reform was, of course, designed to reduce the huge flows of unregulated contributions (so-called soft money) into the parties' coffers, and it certainly has eliminated one big loophole that allowed large contributors to give to the parties. But, as the record fundraising totals of 2004 suggest, the role of big-ticket partisan contributors and the parties remains massive. What is more, many of the dollars that were once raised in soft money have shifted into nominally "independent" organizations closely affiliated with one party or the other, effectively circumventing the soft-money ban contained in the recent campaign reforms while strengthening the pull of deep-pocketed, single-issue groups like the Club for Growth.

Perhaps the most compelling evidence of the power of the party in the electoral arena is the seemingly strange practice of intercandidate giving—in which members of Congress are contributors as well as campaigners. In the early 1970s, the party leadership in Congress ran small campaign-finance operations. But members of Congress jealously hoarded their own funds, establishing huge "war chests" designed to deter potential challengers. In 1978, a bit more than $1 million (in 2000 dollars) was spent by members of Congress and their PACs to help elect other candidates. In 2000, the figure was over $20 million. And although both parties now play the intercandidate game, Republicans play it much better. In 2000, Republican members of Congress and their PACs contributed 50 percent more to fellow candidates than did Democrats. Among the top twenty givers to other campaigns in 2004, all but four were Republicans.

The most influential type of intercandidate giving comes not from run-of-the-mill partisans but from the members of Congress with the most at stake in controlling or capturing a congressional majority, namely, party leaders. House Majority Leader Tom DeLay—despite being under the cloud of thirty-two Texas indictments centered on the possible illegal use of corporate funds by his PAC—spent nearly $1 million to fund other candidates in the 2004 election, barely outpacing House Speaker Dennis Hastert. Between 1990 and 2002, spending by party leadership PACs on both sides of the aisle increased nearly *600 percent:* from a little more than $3.5 million (in 2002 dollars) to more than $24 million. Of that total, more than $14 million—or about 60 percent—was spent to elect Republican candidates.[53]

And not just any Republican candidates. DeLay, as one unflattering recent biography notes, has indeed "spent millions to elect Republicans to the House. But he has also worked (and spent his PAC money) to eliminate Republicans who refuse to get in harness when he needs them."[54] (One such Republican was Marge Roukema: Scott Garrett was the happy recipient of DeLay's support and funds.) The GOP leadership has two goals, not always in complete harmony—electing a majority, and electing a conservative majority. In pursuit of the former, it has sometimes sided with moderates whose defeat risked the loss of a seat. But when, as is increasingly the case in a world of safe seats, the GOP leadership can demand consistency with conservative principles without creating a serious threat of general election defeat, it has proved willing not just to campaign on conservatives' behalf but to put its money where its mouth is.

Brave New World

For the moderate Republicans of days gone by—men and women like Marge Roukema—the growing influence of the base is an unwelcome development. But for the new breed of conservative Republican legislators like Scott Garrett, it is the key to their astonishing ascent in American politics. The transformation of the Republican Party from a motley collection of go-slow conservatives and traditional antistatists into a formidable juggernaut of committed right-wing true believers has been gradual—punctuated by bursts of energy and activity, but driven forward by persistent, slogging progress through election after election. But it is a change that has upended American politics, making the call of the base within the GOP louder and more irresistible than ever before.

Beneath this change, we have seen, lie tectonic shifts in the American political landscape, fueled by the huge and growing inequality of resources and influence in the United States. But the overarching force that has turned these deep shifts into enhanced power for the Right is the transformed identity of the Republican Party. Slowly but seemingly inexorably, the GOP has built a powerful foundation of support in the South and among conservative groups. It has augmented the grassroots mobilization of its most committed supporters with a massive party-oriented fundraising machine and energetic conservative policy network. And it—and its affiliated groups—have greatly stepped up their monitoring and enforcement of politicians deemed less than faithful to the party cause. Taken separately, these shifts may seem small. Cumulatively, they have been profound. In a decentralized political system where efforts at coordination seem perpetually prone to failure, the GOP has managed to make the Republican base the one thing that all Republicans have to worry about.

To be sure, there are still Republicans who refuse to race to the base. But they are getting scarcer. With most Republican-occupied seats safely in the hands of the GOP, the pressures posed by the Right weigh heavily on the minds of even the most moderate of Republicans. More important, old-style moderates cannot hang on forever. They have their own funds, their own state and local organizations, their own constituent-politician relationships. But when they move aside or go down to defeat, the field is open for someone else within the party to step in. That someone, as we have seen, will almost always be farther to the right and more partisan than the politician replaced.

Like a glacier whose slow movement belies the violence with which it can rip through its surroundings, the gradual transformation of the Republican Party has fundamentally altered the terrain of American politics. The creatures that now dominate this transformed landscape also helped create it: the New Power Brokers of the Republican Party. It is to these brokers and their coordinated efforts to transform American governance that we now turn.

5

THE REPUBLICAN MACHINE

More than ever, American politics is being driven from the top. And because the increasingly coordinated efforts of these elites are so central to off-center governance, it makes sense to start at the top of the top: the New Power Brokers in American politics. The New Power Brokers—men like Tom DeLay, Grover Norquist, and Karl Rove—are colorful figures. But this is not just a story about interesting personalities. Who rises to power and how power is exercised are ultimately grounded in political institutions and processes. At root, the growing sway of the New Power Brokers reflects the transformed American political landscape that the last chapter laid bare—and in particular, the growing power of the conservative GOP base. The base stokes the ideological intensity of today's Republican Party. The New Power Brokers direct this fervor toward remaking American public policy.

The New Power Brokers share two revealing characteristics. First, they are ideologues. They hold views that are far, far to the right of most Americans. Second, they are powerful not primarily because they hold positions of formal authority but because of their strategic location at the top of an increasingly organized conservative network. The New Power Brokers straddle the twin worlds of politicians and activists. Each of these worlds brings something important to the conservative table, yet each badly needs the other. The brokers do precisely what their name implies: They broker, facilitating or blocking each side's efforts to connect. This allows them to reward and punish, to craft policy and messages across far-flung institutions, and ultimately to provide highly effective protection to Republicans threatened by popular backlash against the conservative agenda. Much of this, however, takes place with surprisingly little of the usual pomp and circumstance of formal power. Rove, DeLay, and Norquist do not always shy from the spotlight. But a great deal of what they do goes on behind-the-scenes—whether it's strategizing, crafting messages, or assembling broader networks of influence in support of their goals.

Indeed, the position of the New Power Brokers bears more than a passing resemblance to the leadership of a very different political world: Florentine Italy of the fifteenth century. There, the famous Medici family ruled government and finance, but not by virtue of formal authority (the most powerful leader of the family, Cosimo de' Medici, "never assumed lasting public office" and "hardly gave a public speech," according to an illuminating study).[1] Rather, the Medici were powerful because of the network of support they assembled through financial and family ties, particularly deliberate patterns of marriage. The New Power Brokers are not marrying off GOP loyalists, of course (or at least so far as we know). But they are engaging in their own form of matchmaking, linking powerful interests with supportive politicians and mobilized activists. Like the Medici, their power rests on more than the rules of government. It rests on a social structure that extends beyond and below the state. And, as we saw in the last chapter, this structure has increasingly aligned their goals with those of the economically privileged and the ideologically extreme.

How exactly the New Power Brokers achieve their goals varies depending on the task. Sometimes it is a matter of broadcasting a loud and clear message. Sometimes it involves trying to change the news media's topic of choice from something unpleasant or giving an ongoing controversy a new and emphatic spin. At other times, the aims are more narrowly legislative: assembling a coalition in support of an item on the Republican agenda, or consolidating agreement within that coalition behind a specific proposal. Sometimes it is a matter of rounding up votes for a legislative bill or rule of dubious popularity. And sometimes the goal is to provide what we call "backlash insurance," carefully tailored protection for potentially vulnerable Republicans so that they can race toward the base with eagerness and impunity. Each is a distinct challenge. Each requires the mobilization of the appropriate combination of carrots and sticks. But each, fundamentally, requires that diverse and strong-willed actors coordinate to achieve a goal they might otherwise fail to accomplish: shifting policy away from the center and toward the extreme.

An increased capacity for coordination is the nearly invisible foundation of the Republican Revolution—the key not only to their victories but also to their ability to protect Republicans from the fallout those victories might produce. The first half of this chapter looks at how this coordination has arisen and how it works. The second half turns to one of its most important payoffs: the ability to provide backlash insurance that protects Republicans against public outcry for pursuing the wishes of their leadership and the insistent demands of the base.

The Invisible (Right) Hand

In journalistic accounts of politics, personalities loom large. Yet politics is fundamentally about collective action. Executing a multifaceted and ambitious agenda involves a host of complex group efforts. Formulating and sticking to a clear message, controlling the agenda, raising huge amounts of money and then channeling it to the places where it can have the greatest impact, rewarding friends and punishing rebels and mavericks, holding a slim majority together—all of these require that a large number of individuals work together. And not just any people: formidable individuals with sizable egos and diverse and often conflicting interests. In big, disparate coalitions, it is not enough to establish broad and vague aims. Priorities have to be set, strategies formulated and executed, and a message agreed upon and followed.

In American politics, centrifugal tendencies are everywhere. Asked recently to contemplate a House of Representatives without the leadership of the great coordinator, Tom DeLay, a Republican strategist with close ties to the White House commented: "It would be complete and total chaos. The House would descend into 'Lord of the Flies.'"[2]

In fact, American politics has often looked like "complete and total chaos." Our political institutions were engineered in ways that make sustained coordination fiendishly difficult. Authority runs in all directions.

Multiple governing institutions create many points of entry into politics. And because each of our political institutions is organized along different lines, they create distinctive interests. Unifying these outlooks into a coherent, sustained, working majority is often an exercise in "herding cats." As the veteran pol Harry Truman commented after Dwight Eisenhower's election: "He'll sit there all day saying do this, do that, and nothing will happen. Poor Ike, it won't be a bit like the military. He'll find it very frustrating."[3]

Not only does the original design of American political institutions thwart coordination; modern trends in American society and politics are widely held to have reinforced that tendency. After World War II, according to much conventional wisdom, the United States began to shift from "party-centered" to "candidate-centered" politics.[4] Traditional patronage-based party machines gave way to newly empowered candidates who—thanks to primaries and the rise of modern communications technology—could now bypass the party establishment and convey their own unique "brand" to voters. Modern candidates became entrepreneurs, working through television and mass mailings to reach voters while cultivating personal connections with powerful interests, including the rapidly burgeoning assortment of PACs. Candidates built their own reputations, their own coalitions, their own fundraising networks. Party leaders were sometimes helpful, sometimes a hindrance, but mostly just not particularly relevant.

This traditional view, it is now abundantly clear, drastically understates the contemporary power of the GOP leadership, especially in the House. Leaders have assembled a range of tools that give them considerable leverage over the party rank and file. Indeed, among close watchers of Congress, few dispute that authority in the House has become dramatically more concentrated. Over the past three decades, the independent baronies of powerful committee chairs have been crushed. Initially, some of that power was dispersed outward, to subcommittees and individual members of Congress. But the more recent trend, especially since Republicans swept to a majority in 1994, has been breathtaking centralization. Compared to their counterparts of the 1970s, today's congressional leaders possess much more formidable weapons for quelling dissent and advancing their policy ambitions.

One can see the signs of heightened centralization almost everywhere. Perhaps the most transparent evidence is voting records in Congress. "Party Unity" scores measure how often legislators vote with their party when the overall vote reveals a partisan divide. These scores have trended sharply upward since the 1970s, especially since the early 1990s and especially on the Republican side of the aisle. In 2003, they reached the highest levels in the five decades in which they have been tallied, and they dropped only slightly in 2004.[5] These extraordinarily high levels of cohesion in a highly diverse and fragmented society belie the traditional image of the politician as a free agent.

Yet voting unity is only the tip of the iceberg. Numerous other indicators show increasingly coherent partisan efforts. The scale of financial resources generated by party organizations and controlled by the congressional leadership has risen dramatically. Coalitions of interest groups closely allied with the Republican Party have become much more formidable. These coalitions' operations, moreover, have become more tightly coupled. The informal apparatus for developing, coordinating, and broadcasting Republican messages has expanded enormously.

The story of growing political centralization, in short, is not just a story of Congress. The heightened capacity for coordination, so central to the Republican Revolution, transcends this single locale. It reflects the basic development we saw in the last chapter: the emergence of a more tightly networked, fully nationalized, and deeply institutionalized conservative movement.

It is in this respect that the rise of the New Power Brokers is emblematic, for it has helped to consolidate the social and political preconditions for levels of coordination that are unprecedented in modern American politics. The power brokers oversee the upper levels of the conservative movement. Straddling the worlds of politicians and activists, they collect and disseminate (or withhold) information and other crucial resources, including money and access. They facilitate the exchanges that are necessary to develop, refine, and enforce an agenda and a message. Norquist, for instance, uses ATR headquarters to host a Wednesday, invitation-only breakfast meeting that has become a networking center for conservative Washington. The highly popular events bring together members of Congress and their staff with administration representatives, political operatives, lobbyists, media figures, and conservative activists to ex-change information, develop strategies, and refine talking points.

Equally important, the power brokers' authority within these networks makes it possible to focus the energies of diverse interests. The power brokers monitor the activities of politicians and lobbyists, dispensing rewards and punishments based on loyalty and contributions to the col-lective effort. They are the guardians of the *reputations* that elite actors need to continue participating in this high-stakes atmosphere. The power brokers certify politicians to receive the favors of powerful interest groups, and they certify interest groups to receive the largesse that pow-erful politicians can dispense to those in favor.

Of course, the degree of coordination should not be exaggerated. Like any coalition in a huge society, this one has real fissures. Republican power brokers must walk a fine line in marshalling their forces. As the Senate career of Arizona Republican John McCain attests, American pol-itics continues to create opportunities to develop semi-independent seats of power. And of course, fights within the leadership itself can be intense. As we saw in Chapter 3, Republican leaders have to pick carefully how far, and in what directions, they push. And sometimes even heavy pushing comes up short. Sometimes, as in their battles over Bush's energy plan (and probably Social Security as well), Republican elites overreach and must choose between retreat and defeat.

Still, as will become clear, a good deal of what passes for internal divi-sion and dissent is pure theater or sloughed off to issues that the New Power Brokers judge to be of secondary importance. More important, the formidable advantage that Republicans have come to enjoy can be appreciated only in light of the age-old truth that power is always rela-tive. There is a joke about two campers who watch, terrified, as an angry bear approaches their campsite. When one begins to lace on his running shoes, his companion wonders why, since he will still not be able to out-run the bear. "I don't have to," comes the reply. "I just have to outrun you." In a fundamentally uncoordinated political system, even a moder-ate advantage in the contest of coordination conveys a huge edge.

Effective coordination is not perfect coordination. Message control doesn't require that the chorus sing in absolute harmony—just that it is typically louder and significantly less off-key than its competitor. Passing legislation generally doesn't require the vote of every Republican—just the votes of almost all of them. Providing backlash insurance doesn't require protecting incumbents against any possible challenge—just the most serious and immediate challenges. What is needed is not unmatchable coordination—just coordination one's opponents cannot match. And the extent of coordination among Republican political elites, imperfect as it may be, is unprecedented in modern American history. It is certainly far, far greater than anything seen on the Democratic side. Thirty years in the making, the product of deep trends, hard work, and savvy strategies, it represents a remarkable organizational achievement.[6]

Lobbyists, Legislators, and the New Power Structure

The basic contours of these new arrangements can be identified by looking at the lines of influence that run between the central power brokers and their two key constituencies: major lobbyists and Republican politicians. Popular images of Washington politics often give pride of place to the powerful lobbyists who congregate around K Street (and, increasingly short of space, have spilled out well beyond it). Interest groups and their highly paid retainers spend vast sums to try to steer political outcomes in their favor. Indeed, while expensive lobbying has long been prevalent in Washington, it has recently exploded. The cost of direct lobbying—personal contact with lawmakers—has nearly doubled since 1997, to almost $2 billion per year. Indirect lobbying (such as telemarketing and issue advertising) raises the total to roughly triple that amount.[7] Lobbying is a big and rapidly growing business. And it grows, presumably, because people with money think it's worth investing in. They wouldn't be writing bigger and bigger checks unless they expected that the added investment would more than pay for itself.

Most profiles of K Street portray it as a high-powered world in which well-heeled lobbyists run the show, with legislators doing their bidding. At times, elements of the Republican Revolution have seemed to vindicate this common interpretation. A notorious episode following the Republican's electoral victory in 1994 is often taken as emblematic. Tom DeLay galvanized a major deregulatory initiative, dubbed "Project Relief," with the backing of a vast array of business interests. So radical was DeLay's agenda that moderate Republicans were emboldened to speak out. Senator John Chafee of Rhode Island, chairman of the Senate Environment and Public Works Committee, described the proposed revisions to environmental policy as "terrible legislation. When all the artichoke leaves are peeled away, they are out for the Clean Air Act, the Clean Water Act, the Endangered Species Act; that is what they're gunning for." Representative Christopher Shays of Connecticut complained, "We are gutting [the] EPA and gutting environmental laws."[8]

As House Republicans worked on these deregulatory initiatives, reporters commented on the remarkable prominence of business lobbyists. Interest group representatives took up positions in committee staff offices, where they drafted legislative text on office computers, conducted briefings for congressional staff, and generally acted as expert consultants on the details of legislation. The picture was one of powerful interests, with huge financial stakes in proposed policies, dictating to elected officials. Yet DeLay's own comments at the time offer a revealing glimpse at a more complicated relationship. "You've got to understand, we are ideologues," DeLay told the reporter Elizabeth Drew. "We have an agenda. We have a philosophy. I want to repeal the Clean Air Act. No one came to me and said, 'Please repeal the Clean Air Act.' We say to the lobbyists, 'Help us.' *We know what we want to do and we find the people to help us do that.*"[9]

Indeed, there is much to suggest that the New Power Brokers have worked diligently to turn the stereotyped relationship between the lobbyists and the lobbied on its head. The most publicized example has been the "K Street Project," begun shortly after the sweeping victory of congressional Republicans in 1994. Unsurprisingly, DeLay and Norquist were at the center of this initiative, too. The K Street Project was designed to pressure lobbyists to adopt a more pronounced Republican slant in both their campaign contributions and their hiring practices. Using figures compiled by Norquist, DeLay called lobbyists into his office to discuss whether their contribution and hiring practices qualified them as "friendly" to the GOP. "If you want to play in our revolution," he announced, "you have to live by our rules."[10]

Stories about DeLay's efforts to dictate hiring practices on K Street have certainly created waves. In 1996, then-Republican National Committee Chairman Haley Barbour and the House Republican leadership organized a meeting in which, according to a veteran steel lobbyist, they "made it clear to [several large company CEOs] that they were expected to purge their Washington offices of Democrats and replace them with Republicans."[11] In 1999, the House Ethics Committee admonished DeLay for, as the *Washington Post* described it, "threatening a Washington trade association with retaliation last year for hiring a prominent Democrat as its president."[12] DeLay had reportedly held up legislation supported by the Electronic Industries Alliance (EIA) because it had passed over a Republican candidate for its presidency and hired former Democratic Representative Dave McCurdy instead.

The impact of these efforts is hard to gauge. Clearly, however, the Republican leadership has built an unprecedented apparatus for monitoring lobbyist activities. As the *National Journal* reported in 2003, "It is now routine to sound out DeLay, his staff, or those familiar with his thinking, about potential lobbying hires."[13] In the House, Majority Whip (and DeLay protégé) Roy Blunt coordinates this oversight in regularly scheduled meetings with lobbyists. Rick Santorum directs a similar effort in the Senate. Much of this activity is unapologetically public—as, indeed, it needs to be in order to send lobbyists the clear message that the Republican leadership intends.

This activity is designed not simply to tilt the interest group world further toward Republicans. The New Power Brokers are also trying to centralize and coordinate patterns of interaction that previously had been decentralized and uncoordinated. Lobbyists and politicians are encouraged to run their efforts by, and through, the brokers. The following news report of private lobbying activity is telling:

> The assistant who answered Rove's phone was a woman who had previously worked for lobbyist Jack Abramoff, a close friend of Norquist's and a top DeLay fundraiser. One Republican lobbyist, who asked not to be named because DeLay and Rove have the power to ruin his livelihood, said the way Rove's office worked was this: "Susan took a message for Rove, and then called Grover to ask if she should put the caller through to Rove. If Grover didn't approve, your call didn't go through."[14]

Again, these efforts have met with only partial success. But much of that success is likely to remain below the surface, as potential rebels decide that the likely results of disobedience will be unpleasant. Indeed, it is a cardinal feature of power that once it has been institutionalized it often becomes almost invisible; people quietly accommodate to the new realities. As one Republican lobbyist commented, "DeLay wields so much influence over the congressional agenda that antagonizing him over hiring decisions is widely considered self-destructive."[15]

Although much of the leadership's influence is likely to be hidden from view, these efforts appear to have had some real effects. K Street hiring practices get the publicity, but the evidence of shifts in donations is clearer. According to the Center for Responsive Politics, political donations from nineteen key industry sectors were split roughly evenly between the parties a decade ago. Today, the GOP holds a two-to-one advantage in corporate donations.[16] Increasingly, groups "pick" a party rather than minimize risk by giving generously to both sides.

The political scientist Michael Heaney's detailed research on interest groups that lobby on health policy offers a more systematic assessment.[17] Heaney found that health care groups that are identified as more partisan are also perceived as more powerful by their interest group colleagues. They are also more likely to become the leaders within coalitions of groups seeking to influence health policy. We have already discussed the tight network connecting health care interests to the Republican leadership in the development of the Republicans' Medicare drug benefit. Before the bill passed, journalist Nicholas Confessore noted that the upper ranks of the drug industry's lobbying organization, PhRMA, "were stocked with former aides to powerful Republicans, and its political behavior reflects it: The industry . . . now contributes 80 percent of its money to Republicans. PhRMA has essentially become an extension of the GOP." Indeed, as noted in Chapter 3, the network tightened even more after the legislation passed. One of the bill's chief architects, Billy Tauzin, retired from the House to accept the influential position of the head of PhRMA, at a salary estimated to be in the neighborhood of $2 million a year.

In other areas, too, the Republican leadership has successfully changed the way lobbyists do their business with politicians. To an increasing extent, lobbying activity is funneled through centralized channels. The flow of campaign funds is a case in point. The Republican Party has increased the centralization of donations—to leaders and party outlets rather than to specific politicians. Most notorious (and, in legal terms, precarious), was the manner in which many national interest groups discovered a surprising interest in Texas legislative politics after 2000. Corporations like Philip Morris, Sears, AT&T, UPS, and Bacardi gave heavily to the political action committee Texans for a Republican Majority, which DeLay had helped organize to contribute money to state legislative races in Texas. This was, of course, part of his elaborate and ultimately successful effort to gain additional House seats through the off-cycle reapportionment of Texas districts.

The distinctiveness of this new power structure is brought into sharp relief by a comparison with the realities of the Clinton years. Then, Democratic leaders haggled—often fruitlessly—with individual groups over the terms that would induce their cooperation. It was well understood in Washington that interest groups could benefit by holding out or by working with an individual "swing" legislator to maximize their leverage. When the Democrats held a thin majority, lobbyists (and many swing politicians) behaved like cats rather than like cattle willing to run with the herd.

The discussion in Chapter 3 of recent policy battles reveals a quite different pattern: Republicans have been able to leverage their greater control over political access and resources into a stronger bargaining position. Repeatedly, groups are told that loyalty to the coalition comes first. On big initiatives, groups are instructed to provide backing for the leadership's positions at the outset, well before key features of the legislation have been finalized. The central message is blunt: If you support us, we will see to it that you are taken care of. If you hold out or seek to negotiate separate deals with individual members, you can kiss your cause good-bye.

In short, the New Power Brokers have an enhanced capacity to induce organized interests to work through them and to do so on their terms. Leaders do not passively respond to groups; instead, they mobilize them to pursue agendas and tactics crafted by the leadership. Students of Washington are used to the efforts of leaders to "whip" members of their party into line for crucial votes. In the past few years, however, there have been growing efforts to "whip" interest groups, with lobbyists instructed to put pressure on legislators, even on issues far removed from their clients' own concerns. As one lobbyist told a reporter, "I always thought my job is to look out for my client's interests. Suddenly I'm working for the Republican Party."[18]

Bye-Bye Barons, Hello Backbenchers

The success with which the leadership in Congress has restructured its relationship with lobbyists owes much to its altered relationship with Republican members of Congress. Lobbyists accede to GOP elites for a simple reason: In an increasingly centralized political environment, the New Power Brokers control access to those who make public policy. As executives at Westar Energy Inc., a Kansas-based corporation, revealed in private e-mails, contributions to Republican leadership PACs were necessary "to get a seat at the table."[19]

Nothing signals the new realities more clearly than the collapse of the major alternative power base within legislatures—committee chairmanships. One of the first steps taken by the new Republican leadership after obtaining a majority in the 1994 elections was to remove the autonomy of committee barons, their chief rivals for power in Congress. Traditionally, a committee chairmanship was the great prize awaiting those who had worked their way through the ranks and attained the greatest seniority. And with that prize came power, from control over committee staff to considerable discretion over the agenda and the alternatives within the committee's jurisdiction.

Within weeks of Newt Gingrich's ascendance to the Speakership, however, the power of the congressional barons was effectively broken. Committee chairmanships were limited to six-year terms. Explicit rules announced that seniority would not determine chairmanships. Marge Roukema was not the only long-serving member of Congress denied the traditional prize for lengthy service in Congress. Gingrich overrode seniority to handpick new chairs on three crucial committees. Although chair-rigging has not been used solely (or perhaps even chiefly) to discipline moderates, chairmanships can be held hostage to loyalty. In what

Congressional Quarterly called "a high-profile delivery of leadership pay-back," Christopher Shays of Connecticut was denied the chairmanship of the Government Reform Committee in January 2003 after he used pro-cedural rules to force a vote on campaign finance reform.[20] Two months after the Republicans' successful patriotism-draped campaign of 2004, GOP leaders ousted Christopher Smith as chair of the Veterans Com-mittee, reportedly because of his overzealous advocacy on behalf of veterans.

The subservience of committee chairs is now well institutionalized. Although some chairs continue to wield independent power, the days when they gained that power solely on the basis of their service or expert-ise are gone. All candidates for committee chairmanships must audition before the House Republican steering committee, largely controlled by the leadership. There, candidates are grilled on their fealty and on their capacity to advance (and help finance) a coordinated agenda. The com-petitive nature of these tryouts sends a clear signal: In the Republican House, a chairmanship is not an entitlement; it is a reward for loyal ser-vice. The forum, which participants describe as tough and intimidating, makes it evident who works for whom.[21]

At the same time that they have weakened committee chairs, Re-publican leaders have assembled resources that increase their sway over the congressional rank and file. These resources include both carrots and sticks. The sticks, of course, receive the most attention (even though their use may signal a momentary breakdown of coordination rather than its success). Party leaders make it abundantly clear that politicians will pay dearly for real, as opposed to theatrical, disloyalty, particularly if it occurs on an issue the leadership sees as critical.

These threats cannot be ignored. As power within Congress flows toward the leadership, the implications of disfavor grow. As decision-making circles become tighter, access to these circles becomes more valuable. And the leadership controls access—to committee chairman-ships, to participation in conference committees, and to the various informal venues in which agendas and proposals are hammered out. The price of disloyalty can be exclusion from these arenas, and in today's centralized Congress, the credible threat of exclusion is a hefty stick.

Nor does the leadership's power stop at the walls of Congress. Beyond those walls, the leadership's growing ties to a highly networked community of well-resourced activists are crucial. Funds from party leaders, and from those groups they directly control, can be withheld. Groups essential to Republican candidates can be sent the message that a particular politician is not reliable.

As we emphasized in the last chapter, the ultimate weapon is the threat of an electoral challenge launched by the base against an uncooperative colleague. Revealingly, in today's Washington, "primary" has been changed from a noun to a verb, as in "We'll primary you." This might be seen as an empty threat. After all, attacking a candidate from the right runs the risk of endangering a Republican seat, especially since disloyalty is most likely to be on display precisely in the swing districts where Republicans have most reason to fear a general election loss. And indeed, leaders fearing such an outcome may choose to defend the moderate—as they did, for instance, when Arlen Specter was challenged from the right by Patrick Toomey. But the leadership may also wish to send a message to other potential defectors, especially if it feels it may have a seat or two to spare or has confidence in its ability to manage any general election challenge. DeLay, for instance, has contributed to the Club for Growth, which makes no secret of its willingness to target moderate Republican incumbents.[22]

Of course, the wielding of power need not lead to open and bloody political fights. Anticipating the consequences, potential "rebels" usually decide that passivity is the wiser course. Indeed, the role of Republican moderates over the past decade has rarely transcended the theater of feigned conflict. Centrist Democrats in the House, increasingly frustrated in their efforts to forge compromises across the aisle, derisively joke that a House Republican moderate is someone who throws a ten-foot rope to a drowning man twenty feet offshore. One disgruntled Democrat opined that moderate Republicans "will be with us as long as their votes are irrelevant to the outcome. [They] are reverse Houdinis. They tie themselves up in knots and then tell you they can't do anything because they're tied up in knots."[23]

In the end, if moderates like Marge Roukema find the price of loyalty too high, they may choose to leave quietly rather than continually struggle to find space for marginal assertions of independence. Thus the leadership's final weapon against unreliable moderates is patience. Given the flexibility of the instruments available to them, the votes of every member are rarely necessary. Moderates and rebels, especially if they play an active role in trying to spread disloyalty, can be excluded, harassed, and marginalized until their seat falls open. Then, the networks that link party leaders and powerful conservative interests can reassert themselves, and the race to the base can resume. In his inimitable way, Grover Norquist summarizes the big picture: "What do these so-called moderates have in common? They're seventy years old. They're not running again. They're gonna be dead soon. So, while they're annoying, within the Republican Party our problems are dying."[24]

Backlash Insurance

The midterm election of 1982 was the first in which Marge Roukema ran for reelection. It was also a year in which Democrats gained twenty-six seats in the House. The win was neither unusual nor entirely unexpected. Just two years earlier, Republicans had gained *thirty-three* seats in the House. And the reasons for thinking a big shift the other way would occur in 1982 were strong. The economy was on the rocks, the Reagan Revolution seemingly adrift. Most important, Democrats had seized on the Reagan administration's momentary embrace of cuts in Social Security benefits, relentlessly hammering Republicans on the issue throughout the fall. The image of Republicans heartlessly casting wheelchair-bound seniors into the gutter dogged the GOP until Election Day, when it lost ground in nearly every region. As Reagan's budget director would later recall, "The centerpiece of the American welfare state had now been overwhelmingly ratified and affirmed in the white heat of political confrontation."[25]

Simply put, the Democratic attacks worked. Americans were angered, Republicans got clobbered, and would-be Social Security reformers went back to the drawing board (where they would plot the long, circuitous path of reincarnation that would finally result, more than two decades later, in a concerted presidential push to upend the program). The biennial electoral contest had done what it was supposed to do—discipline a party that many voters felt had strayed too far from their idea of what their government should be doing.

All of which prompts a key question: Even if the call of the Republican base and the power of the Republican leadership have increased, why have rank-and-file conservative politicians so obediently heeded their new marching orders? After all, despite the power of the base, there remains at least one potent problem with appearing extreme in American politics if you hold elected office—voters may decide that you shouldn't hold it anymore. Granted, the base is now louder and better organized. Granted, the New Power Brokers run the show more tightly. But just as the most painstakingly designed consumer product is still a failure if no one buys it, the most powerful base is impotent if no one wants to elect (and reelect) the folks who represent it. How then did the base and GOP leadership get away with peddling a product that, on careful reflection, few middle-of-the-road voters appear to want?

The answer brings us to the key carrot that the New Power Brokers can employ in lieu of sticks—what we call "backlash insurance." The purpose of backlash insurance is to give politicians strong guarantees that their excursions into off-center territory will not lead them into the wilderness of electoral defeat. As congressional authority has become more centralized and the conservative network more dense, Republican leaders are increasingly well equipped to offer skittish moderates a range of reassurances. Employed as circumstances dictate, these formidable forms of backlash insurance can effectively inoculate moderates against the danger that, in racing to the base and obeying the party leadership, they will be exposed as extremists.

Backlash insurance is provided in four main ways: by coordinating the message of the governing coalition and controlling the agenda of political debate; by using congressional procedures to provide much-needed cover for vulnerable incumbents; by designing laws so that their costs and risks are obscured and their privileged beneficiaries are activated to fight for more benefits down the line; and by aiding embattled Republicans, and attacking their challengers, on the electoral battleground. But these tools of backlash insurance all share the same goal: to shield incumbents from electoral accountability when they race to their base.

Insurance Policy #1: Controlling the Agenda

Perhaps the most ubiquitous form of backlash insurance is simply control over the policy agenda. The enhanced coordination of the Republican coalition means the New Power Brokers can pick carefully which issues national politicians are forced to address as well as which ones they can avoid. Issues that would subject "moderates" to significant cross pressures—such as a vote on the minimum wage, unemployment benefits, or a patients' bill of rights—can usually be kept from coming up for serious consideration at all.

Those who follow politics closely know the importance of agenda setting. Agenda access is the great bottleneck of politics. At any moment, a huge number of issues compete for a hearing. Only a handful receive sustained attention from elected officials. The number of issues that actually register with the mass public shrinks even further. Political elites thus battle tenaciously to put their most prized issues atop the agenda. If they succeed, they can throw a blanket over issues that divide their coalition or that play to their opponents' strengths. Exercising broad agenda-control can keep potentially popular but unwanted initiatives off the table.

Agenda control, however, is not just about focusing political discussion on the preferred issue. Equally important is the ability to determine which of the possible alternatives for responding to a particular issue will be considered. We have already discussed several examples of the political repercussions of controlling the alternatives. Most telling was the battle over impeachment. Having helped set the agenda by focusing attention on Clinton's behavior, Tom DeLay and his allies had to wage another critical battle. They worked furiously, and often ruthlessly, to make sure that the most popular alternative, censure, remained out of reach. Removing this option, which was favored not only by the public but by a bipartisan majority in the House, cleared the way for an up-or-down House vote on impeachment, which the Republican leadership won.

Last, agenda control extends to "framing"—that is, determining which of many possible dimensions of an issue will command attention. Politicians and their allies focus relentlessly on crafting and hammering home their "message" for a simple reason: In politics, who wins typically depends not just on which issues and alternatives people are talking about but how they are talking about them.

Most issues, after all, are complex, involving a range of potential considerations. What position people take on an issue often depends on which aspects of the issue receive their attention. An evocative but by no means atypical example is the difference between asking voters whether too little is being spent on "welfare" (which almost nobody supports) and asking whether more should be spent on "assistance to the poor" (which sizable majorities endorse). It might be thought that this is minor stuff, since voters know what issues they care about and what they think about those issues. The evidence to the contrary is overwhelming. During the protracted debates over welfare reform in the 1990s, the political scientist R. Kent Weaver found that virtually any alternative to the status quo polled extremely well.[26] As long as proposed alternatives shared the characteristic of "ending welfare" voters registered enthusiasm—even when each of the different proposals would have put vastly dissimilar arrangements in place. Similarly, slight changes in the wording of poll questions, designed to "prime" one set of considerations over others, can lead to radically different voter reactions. In the mid-1970s, for example, between 44 percent and 48 percent of Americans said they would "not allow" a speech by a communist. When a similar group was asked if they would "prohibit" a speech, the number who said yes was cut in half—presumably because "prohibiting" a speech somehow sounds more intrusive than "not allowing" it.[27]

These are entertaining examples, but do things like this really matter in politics? Judging from the activities of political professionals, they do, and greatly. The power of controlling agendas, alternatives, and framing is strongly signaled by the actual behavior of political elites—the strategic actors most knowledgeable about and most intensely focused on the political world. Aside from fundraising, which is now itself primarily a tool for crafting and controlling political agendas, nothing attracts the energies of political elites as much as the development and dissemination of their "message." Just as pollsters can prime those responding to their surveys, political elites work intensively to prime (or "spin") the reception of political and social events.

Indeed, political consultants have reached new heights of sophistication as they seek to sell politicians and their agendas in the way Madison Avenue tries to sell soap. The central tool of the trade remains polling. Once, polls were used infrequently and almost exclusively to determine what people actually thought about key issues. Today, polls are ubiquitous and routinely used to determine how people can be made to think differently. And increasingly these efforts go beyond polling to include focus groups and other opinion laboratories designed to carefully test-market not just proposals but the specific wording that most effectively frames crucial political debates.

A central aspect of agenda control is the capacity to speak with a loud and consistent voice. In a vast and complicated society, communication can easily degenerate into a Tower of Babel. To speak loudly and consistently usually requires speaking in unison—which is where the Republicans' tools of coordination become so crucial. On Capitol Hill, the amplification of the Republican message can be accomplished by controlling the legislative agenda and alternatives. Beyond the Capitol, the Republicans' impressive means of coordination can be used to improve the chances that issues and ideas entering public debate are framed in the most favorable way. From White House memos like the one we saw in the tax-cut struggles covered in Chapter 2 ("Roll-out events like this are the clearest examples of when staying on message is absolutely crucial") to Republican pollster Frank Luntz's call for a "New American Lexicon" that ensures all Republicans are deploying the same "words that work," the dissemination of GOP talking points has never showcased greater political skill or cohesion.[28] The enhanced coordination of Republican elites has allowed them to become unrivaled practitioners of a new sort of language arts.

Insurance Policy #2: Rigging the Legislative Process

Centralized power in Congress also allows the legislative process to be carefully scripted to eliminate unpleasant scenarios, such as the discomfort that many Republicans would have felt had they been forced to choose openly between censuring or impeaching Bill Clinton. Using its ironclad control of the House Rules Committee (where the Republican majority is nine to four), the party leadership increasingly employs "closed rules" on important legislation. This makes it impossible for Democrats to offer the amendments that would put politicians in the awkward position of voting against proposals favored by moderate voters in their district. The systematic research of political scientist Robert van Houweling shows not only that the use of closed rules has greatly increased but that the pattern of usage strongly points to the leadership's desire to protect moderates from awkward votes.[29]

In the Senate, Republicans face a more serious challenge. Because closed rules are not allowed, Democrats retain the prospect of forcing votes on more moderate alternatives. As we have seen, this possibility does not arise to the same degree in the budget process, where amendments and debate are strictly limited. But on other legislation, Senate Democrats can use the powers of the minority embodied in Senate rules to moderate legislation, or to expose Republicans if they accede to more right-wing proposals.

Republican leaders, however, have developed a devastating strategy for circumventing this obstacle: aggressive use of conference committees. Passage of a more moderate alternative in the Senate simply opens the door for a conference between House and Senate. And these conferences have become the leaders' private playground, presenting unrivaled opportunities for moving policy outcomes as far to the right as possible. As van Houweling's research documents, in recent years there has been a rapid increase in the use of conference committees for highly partisan purposes. Membership of the committees is stacked with supporters of the leadership. At the same time, even within these committees more and more of the real work is done in secret settings—among a small group made up of the GOP leadership, hand-picked legislators, and administration officials, including Vice President Cheney. Potential troublemakers are simply excluded. For example, only the two most accommodating Democratic senators (Louisiana's John Breaux and Montana's Max Baucus) were allowed to participate in the meetings where the Medicare bill was fashioned, and no Democrats participated in meetings over the energy bill.[30]

Rules governing conferences are so flexible, moreover, that Republicans have been able to craft bills that differ in crucial respects from those initially passed in either chamber. (The "scope rule" that governs what issues conferences can address says only that the conference report must be relevant to *something* in either the House or Senate version of the bill.) Tightly controlled and carefully orchestrated, conferences have been run with increasing skill to implement an intensely partisan agenda. All of this marks a profound break from traditional practice. Questioned about the decline of conferences as a venue for bipartisan, cross-chamber compromise, Senator Rick Santorum responded: "This idea that somehow or other . . . everybody has a seat at the table all the time, it's just not the way this place operates. The majority means something. It means that you win."[31]

The availability of conference committees offers the Republican Senate leadership a close approximation to the closed rules that operate in the House to exclude potentially troublesome amendments. This is because once a conference (heavily stacked in favor of Republicans) has crafted an agreement, it is subject to a straight up-or-down vote in each chamber. Even in the Senate, no amendments are allowed.

In fact, conference committees can sometimes offer even better backlash insurance than closed rules. This is because conferences create opportunities for Republican senators to simultaneously stake out "moderate" positions and pursue extreme policies. When legislation first comes before the Senate, senators are free to take "moderate" positions on elements of the legislation. Many of these positions, however, will ultimately not matter, because the leadership, via the conference, controls the presentation of alternatives at the crucial final stage. Thus Republican "moderates" were able to cast "independent" votes on the initial tax bill in 2003 before "reluctantly" falling in line for the final vote on the conference committee's proposal—which in key respects was *further* from their own stated preferences than President Bush's proposals, which they loudly rejected as unacceptable at an earlier stage. With conference committees, senators get to join their House colleagues in having their cake and eating it, too, as the leadership lets them happily engage in cheap, which is to say meaningless, moderation.

Despite this impressive set of agenda-control techniques, the urge to venture off center may still leave some Republicans facing politically dangerous votes. So should awkward matters need to come up for a vote, the leadership has refined an additional clever stratagem called "catch and release." Moderates feeling pressure to vote against a bill are "caught" until the leadership is confident it has the votes for passage. Once victory is assured, nervous Republicans are "released" one by one to vote their "conscience." Releases can be granted to the members who face the greatest pressures or to those who haven't had a good opportunity to express their "independence" lately. The beauty of the technique for political extremists needs to be underscored. Once again, it permits cheap moderation. Off-center policies can provide useful opportunities to burnish moderates' reputations, but only once it is assured that their votes won't matter.

Insurance Policy #3: Policy (Mis)Design

The power of Republican leaders extends beyond controlling how issues and alternatives come to a vote. Centralization and coordination also facilitate the third powerful source of backlash insurance: control over policy design. Our review of Republican policy initiatives has revealed how, time after time, proposals are carefully crafted to maximize the gap between moderate appearance and extremist substance. The upfront loading of middle-class tax cuts, the hiding of big corporate giveaways behind the label of "prescription drug insurance," the casting of a fundamental transformation of Social Security as a modest "modernization," the behind-the-scenes undermining of health, safety, and environmental law—all of these are notable not only because of what they say about Republican intentions but also because they hide those intentions so well. The new rules for Republican radicals that we outlined in Chapter 3, from "Run from Daylight" to "Starve the Beast—Later," express an abiding GOP aspiration: to advance off-center ambitions without making those ambitions apparent.

This aspiration can be aided by the use of poll-tested rhetoric and focus group-formulated language (what political scientists Lawrence Jacobs and Robert Shapiro nicely term "crafted talk").[32] But now policy design itself has become thoroughly politicized. Features of legislation themselves are subjected to careful strategic vetting to determine which components will "prime" voters in the appropriate ways. Armed with this information, GOP elites design laws not to *respond* to public opinion but to manipulate and shape it to maximize political gain. Policy complexities are exploited and magnified to increase the size of subsidies for privileged groups. Time bombs calibrated to reconfigure the future political agenda favorably are quietly slipped into law. And then, using all the tools of coordination, these hopelessly complicated designs are hurried through Congress with no time for analysis or reflection—which is exactly how the designers want it.

The political use of policy design is nothing new. All elected officials try to make their policies popular and politically sustainable. What is new is the *degree* to which policy design has become politicized, the *amount* of manipulation that takes place, the *frequency* with which these strategies are exploited, and the *exclusiveness* of the main beneficiaries. For those who say, "This has always happened," we have a simple response: "Yes, but not like this." As with the use of procedural legerdemain, the increasing manipulation of voters through policy design has precedents in past efforts by Democrats as well as Republicans. But current practice far exceeds what has been done before in both ubiquity and extent.

Consider once again the sunset provisions of the tax cuts—provisions that supposedly terminate tax cuts at a certain date in the future but which in practice are designed solely to make the tax cuts look smaller (and hence less threatening to popular programs and the budget) than they really are. (The reality that the sunset provisions were never intended to take place is underscored by Republicans' current claims that failing to extend the tax cuts will amount to the "biggest tax increase in American history"—a tax increase that they supported in 2001 and 2003 when they put the sunset provisions into law.) As we pointed out in Chapter 2, drawing on the research of two respected Brookings Institution economists, previous budgets had included a few small sunset provisions, but the net effect was marginal. As late as 2001, the cost five years down the line of extending budget items set to expire was less than $10 billion. In 2003, the comparable figure was almost $140 billion— and the cost ten years out was a stunning $430 billion, or nearly 2.5 percent of the nation's economy. To say "this has been done before" about these policy manipulations would be like saying "this has been done before" to the builders of the Great Wall of China because peasants had already built fences.

In engaging in these extensive manipulations, Republican elites are responding to a simple reality: The prospects for electoral backlash are heavily dependent on voters' knowledge both of what politicians do and of what those actions mean for their own well-being. As the political scientist R. Douglas Arnold has persuasively argued, electoral retribution against incumbents for their policy choices requires that the policy's effects are *discernible* by voters, *traceable* to the policies themselves, and that voters can determine who should be held responsible.[33] These conditions are not easily met, and at every stage, formidable cognitive hurdles can be built to thwart voters from making the necessary connections.[34]

For example, those who design policies can affect their traceability— the degree to which voters can ascertain their effects and link them back to specific decisions—by increasing the uncertainty, length, and complexity of the causal stages that lie between a policy's enactment and its perceived outcomes. Ideally, politicians hope to design initiatives for which the benefits are easy to perceive and the costs are hidden. Time lags and phase-ins are helpful in this regard, so policy makers often front-load benefits and back-load costs. With such features, they can tailor even relatively straightforward initiatives to make it very difficult to recognize true effects.

Indeed, all of the knowledge that voters need to exercise control can be filtered and shaped through the design of policies. The policy world is a complex environment, in which those who are able to control and coordinate the design of policies have tremendous power. Whether citizens are mobilized politically and whom and what options they support frequently turn on how elites fashion the complex instruments of governance. And these instruments can be used not only to exploit limitations in voter knowledge but also to take advantage of vast inequalities in political knowledge that distinguish ordinary Americans from the most privileged. Time and again, Republican policy initiatives have been designed in ways that systematically place meager or doubtful benefits for average Americans prominently in the foreground while quietly showering the bulk of their largesse on the attentive and well off.

The use of policy design under the New Power Brokers is the apotheosis of the "anything goes" logic of political warfare. In the age of big government, the temptation to use policy to undermine political accountability is powerful and ever present. But that temptation has traditionally been tempered by two countervailing realities: the need to seek compromise with those who do not share your goals, and the desire to draw on expertise that is not narrowly political. The increasing coordination, conservatism, and power of the Republican coalition have largely done away with the first inconvenience. Republican elites have dispensed with the second on their own.

We can see how far current elites have moved from past practice in the evident shock and dismay of one of the few policy experts to go on record after having spent time in the Bush White House, John DiIulio. As DiIulio noted in his confessional memo, "In eight months, I heard many, many staff discussions, but not three meaningful, substantive policy discussions. There were no actual policy white papers on domestic issues. There were, truth be told, only a couple of people in the West Wing who worried at all about policy substance and analysis. . . . Every modern presidency moves on the fly, but, on social policy and related issues, the lack of even basic policy knowledge, and the only casual interest in knowing more, was somewhat breathtaking." But perhaps DiIulio's most revealing revelation was who was in charge of policy design in the Bush White House—not the Office of Management and Budget, not the White House policy staff, and certainly not the executive departments. Rather, all policy ran through one man, Karl Rove. "Little happens on any issue without Karl's okay, and, often, he supplies such policy substance as the administration puts out," wrote DiIulio. The reason? "The Republican base constituencies, including beltway libertarian policy elites and religious right leaders, trust him to keep Bush '43' from behaving like Bush '41' and moving too far to the center or inching at all center-left."[35]

Insurance Policy #4: The Republican Rescue Squad

Yet what if all these tools of backlash insurance are not enough? What if the eagerness to pursue off-center policies is such that even this impressive set of protections is not sufficient to make potentially vulnerable supporters feel safe? All is not lost. For Republican elites can offer one last set of reassurances linked to the formidable resources they can mobilize. "If you're in trouble," they can say, "we will provide the money you need to crush a potential opponent."

The key to this promise, as we discussed in Chapter 4, is a striking development of the past decade that has affected both parties, but especially Republicans: the rise of a more centralized financial apparatus. Here one must include both the huge amounts of money parties can provide directly *and* the money they can leverage by calling on party supporters in the lobbying world. In combination, these resources constitute a crucial additional layer of insurance against any trouble vulnerable incumbents might face.

In the last chapter, we saw that more and more incumbents reside in districts where electoral challenge is a remote possibility outside of party primaries, and we reviewed some of the reasons for this. Perhaps the most worrisome cause of the trend—worrisome because, by placing politicians in the position of picking voters rather than the other way around, it so grievously undermines true electoral accountability—is partisan gerrymandering. Redrawing district boundaries to ensure that Republicans enjoy consistently safe margins is a powerful form of backlash insurance, and one of the Republican rescue squad's most potent weapons against the potentially moderating influence of electoral competition.

Yet even representatives in districts where presidential election results suggest potential vulnerability rarely face serious threats. A careful analysis by three Emory University political scientists suggests that financial advantages are a big part of the reason. The cost of running a competitive campaign has roughly tripled in the past decade, raising the bar beyond the reach of many potentially viable challengers. In 1972, according to the Emory University researchers, more than half of experienced challengers in promising districts were able to wage financially competitive campaigns. By 2002, however, fewer than a seventh could do so. In fact, "even those challengers with the greatest potential for running competitive campaigns are having more and more difficulty raising the funds necessary. . . . As a result, competition is now confined to open seats and a handful of races involving exceptionally vulnerable incumbents and/or exceptionally well-financed challengers."[36]

Nothing Succeeds Like Success

Backlash insurance is a product that seeks its own obsolescence. The better it works, the less it's needed. The high level of loyalty Republicans leaders have commanded reflects their enhanced capacity to protect their members. And the more loyalty Republican leaders command, the easier it is for them to protect the party rank and file against the unwanted interference of moderate voters. Republican leaders have increased their power precisely because they have attenuated the connection between off-center forays and the risk of electoral backlash. And they have weakened the "electoral connection" precisely by virtue of the fact they have increased their power to shape the agenda and actions of their party.[37]

Most political analysts have missed the true scope of this crucial development because they have failed to fully appreciate the increasingly networked character of the modern conservative movement. The GOP coalition is not simply the sum of its parts. Looking only at Congress, or only at lobbyists, will not reveal the full picture. Instead, the power of Republican leaders, and of others at the top of the new GOP hierarchy, results in large part from their increased role in linking these realms. Top Republican leaders are, quite literally, brokers. And their power is multiplicative, not additive. The more they can control the behavior of legislators, the more they can control the behavior of lobbyists. And the more they can control the behavior of lobbyists, the more they can control the behavior of legislators. Each link in this complex chain of power holds together because the leaders—and only the leaders—can deliver.

For this reason, simply adding up or comparing the power of elements of the conservative movement largely misses the point. What has changed is the ability of all these actors to operate in a more coordinated fashion. In a real sense, the power of conservative leaders, rank-and-file Republican politicians, and interest groups have all increased simultaneously. Centralization and coordination permit the common and energetic pursuit of a conservative agenda—without excessive and unwanted distractions from voters, the media, the opposition, or centrist GOP incumbents. Indeed, these great "guardians" of the center have repeatedly been sidestepped, bought off, outfoxed, or overridden, as the next chapter makes abundantly clear.

6

THE CENTER DOES NOT HOLD

The "center" is the lodestar of American politics, the ultimate destination of all politicians who want to get things done. In virtually every election or policy debate, political deal-makers eventually head for the center. They do so for a simple reason. In American politics, power rests in the middle—with swing voters in the electorate and with moderates in Congress. To flee the center is not to forge a new trail. It is to rush headlong over a cliff.

Or so the conventional image of American politics suggests. In fact, Republicans have blazed an off-center trail while keeping their feet planted on terra firma. We have watched in previous chapters as coordinated GOP leaders and their followers raced to their base in hot pursuit of an off-center agenda, generously deploying backlash insurance as they went. Still, a question remains: How have Republicans overcome the many political forces that traditionally hold such extremist ambitions at bay? To be sure, as the last two chapters have shown, Republicans have new reasons to race to their base and new tools to get away with it. But how are these incentives and strategies powerful enough to overcome the once-formidable pull of the center?

After all, the checks and balances of American politics are not simply institutional. They consist, in addition, of crucial "guardians" of moderation—voters, the opposition party, the media, and electorally vulnerable politicians. According to our received view of American politics, these guardians should have been galvanized into action by the off-center drift of politics and policy, assuring a return to the hallowed middle ground. Understanding why this hasn't happened gives us deeper insight into the Right's new might.

Homo Apoliticus

The ultimate guardian of the center is supposed to be the American people. If American politicians are heading right but American citizens are not, then at the next election those politicians will be shown the door. Indeed—as optimistic as this view may seem by this point—a large body of political science research and theory asserts that democratic accountability in the United States is surprisingly strong. We say "surprisingly" because no serious student of politics believes that Americans are the über citizens of democratic theory. Analysts have long known that most Americans generally pay little attention to politics and have limited political knowledge. To take just a few examples, less than a third of Americans know that a member of the House serves for two years or that a senator serves for six. In 2000, only 55 percent knew the Republicans were the majority party in the House. Just two years after the impeachment trial in the Senate, only 11 percent could identify William Rehnquist as Chief Justice of the United States. And awareness of essential facts related to policy debates is typically even less impressive than basic civics knowledge. Roughly half of Americans think that foreign aid is one of the two top expenditures in the federal budget (in reality, it consumes about 1 percent of the budget). In 1980, in the midst of the Cold War, 38 percent of Americans surveyed believed that the Soviet Union was a member of NATO—the anti-Soviet defense alliance. Two years after the huge 2001 tax cuts, as we saw in Chapter 2, half of Americans were unable to recall that taxes had been cut at all.[1]

And yet, many professional analysts have remarkable faith in that object of traditional skepticism: the American voter. These analysts largely take for granted the limited attention and knowledge of everyday citizens. They argue, however, that citizens make surprisingly efficient use of what little information they have and that electoral systems, in aggregating citizens' views, further sort bad information from good. Employing mental cues and shortcuts, such as signals from social acquaintances or public figures, voters can produce outcomes not so different from those that would emerge if they were fully informed. Voters do not need to read the legislative fine print or even the bold print to know where they stand on issues they care about. It is enough to know how visible figures or groups they trust (or loathe)—from Ted Kennedy to the National Rifle Association—are aligned on the issue at hand.[2]

What is more, voters don't act alone. Their views have impact only though elections and other processes of social aggregation. And these processes, according to many researchers, have strong rationalizing qualities that enhance the electorate's power. An analogy is the stock market. Market watchers generally have great respect for the stock market as a repository of what is known about the value of companies. This is not because those who invest in the stock market are necessarily well informed and savvy. It is because when the judgments of millions of individual investors are combined, mistakes tend to cancel out. Some people overestimate, others underestimate. But over millions of decisions, this "noise" gets filtered out, and the average price comes remarkably close to capturing the real value of a company.

Optimistic analysts of American politics believe that the electoral "market" closely resembles the stock market. Just as the Dow Jones may be an accurate store of widely dispersed information about the economy, aggregation of public views—in opinion surveys and in elections—filters out weak spots in voters' political knowledge while magnifying areas of strength. Individuals may be inattentive, ill informed, and often irrational. The voting public as a collective entity, however, is attentive, informed, and rational.[3]

These are powerful and creative arguments. Unfortunately, they also rest on shaky foundations. Voters *can* discipline politicians. But to do so effectively, they need important resources that are too often lacking. The most crucial is knowledge: knowledge of what politicians do, and knowledge of what those actions mean for citizens.

Return to the analogy of the stock market. The magic of aggregation works only if mistaken understandings are distributed randomly, so they will tend to cancel out. One person's overestimate is offset by someone else's underestimate. But what if highly resourceful elites are working nonstop to produce *consistent* distortions in voters' understandings?

What if these elites are trained to identify the precise weak spots in public perceptions? And what if they employ teams of specialists, adept at developing the best strategies for exploiting those vulnerabilities? In these circumstances, the analogy may not be an idealized, distortion-free marketplace. It may be the markets beset by economic scandals during the late 1990s, which came to be symbolized by Enron. In the case of Enron, insiders possessed enormously more information about their companies than outsiders did. And they developed a range of sophisticated techniques designed specifically to prevent the sending of clear signals about the value of their companies, allowing them to pick the pockets of average investors.

American government has not turned into Enron. But as our discussion in the last chapter indicates, the systematic efforts of political elites to distort public perceptions of their activities bear more than a passing resemblance. And as was true in recent financial scandals, the goal of many of these efforts is not simply to exploit limitations in knowledge in general but to exploit limitations in knowledge precisely among those who would be most likely to be angered if they were aware of what was going on.

Indeed, this tailored disinformation strikes at a second fundamental weakness of optimistic claims about how opinion leaders and social aggregation protect ordinary voters. These arguments typically assume that even if particular individuals are likely to remain ignorant, "good" information will be relatively equally distributed among voters with differing preferences. This assumption, however, is unwarranted. Study after study finds that the politically active, far from identical in their preferences or characteristics to the politically inactive, are notably more extreme. As Steven Rosenstone and John Mark Hansen sum up the evidence, "The . . . decline of citizen involvement in elections and . . . in government has yielded a politically engaged class that is not only growing smaller and smaller but also less and less representative of the American polity."[4] Furthermore, voters who know little about one issue are likely to know little about another. Lack of political knowledge is self-reinforcing and cumulative. As the dean of American public opinion studies, Philip Converse, observes: "With information as with wealth, 'them that has gets,' and there is no comforting system of progressive taxation on information to help redress the drift toward glaring inequalities."[5]

As we saw in Chapter 2, the politics of tax cuts vindicates these concerns. The better informed were precisely the groups that stood to gain from the lower-profile elements of the tax cuts. Had accurate information about the tax cuts been more widely and equally distributed, the political dynamics would have been very different. Indeed, research by Princeton political scientist Larry Bartels reveals that the more people knew about the tax cuts, the less favorable their views became. Richer Americans were both more favorable to the tax cuts and better informed. But once the effect of income was factored out using standard statistical techniques, greater knowledge produced greater opposition, not greater support.[6]

The bottom line is that voters have strategies to compensate for their informational limitations, but coordinated and powerful elites have at least as many strategies to prey on those limitations. Still, voters don't have to grapple with these elites completely on their own. They have at least three powerful allies in their struggle: the opposition, the media, and vulnerable politicians. Confidence in the sway of the center often rests on faith that these three groups of "counter-elites" will act as guardians of moderation. This faith is not without foundation. But, unfortunately, its foundation is much less solid than commonly thought.

The Loyal Opposition?

In democracies, a major protection against partisan aggrandizement is the challenge of the opposition. Rather than try to limit ambition, democracies seek to check ambition with counterambition (in the political scientist Robert Dahl's terms, they place *contestation* alongside *participation* as a means of ensuring responsiveness).[7] What thwarts elite dominance is fierce competition among *teams* of elites for public office. Those who rule always face challenges from those eager to replace them. Opponents hunt for any opening to swing the electoral balance in their favor. Off-center policies create just such an opening.

In the purest vision of such contestation, the governing coalition has little capacity to control the agenda or dominate the framing of issues. Their opponents will always counter, raising alternative issues, alternative proposals, and alternative ways of understanding the matter at hand. And since, in general, each side should be about as skilled and ambitious as the other, each is likely to identify and exploit the most powerful options available. Like contesting car companies, each side seeks to offer the voters the best vehicle. And just as competition among car companies allows consumers to get better automobiles at lower prices, competition between parties means that voters get better representation with less effort. The nonstop efforts of dueling teams to sell their wares leave the voter in the driver's seat.

To be sure, the United States has rarely featured no-holds-barred competition between cohesive and unified partisan teams. Still, as the parties have grown more distinct and cohesive, something close to team-based party competition has come to seem more the norm. And sometimes it has even worked. When control of Congress and the executive branch resides in the hands of different parties, as they did during the Reagan years and after the Gingrich-led Republicans won control of Congress in 1994, competing parties may battle each other to a draw. Democrats confronting Reagan, for example, were able to prevent many of the Great Communicator's proposed cuts in social programs in the 1980s. Republicans, for their part, had little trouble blocking Clinton initiatives that diverged from the center, even before they captured Congress in 1994. And in the dramatic clash over the budget in the mid-1990s, Clinton and the GOP Congress repeatedly jousted before, exhausted, they settled on a compromise in 1997.

But the battle is not always so even, especially when one side controls all the major venues of government and has a strong capacity to coordinate the activities of its coalition. Since the 2000 election, the opposition Democrats have worked energetically to contest agenda control, but they have faced formidable obstacles. Decrying their evident ineffectiveness, today's Democrats typically lament the loss of their own Great Communicator, Bill Clinton. But of course what was lost was not just a single highly skilled politician. Democrats also lost the most valuable site for developing and deploying a political message: the White House.

Possessing an effective spokesman and the bully pulpit, Democrats were able to compete with the Republicans' coordinated message machine in the 1990s. Without these advantages, the Democrats' weaker capacity to coordinate around a powerful message has been all too apparent.

For, clearly, even when Democrats did have a stronger institutional position in the 1990s, they proved much less capable of coordinating around key initiatives than Republicans have in recent years. Although Congress began to move toward greater centralization well before the Gingrich revolution, the capacity of the Democratic leadership to construct and impose an agenda was strikingly limited in comparison with subsequent Republican efforts. The contrast between Bush's first two years and Clinton's is telling. The Clinton administration's top priority—health care reform—foundered on the shoals of internal party divisions, before Republicans and mobilized conservative forces delivered the coup de grâce. Far from following the dictates of the Democratic leadership in the House, committee barons battled furiously over jurisdiction. Squabbling Democrats were never able to get legislation to the floor of the House, much less move it successfully through a Congress nominally under their control. Congressional Democrats seeking to establish independent political stances opportunistically triangulated between the two parties. These independent and highly publicized efforts fueled perceptions that Clinton's proposal was extreme while making it easier for conservatives and organized interests to block the plan without the threat of seeming extreme. Even supportive interests played fast and loose, holding out for a better deal as the momentum behind the initiative was hopelessly lost.

Although the two parties have both become more cohesive, there remains considerable truth to the old Will Rogers joke about the Democratic Party's basic organizational deficiencies. ("I am not a member of any organized political party; I'm a Democrat.") In crucial areas, from fundraising to congressional leadership to the fervor of the base, the Democratic Party is both less centralized and less networked than the contemporary Republican Party. Individual Democrats, when they have enjoyed power at all, have much more jealously hoarded their autonomy than have the Republican rank and file—a reality on display repeatedly in Clinton's two terms. Moreover, big money is a strong unifying force for Republicans, but it introduces considerable cross-pressures for Democrats. Important elements of the standard Democratic agenda, especially on economic issues, coexist awkwardly with the realities of contemporary political finance, which require that Democrats seek support from deep-pocketed business contributors. As we will see in the Conclusion, there are exceptions to these generalizations. But they are just that: exceptions. Democrats still have a hard time escaping the Tower of Babel.

If Democratic elites tended to act like cats at the best of times, the loss of institutional control has only accentuated these tendencies. Republicans have repeatedly used the resources at their disposal to break Democratic unity and, with it, the capacity to develop a coherent message. Moderate or vulnerable Democrats, after all, are scarcely immune to some of the techniques that Republicans use to pacify GOP moderates. Agenda control allows the majority to pick issues, design alternatives, and frame debates in ways calibrated to peel off isolated Democrats. Indeed, all of the tools of backlash insurance that we discussed in the last chapter can have the effect of placing key Democrats in extremely difficult positions. Backed by effective marketing and forced to the agenda as up-or-down votes, certain policy labels are hard to resist, even for elected officials fully aware that what's actually inside the package is distasteful. Under these circumstances—as we saw on tax cuts and prescription drug legislation—some Democrats simply find it hard to say no. And, of course, these Democrats often realize that, given Republican unity, their resistance will not stop legislation from passing anyway.

Republicans may actually have to bargain if they need a Democrat or two (perhaps to clear a committee hurdle in the Senate or overcome a particularly thorny "poison pill" that Democrats manage to get on the agenda). But in many cases there are several prospects to provide the needed votes. Thus the bargaining may well take the form of a reverse auction (that is, an auction with many sellers and one buyer): Who is willing to provide their vote at the lowest price? We have seen occasions where relatively small "side payments" to wavering Democrats were sufficient to give Republicans a victory. In fact, this scenario typically produces the New Power Brokers' ideal "bipartisan" bill: one advancing an off-center agenda that is passed with overwhelming Republican support and a handful of largely symbolic Democratic votes. Of course, if Democrats could evince the same coordination that Republicans do, reverse auctions of this sort would be difficult to pull off. But keeping potentially wayward party members in check is hard enough for any party out of power, and it is particularly hard for the Democrats.

One reason why it is so hard is that there are actually some significant rewards—both political and material—for becoming the occasional Democrat who crosses party lines. Just as moderate Republicans can gain by staging carefully crafted "revolts" against their leadership (revolts that, in the present Congress, are rarely more than symbolic), moderate Democrats can gain by showing their "independence" on issues they loudly trumpet as crucial to the nation's future. Former Senator John Breaux of Louisiana and current Senator Joe Lieberman of Connecticut made names for themselves with their eagerness to assume this mantle. What makes these moments of statesmanship so valuable for Democrats like Breaux and Lieberman is not just that they get cast in the spotlight as defenders of the bipartisan way (even when their participation provides the only evidence of bipartisanship). Equally valuable, the dealmakers get to nudge policy in directions that advance their political needs. Such nudges, however, have in recent years almost never gone beyond marginal adjustments to primarily Republican-crafted bills. Cheap moderation has its counterpart in cheap bipartisanship.

Sometimes the reward for cheap bipartisanship is merely the opportunity for an ostentatious show of above-the-fray leadership. But at other times, it is the opportunity to please a local interest crucial to one's political standing and future. Tom Daschle's embrace of the Republican-backed energy plan because it supported greater reliance on the corn-based fuel additive Ethanol—a big home-state cause—is a case in point. When Republicans only have to peel off a few votes to pass an industry-favorable bill, it does not take great ingenuity to figure out which Democrats have the most at stake in the matter: those who are elected from places where the favored industry provides jobs and campaign dollars. As the journalist Jonathan Chait pointedly complains, "Noxious laws enjoy support from a coalition of all the Republicans plus a rotating handful of Democrats who have ties to interested parties. Almost all the Democrats are on the side of the angels on almost every issue. But it doesn't take many Democratic defectors to give the Republicans a majority."[8]

A second reason that Democrats have great trouble keeping their troops in line brings us back to the Great Compromise of Senate apportionment. We noted in Chapter 1 that the two-senator-per-state rule generally advantages Republicans in the battle for Senate seats. But alongside that straightforward advantage lies another enormous benefit that the Senate's territorial organization confers on Republicans—the omnipresence of Democrats elected from "red states" that Republican presidential candidates routinely win. Although Bush lost the popular vote in 2000, for example, he won thirty of the nation's states. In 2004, while winning just 51 percent of the popular vote, he raised the total number of states he carried to thirty-one—or 62 percent of the nation's states. It is hard to paint a clearer picture than this of the degree to which Republican presidential standard-bearers are advantaged in smaller states.

Many Democrats in the Senate are from these less populated "red states." After 2000, twenty of fifty Democratic senators were elected from states Bush had won in 2000. After the elections of 2004, the number hailing from a state won by Bush in the last election fell to sixteen of the Democrats' reduced ranks of forty-four. These senators are the politicians to whom Republicans come calling when they need Democratic votes. During the tax-cut debate of 2001, for example, President Bush campaigned strenuously for his proposal in Senator Max Baucus's home state of Montana. The reason was not that Bush needed to court Montana—he received nearly 60 percent of the vote there in 2000. And he was certainly not going to change American public opinion by focusing on a state with a population just slightly smaller than that of Detroit. Bush's goal was instead to frighten Baucus into signing onto the agenda of a president who had crushed Al Gore in Baucus's backyard. Revealingly, every one of the Senate Democrats whom Bush singled out for special praise at the signing ceremony for the 2001 tax cuts—Baucus, Breaux, and Zell Miller of Georgia—came from states that Bush had won handily in 2000.

It is worth emphasizing the obvious point that Bush's ability to win states represented by nearly two-thirds of the country's senators does not mean, by any stretch of the imagination, that Bush enjoys the support of two-thirds of the American people. Rather, the Senate's structure gives an important bargaining advantage to the party best able to appeal to lower-population states. Even as Democratic senators have held on in many of these sparsely populated regions, they have seen their party's presidential standard-bearers go down to crushing defeats. These results put them on constant notice that their own future may be less than wholly secure if they provoke the concerted attacks of the president who won their state. Of course, a similar logic applies to Republican senators from states won by Democrats. But thanks to the small-state bias of the Senate, there are many fewer such states. After the 2004 election, only nine Republican senators held seats in states won by John Kerry.

All this underscores how difficult it is for the contemporary Democratic Party to maintain enough party discipline to prevent legislation from passing in the face of coordinated Republican offensives. To many liberal pundits, this points to the need for Democrats to follow the Republicans' lead and adopt the disciplined mode of operation of a parliamentary-style party. Democrats should not attempt to participate in governing, they argue, since Republicans exclude them from any real power. Instead, they should act as a loyal opposition—focused, unified, and committed to bringing down the party in power. In fact, limited steps in this direction have already occurred. Party unity scores have risen on the Democratic side, and party leaders have argued that Democrats' only chance of real influence is to stick together rather than seek out individual compromises. The narrow margins in Congress make a firmly oppositional stance more attractive, since bringing down those in control looms as a realistic prospect.

Yet the United States is *not* a parliamentary democracy, and it's unrealistic to expect Democrats to act as though it is. Republicans have built a centralized, unified party through decades of network building. Their unity is enforced through the exercise of political authority and the capacity to dispense and withhold benefits from the rank and file. In the United States, these tools are much more plentiful for the majority party than they are for the minority party, and they are far better developed on the Republican side of the aisle than they are on the Democratic.

In the American political system, the road of loyal opposition is lonely and often unrewarding. Unlike in a parliamentary system, there is no "leader" of the opposition who can consistently command attention. Instead, jostling among competing contenders for that title is inevitable. Journalists, moreover, pay attention to those with power, particularly the president. A Democratic National Committee study showed, for instance, that in a three-month period in 2002, CNN carried 157 Bush administration events but only 7 Democratic leadership events.[9] This huge imbalance is notable not because it reveals partisan media bias—as we will show in a moment, partisan bias is not the most interesting issue raised by the media's current operation. It is notable because it shows how hard it is for the minority to gain critically needed attention.

Democrats have trouble attracting attention in large part because it is so hard for them to take the initiative. They cannot force a "vote of no confidence," the parliamentary nuclear option that can topple the party in power. They cannot force consideration of bills, or conduct hearings. Almost always in Washington, Democrats are forced to engage in battles, and on terms, that the Republicans choose. Watching American politics today, as the columnist Ronald Brownstein notes, is "like watching a baseball game where one team is always at bat, or a basketball game where one team always has the ball."[10] Under these circumstances, the temptation of individual Democrats—especially individual Democrats from states that routinely vote Republican in the presidential arena—to defect from the opposition coalition is constant and frequently overwhelming. And even a few defections may allow Republicans to describe their initiatives as "bipartisan." The loyal opposition is too often the languid opposition.

The Fourth Estate

In the United States, the news media is seen as a crucial watchdog over the political establishment, not least by reporters themselves. As two veteran editors of the *Washington Post*, Leonard Downie, Jr., and Robert Kaiser, summarize this widely held aspiration: "Accountability is an important check on . . . power. Our politicians know that informed voters can throw them out of office . . . Good journalism is a principal source of the information necessary to make such accountability meaningful. Anyone tempted to abuse power looks over his or her shoulder to see if someone else is watching. Ideally, there should be a reporter in the rearview mirror."[11]

Indeed, since most of what Americans know about politics is gleaned from the media, reporters seem especially well placed to guard against political gambits that depart from citizens' wishes. If the media's watchdog role is as integral to contemporary society as many in the news business believe, then politicians who want to head off center should be checking their rearview mirrors often.

Yet the information and communications revolutions of the past few decades have not been kind to this watchdog role. Nor have the political transformations that we have tracked in this book. Over the past decade or so, political elites have not only refined their techniques for dealing with voters; they have also refined their strategies for managing the media. As Republican efforts to move off center have become more aggressive and coordinated, the news media have found themselves increasingly ill equipped and overmatched. Far too often, they act like lapdogs rather than watchdogs in the political battles waged through their outlets.

Discussions of the media's role in American politics typically focus on one big issue: partisan bias. The evidence on this score is mixed. Most journalists describe their political orientation as centrist, although their voting choices lean Democratic. In response to specific questions about policy, journalists are left of center on social issues like affirmative action, gay rights, and abortion, and right of center on economic issues like taxes, deregulation, and Social Security privatization. Publishers, not surprisingly, lean right. And, historically, so too have editorial pages. The Pew Charitable Trust's Project for Excellence in Journalism conducted a careful content analysis of the 2000 campaign and found that stories about Bush were twice as likely as those about Gore to have a positive slant. Given these decidedly mixed results, it says a good deal about the Republican machine's success that the dispute today is not *whether* there is "liberal media bias" but how extreme that bias is. (Our Google search for "liberal media bias" yielded more than 47,000 hits, compared to 710 for "conservative media bias.")[12]

No doubt there are interesting observations to be made about partisan bias in the media. To understand the media's place in politics, however, this is the wrong place to begin. It is the conventional media's other biases that have contributed the most to its weakening watchdog role.

The first of *these* biases is the simplest: The news media is in the entertainment business rather than the information business. And in the contemporary entertainment world, "eyeballs" are subject to fierce competition and easy distraction. For those in the news media, this puts a premium on drama and brevity. The amount of political news has steadily declined in the major media outlets. And what stories there are have become shorter and more personality-focused. The changes are especially dramatic on the major television networks, which from the 1960s until a few years ago were the principal source of news for most Americans. Television news has never been a very good forum for the transmission of large amounts of information. An edition of the *New York Times* or *Washington Post* contains about a hundred thousand words—more than this book. The NBC nightly news averages about thirty-six hundred words. Even in the heyday of network news, the text of Walter Cronkite's broadcast would cover about half the front page of a top daily newspaper.[13]

But over the past few decades, these news broadcasts have been transformed. Changes in the media environment, particularly the spread of cable, have transformed the networks' news operations from relatively cozy monopolies into increasingly fierce competitors for a shrinking share of the audience. Between 1981 and 2001, the three network news broadcasts lost about 40 percent of their audience. When asked in 2000 to describe the mission of *NBC Nightly News*, Tom Brokaw's two-word answer was "to survive."[14]

This economic and technological upheaval has dictated a sharp turn from "hard news" toward entertainment. Every story has to grab the viewer immediately, because a single dull moment risks the dreaded click of a remote control. As a result, stories have become shorter, and the emphasis has shifted to those that can best exploit the visual power of television: scandal, crime, celebrities, natural disasters, and "soft" news items like personal health and personal finance. What has been squeezed out is hard news, especially concerning relatively complex issues of policy or politics that require many words to explain and typically yield poor visuals. During the presidential campaign of 1968, candidates could expect to speak on camera for an average of forty seconds without inter-ruption; two decades later, the average is just *nine* seconds. Not surpris-ingly, detailed discussions of policy that would allow voters to get a better sense of the stakes in ongoing political conflict fare especially poorly in this environment.

The print media performs a little better, but not much. There is a lot of wonderful reporting around—our book could not have been written without it. And careful, critical reading of the best national pa-pers can yield a great deal of information about politics and policy. Few Americans, however, get their knowledge of public affairs this way, and fewer do every year. Although by the early 1960s the majority of Americans already got their news mostly from television, 81 per cent of American adults still said they were regular newspaper readers. In 2000, only 55 percent did. As with television, the content has changed. At the beginning of the 1960s, most newspapers were independently owned, but today four-fifths are owned by chains. With consolidation has come a more relentless focus on profits and a stronger message from the top that newspapers are simply another commodity. From this vantage point, intensive reporting can look like an unnecessary expense. Instead, editors are induced to push their newspapers in the same entertainment direction that the networks have taken. In the words of John Carroll, the executive editor of the *Los Angeles Times*, "fewer and fewer news-papers carry significant national reports; some pretty major American dailies have just about eliminated them." As Downie and Kaiser, the *Washington Post* editors, conclude: "The sad truth is that only a handful of American papers give their readers enough news to make them well-informed citizens of the country and the world."[15]

Certainly most newspapers provide very limited information related to the content of policy—information that we have demonstrated is cru-cial for accountability. Consider how *USA Today*, the nation's largest circulation daily, covered the Bush tax cuts in 2001. We and a team of researchers examined every story written in the newspaper on the 2001 tax cuts. Recall again that this was the president's top domestic priority and the most important piece of domestic legislation in two decades. The stakes for Americans were huge. Appropriately, *USA Today* ran 78 stories about the tax cuts, many of them on the front page. But of those 78 articles, only 6 were primarily about the content of the legislation. Only *one* was about the remarkable distributional effects of the proposed changes in policy. Instead, the focus of reporting was the political saga: the president's efforts to rally support, the tactics of opponents, and the slow but steady march of the Republicans' agenda through Congress. The bastion of detailed reportage, the *New York Times*, performed noticeably better, but the same bias was evident. The *Times* ran 126 stories, almost a third on the front page. But almost 60 percent were principally on the politics of the plan, whereas only 7 stories focused on distributional issues.[16] And, of course, most Americans are not getting their news from the *New York Times*.

In short, the tilt on display in the conventional news media is not so much left or right as it is away from political substance and toward political theater. Since the news media are in the entertainment business, the temptation to cover government like sports is hard to avoid. Yet it dovetails perfectly with the efforts of political elites to structure policymaking in ways that shed as little light as possible on their most extreme initiatives.

The second fundamental bias in contemporary journalism is a turn within the conventional news industry to "he said–she said" coverage of political life. In part to counter potential accusations of bias (from increasingly aggressive monitoring operations at both ends of the political spectrum), print and broadcast journalists alike have taken refuge in a style of objectivity that leans heavily on giving each "side" (all stories having exactly two) a platform for saying their piece. Thus news reports consist of dueling sound bites. Efforts to analyze the veracity or relevance of these claims, or to place them in context, are either left to the end of the story or left out altogether. To a remarkable extent, this style of reporting inverts the media's watchdog role, since it guarantees that stories will broadcast a message of political elites' choosing. True, this is done with a counter from the "other side." But the approach greatly enhances elites' capacity to use the press to disseminate inaccurate information or misleading arguments. These stories typically give the agenda setters the chance to go first. The inevitable, almost pro forma criticisms from obviously partisan opponents have little of the impact that tough analysis of a politician's misleading or inaccurate statements might have. Instead, the reader or viewer is likely to be left with the impression that each side has equal validity, even when, on close reflection, one side is advancing demonstrably false claims.

A third and final bias is also eroding the news media's watchdog role: a strong "herd mentality." Media analysts have long noted the tendency for conventional news reporters to jump on whatever the news band-wagon of the moment may be. But with dwindling resources and greater emphasis on finding the most entertaining stories, this proclivity has only become more acute. The problem of agenda setting that we discussed in the last chapter arises in the media as well. At any given time, only a few stories and a few frames for those stories tend to dominate conversation. Almost all the networks and almost all the newspapers quickly focus on the same territory. When partisans talk about "winning the news cycle," this is what they mean—that out of the many possible subjects of discussion, news reports of that day have concentrated on the issues and frames that help their side.

It is this herd mentality, coupled with the "he said–she said" orientation of the news and the emphasis on simple and exciting storylines, that creates such a strong link between effective coordination and success in the media. Through relentless repetition of key "talking points," partisans seek to exploit these herdlike characteristics of the news. Where they succeed, the media morphs from a watchdog into a giant amplifier. Of course, neither left nor right is able to do so consistently. But like the campers running from the bear, the more coordinated side is likely to have greater success.

Here one emerging element of organized bias in the media does warrant mention. Over the past two decades, conservatives have succeeded in building a substantial media empire. The outlets range from money-losing newspapers bankrolled by conservative ideologues like the *Washington Times* and *New York Post* to Fox and the Fox News Channel to a range of "news" and "public affairs" shows on various cable networks and talk radios stations that lean heavily to the right. Compared to the audience for traditional news outlets, most of this empire is still relatively small. Yet Fox has tremendous and growing reach, and if one extends the picture to take in right-wing talk radio, the audiences are often enormous. In 2002, for instance, 17 percent of Americans described talk radio shows as part of their "regular news consumption."[17] Although these shows obviously attract partisans who already share their viewpoint, the political scientist David Barker—in his book *Rushed to Judgment*— finds that the most powerful of the conservative talk radio hosts, Rush Limbaugh, does seem to change minds. Barker also found what other studies have also indicated: Those who get most of their news about politics from conservative media outlets may be hearing a great deal about politics, but what they are told is heavily slanted toward Republican interpretations, even on issues—such as the size of the deficit or whether Weapons of Mass Destruction have been found in Iraq—on which there are correct (but politically inconvenient) answers.[18]

In addition, the expanding conservative media empire has two characteristics that magnify its significance: It is strongly ideological, and it is closely coordinated with conservative political elites. Juxtaposed with the painfully neutral "he said–she said" reporting of the mainstream press, the intense partisanship in these emerging venues is bracing. There is simply nothing on the other side remotely like Fox News, where a former high-level Republican political operative and practiced practitioner of political spin, Roger Ailes, has served from the outset as CEO.

Nor is it simply that these "news" or "public affairs" operations are intensely partisan. They are also deeply enmeshed in coordinated conversations aimed at developing and disseminating successful political messages. Gingrich was quick to understand the possibilities. According to a *U.S. News and World Report* story in 1993, "Limbaugh stays in private contact with key Republican operatives and, as a result, his on-air comments regularly promote party policy and strategy. . . . Gingrich . . . calls the arrangement a 'very loose alliance,' but concedes there is a 'very close symbiotic relationship' between party leaders and Limbaugh."[19] Ailes was caught giving private advice to President Bush even as he ran a "fair and balanced" news operation. Right-wing media outlets as well as Bush aides join in the weekly meetings in Grover Norquist's office. In the words of the *Wall Street Journal*'s John Fund, also a prominent player in conservative circles, "all of the trains run through Grover's office."[20]

Even without the growing conservative media world, however, the news as currently configured creates big advantages for political actors

who are sufficiently coordinated to set the agenda for mainstream coverage. All the elements of bias in the new media environment—its focus on
entertainment, its reliance on "he said–she said" reporting, and its tendency to jump on the news bandwagon—create excellent opportunities
for amplifying conservative talking points. In the words of David Brock,
once a leading participant in what he calls the "Republican Noise
Machine" and now perhaps its toughest critic, "The American media as
a whole has become a powerful conveyor belt for conservative-generated
'news,' commentary, story lines, jargon, and spin. It is now possible to
watch a lie move from a disreputable right-wing Web site onto the after-
noon talk radio shows, to several cable chat shows throughout the
evening, and into the next morning's *Washington Post*—all in twenty-
four hours."[21] It is the structural biases created by the media's competitive environment and standard operating routines, rather than a leftward
or rightward tilt, that are the most serious impediments to the media's
watchdog role. But these biases are not themselves neutral. For the
watchdogs are themselves being watched. From detailed observation,
coordinated political elites have learned how to turn these biases to political advantage.

Canaries in the Coal Mine

If the media are not up to the task, there is one remaining guardian
of moderation seemingly poised to slow down the off-center express: the
Republican Party's most vulnerable and moderate politicians. In the image
of American politics that most professional analysts of politics were tutored
in, these middle-of-the-road legislators are decisive. Not only do they sit on
the fault lines of a competitive political system, warning those on either side
about potential fissures. But, in addition, the structure of decision rules in
Congress should, in theory, place power firmly in the hands of these moderate legislators. If party leaders need fifty votes, they need to attract their
most centrist party members. If they need sixty to overcome a Senate filibuster, they usually need to cross over and court moderates on the other
side of the aisle. They may decide not to make the effort, but if they don't,
then stalemate should ensue. When the moderates have effective power,

government may not do what middle-of-the-road voters want. But at the very least it should not do what middle-of-the-road voters *don't* want.

In this sense, moderate politicians are like the proverbial canary in the coal mine, acutely sensitive to any change in the atmosphere. Indeed, they have to be, since they are unlikely to survive any serious political backlash. When danger lurks, however, these political animals (unlike canaries) do not just pass out. Rather, their voices rise in alarm, pleading with those carrying their cage to turn around. Failing that, they will do whatever they can to escape, leaving their masters behind if need be and flying to a safer perch. And if they don't escape, they will expire. But even in death, they are servants of moderation, for if enough of them go down to defeat they will take their coalition's majority with them. Through all these channels—what the economist Albert Hirschman once called "voice" (lobbying the leaders), "exit" (rebellion), and "loyalty" (electoral suicide)—moderates should keep a majority firmly rooted in the center.[22]

Or so it is often assumed. In the last chapter, we explained why the dwindling circle of Republican moderates cannot be relied on as a guardian of the center. Whether because they have so little effective power or because they are really, underneath it all, sympathetic to most of the Republican agenda, today's moderates rarely stage more than feigned displays of independence. When they vote against a bill, their votes are usually not needed. When they speak of forging compromise deals, they are usually just forging symbolic victories that are quickly and quietly reversed by the leadership at the next available juncture. When they threaten to do more than act symbolically, the leadership threatens back, and so few moderates do more than act symbolically. The strategies for coordination and backlash insurance we discussed in Chapter 5 have their most powerful effects on these supposed guardians of moderation within the Republican coalition. Through control over the political agenda and the congressional process, through the deployment of money and the marshaling of interest-group power, and through the redrawing of district lines and the deliberate use of policy design to hide true intentions and effects, the conservative coalition has put the moderates on an ever shorter leash. It is a leash fewer and fewer GOP centrists have been willing to pull against.

Ultimately, moderates only have strong incentives to abide by their constituents' wishes when their constituents have real electoral power. Otherwise, these centrist politicians find it nearly impossible to resist the demands of their leaders and the call of the base. By coordinating so skillfully and providing extensive backlash insurance, the New Power Brokers have managed to keep the air safe for their Republican canaries.

Crumbling Checks and Balances

In our complex political system, the demands on voters are often overwhelming, the gaps in their awareness and knowledge both inevitable and predictable. Political elites know this, and they respond in ways that exploit these gaps. Agendas are painstakingly crafted and ruthlessly enforced. Messages are carefully calibrated to influence popular perceptions. Policies are expertly designed to exploit weaknesses in voters' ability to get and use information. Costs are hidden; benefits are structured in ways that confuse; policies are engineered with long lag times, confusing provisions, and ticking time bombs—all for one purpose: so that conservative elites, not ordinary voters, will set the future political agenda.

These strategies work, of course, because voters are often poorly informed. But the limited political knowledge of citizens is not the core problem. It is not as if most voters had a much higher level of knowledge twenty or thirty years ago. The problem is deeper. In our increasingly unequal society, in which government activity is not just extensive but extensively complex, voters have proved no match for a mobilized and coordinated conservative movement capable of managing the agenda and shaping and distorting the flow of information to citizens.

The other vaunted guardians of moderation have not proved up to the task either. Because reporters can plausibly claim a stance as disinterested observers, Americans have tended to put their faith in the media. And the press, at its best, fulfills that faith. As Downie and Kaiser of the *Washington Post* remind us, "When journalists use resourceful reporting and vivid presentation to hold the powerful accountable for their acts, they fulfill their highest purpose. They help encourage the honest and open use of power, and they help make America a fairer society."[23] But a system that relies on the media as the primary guardian of responsiveness inevitably leaves voters vulnerable. The establishment media are in the entertainment business, not the information business; they are constrained by a pack mentality and conventions that place "he said–she said" balance ahead of tough, critical reporting; and when it comes to shaping news cycles, they are no match for the new conservative media world. All of these features of today's news environment generate fundamental biases that coordinated elites can effectively exploit.

While the public sees journalists as a powerful assurance of responsiveness, political scientists typically look elsewhere. In the standard view of political competition, politicians check other politicians. Because team-based party competition has become more common, responsiveness rests increasingly on the strength and strategy of the opposing team, or at least the ability of wavering members of the winning team to rein in their teammates. But the loyal opposition is beleaguered and scattered. Meanwhile, the canaries in the electoral coal mine, moderate Republicans, have dwindling resources and incentives to challenge their more radical colleagues. The guardians of moderation need help. In the next—and final—chapter of this book, we show how they might get it.

CONCLUSION: MEETING THE CHALLENGE

They met over the course of four years, in places as far apart as New York and Seattle: a dozen or so political scientists—some with extensive government experience, others pure academics—drafted to examine the state of American politics. They disagreed on much, but they knew something was wrong. "In an era beset with problems of unprecedented magnitude at home and abroad," they argued, American government was adrift. The responsibilities of the state had exploded; the number of interest groups pressuring politicians had skyrocketed. But the nation's democratic institutions were not up to the challenge. "Coherent public policies do not emerge as the mathematical result of the claims of all of the pressure groups," the committee complained. For the public to receive proper representation, the opposition party had to act as "a critic of the party in power, developing, defining, and presenting the policy alternatives which are necessary for a true choice in reaching public decisions." The committee presented its recommendations in a ninety-nine-page report, ratified by the American Political Science Association and published to much attention and criticism—in September 1950.[1]

The report of the Committee on Political Parties, "Toward a More Responsible Two-Party System," might seem of merely historical interest today—if its recommendations had been as completely ignored as most such statements are. But whether the committee's impassioned call resonated beyond the confines of political science or, more likely, the forces of history simply pushed in the direction the committee wanted to go, much of what the report demanded did in fact come to pass.[2] The report's key claim was that American political parties were far too weak. "Historical and other factors have caused the American two-party system to operate as two loose associations of state and local organizations, with very little national machinery and very little cohesion," the committee wrote. "As a result, either major party . . . is ill-equipped to organize its members in the legislative and executive branches into a government held together and guided by the party program." In Congress in particular, there was little of "the kind of unity within the congressional party that is now so widely desired." Members of Congress were "orphans of the political system, with no truly adequate party mechanism available for the conduct of their campaigns."[3] All this, the committee insisted, could and should change.

Be careful what you wish for. Over the past three decades—first gradually and below the radar screen, but in the past decade with growing speed and ever more obvious effects—the parties have become stronger, more national, more unified, and much more distinctive. As we have seen, however, the effects have not resembled the happy consequences the committee confidently forecast. With the British parliamentary system in mind, the committee foresaw fierce competition for middle-of-the-road voters by highly responsive and accountable parties. These national parties would not necessarily "differ more fundamentally or more sharply than they have in the past," the committee projected. Rather, "the clarification of party policy may be expected to produce a more reasonable discussion of public affairs, more closely related to the political performance of the parties in their actions rather than their words."[4]

Today, of course, this sunny vision seems as distant as a 1950s home economics class. Swing voters are in the center of the political spectrum, just as they were in the 1950s, and an electoral map would show Republicans and Democrats much more closely matched than they were at the end of World War II. But the consequence of this tight party competition has not been a "reasonable discussion of public affairs." It has been relentless partisan warfare and a governing party committed to extreme policy ends.

Members of the Committee on Political Parties would have been even more surprised to discover which of the two parties seized on its call for greater coordination and coherence. The committee implicitly assumed that liberal Democrats would benefit from the hardening of party differences, because liberal Democrats were suffering at the hands of a powerful cross-party alliance of conservative Southern Democrats and Republicans. But the rise of truly national parties has ultimately redounded to the benefit not of liberal Democrats but of conservative Republicans. It is Republicans who have built the strongest, best networked, and most disciplined national party of the postwar era. And they have done it not by appealing to the center but by racing toward their base.

A greater irony: The committee argued that weak parties were outdated because of the arrival of big government. The role of the state had become so large, complex, and important that competition among clearly specified party programs was necessary to produce accountability. But as we have seen, the essential ingredient in today's off-center politics is the ability of the Republican Party to manipulate the ever more extensive and complex range of modern public policies to achieve enduring political advantage. A strong party (still more irony: the avowedly *antigovernment* party) has used the tools of big government and the complexities of modern public policies to protect itself against true accountability. And these instruments of backlash insurance have worked remarkably well. In the past few years, Republicans have proceeded at such speed on so many fronts that even those who make the study of politics their full-time job are left dizzy. The growing coordination of Republicans and their allies has produced strong leadership. But it is strong leadership directed to the advantage of the privileged and the powerful—the very interests whose influence the committee hoped strong parties would curb.

What the committee coveted, in short, was responsible party government. What they got—along with the rest of us—was *irresponsible* party government. Parties (or at least one of them) increasingly have the power to act. But they have acted with the impunity that comes when such actions are not disciplined by accountability. A strong party system was supposed to have greatly increased the responsiveness of our political system. Instead, the growing concentration of economic and political resources and the growing use of innovative tools of backlash insurance have left ordinary voters with limited sway over our nation's course.

The report of the Committee on Political Parties offers a cautionary lesson. Political reform is not easy. Nor can its results be perfectly predicted. Books on American politics typically end with a laundry list of specific reforms or a magic bullet that will supposedly cure all. But reformist prescriptions need to be grounded in clear diagnoses of what has gone wrong. Equally important, they need to address the basic problem of reform: creating an effective political movement to achieve it. We have argued that the big change in American politics is a divorce between the moderate center of American opinion and the policy goals and achievements of the nation's political leadership. And we have traced this disconnect to two intertwined forces: the growing pull of the Republican political base, and the increasing ability of Republican political elites to craft their appeals and policies to undercut the normal process of electoral accountability. These two forces have in turn been built on a third: the growing inequality of political resources and organization between the extremes of the political spectrum and ordinary voters—between the rich and radical and the rest. In this chapter, we turn to the fundamental question of what can be done about these troubling developments.

Our prescriptions are informed by our diagnoses. The power of the center needs to be reestablished, and the ability of the extremes to hide their off-center aims needs to be reduced. The first and most pressing issue, however, is how any of these prescriptions might be achieved. The nasty reality is that the very circumstances that call for reform are the biggest obstacle in its path. Off-center politics originates in profound and growing power inequalities that have accumulated over a long period. What is more, these imbalances are now protected by broad if imperfect control of all the main instruments of political authority. Before we get to shopping lists or magic bullets, we need to take a cold, hard look at the challenge of reform—and how the barriers to it might be overcome.

The Four Great Obstacles to Reform

In American politics, change is hard—which is why the Republicans' success in transforming public policy is impressive. But when the goal is to replace key elements of the political system itself, change is even harder, thanks to four special obstacles that stand in the way of political reform.

The "You Can't Get There from Here" Obstacle. There is an old story about a young man who gets hopelessly lost driving the back roads of New England. For hours, he stubbornly forges on. At last, exhaustion trumps pride. Spotting a remote general store, he approaches an elderly gentleman and politely asks for help. After long study of the young man's directions, the older man looks up and says, "If I wanted to get to *there,* I sure wouldn't be starting *here.*"

The design of American political institutions is a lot like those New England back roads. A lot of *theres* are very unlikely to be reached from *here.* Many ideas that sound nice in an op-ed piece or academic seminar are pretty much out of the question. They run afoul of the basic rules governing reform, well-established precedent, or deeply embedded aspects of American political culture.

The first barrier—rules against new rules—is the biggest hurdle. Many basic procedures of American politics are essentially locked in place by other rules. Consider, for example, the interwoven legacies of the Great Compromise at the nation's founding. The Constitution guarantees the strong empowerment of states in our national government. Interested in changing the apportionment of the Senate, so that some senators don't represent *seventy times* as many voters as others? Nonstarter. The Constitution declares, "No State, without its Consent, shall be deprived of its equal Suffrage in the Senate." Thinking of constitutional amendments to reduce some of the biggest disadvantages faced by populous states, such as the small-state bias in the electoral college? Think again. Amendments require a two-thirds vote in the Senate, followed by approval of three-quarters of the states. They can be blocked, in other words, by senators from just seventeen states (representing, in 2000, a little over 7 percent of the population). Failing successful resistance in the Senate, they can be blocked by thirteen state legislatures (representing *less than 4 percent* of the population).[5] The disproportionate influence of small states, with its potential to empower small minorities and its key advantages for the GOP, is here to stay.

Other obstacles rest on precedent. In many instances, the Supreme Court has sent strong signals that particular political reforms will not pass constitutional muster. For example, *Buckley v. Valeo*—the famous Supreme Court case that equated campaign spending with free speech—has not prevented campaign finance reform, but it has seriously constrained what reform can do. Because of its broad conception of spending as a form of free speech, the Court's decision rules out a variety of approaches to campaign finance that have successfully curbed the influence of big donations in other democratic societies.

Finally, as the great democratic theorist Robert Dahl has emphasized, deeply institutionalized features of our political culture make certain kinds of reform improbable.[6] However politically disenchanted Americans may be, they are enormously proud of their political institutions—in many respects, justly so. Overwhelmingly, Americans say their form of government is the best in the world. Constitutional obstacles aside, the United States is simply not going to become a parliamentary democracy with clearer lines of electoral accountability. It is not going to elect national legislators using proportional representation (in which congressional seats are allocated according to the national party vote, not the results in any particular district). Reforms that fail to strike chords in our political heartstrings are not going to be popular destinations.

The "Fox Guarding the Henhouse" Obstacle. Even if the *theres* are potentially reachable from *here,* the question remains: Who is going to make the trip? By now, you have been inundated with stories about a coordinated set of canny political operatives with extreme views and formidable political weapons. Now, why would those canny political operatives voluntarily give up those formidable weapons? They won't. They will fight tooth and nail to hold on to their advantages. They will exploit every ounce of their resources and capacity for coordination. They will deploy every instrument in their toolkit. The foxes are guarding the henhouse.

Consider by way of illustration a typical reform goal, one that we endorse later in this chapter: lowering the barriers to participation among the less engaged (who also tend to be the less extreme). One way to do so is to encourage voter turnout, and it is well documented that same-day voter registration is an effective way to raise turnout. In the 2002 election in California, turnout hit a new low of 29 percent. In that election, voters were given a chance to address this severe problem in the form of a ballot initiative that would have authorized same-day registration. Political scientist Thomas Patterson reports what happened: "By three-to-two, they voted 'no.' . . . They accepted the argument—trumpeted statewide through an opposition campaign backed by conservative groups—that Election Day registration would produce massive voter fraud. In reality, voting irregularities are virtually nonexistent in states that have Election Day registration."[7]

Foxes won't give up the henhouse without a fight. Facing serious threats, they will seek to divert the agenda, frame debates in unfavorable ways, and throw up procedural roadblocks. Forced to retreat, they will substitute purely symbolic or loophole-ridden alternatives. If all that fails, they will try to use their control of other institutional channels (executive agencies, the courts, state governments) to squeeze the life out of reforms when it comes time to implement and enforce them.

There is also the danger that reform movements might simply replace one set of foxes with another. The minority party may lead the call for reform. But once they have turned the tables, what is to stop them from losing enthusiasm for their erstwhile goals? We have seen this before—very recently, in fact. When was the last time you heard Republicans talking about their old rallying cry of term limits? These days, it comes up only when Republican leaders are going after insufficiently loyal GOP members of the House ethics committee—that is, those who seem interested in an ethics committee that actually functions. Reform requires getting by the current foxes without creating a new band of them, and that means that serious political reform calls for serious political momentum that extends beyond one narrow slice of the nation's political class.

The Catch-22 is this: A big push back to the center must precede political reforms designed to produce a big push back to the center. We cannot expect to "bootstrap" reform—to pull ourselves up by our present constellation of political forces. We need to consider some of the possible sources of political momentum that don't begin with the introduction of reform from the top. Major reform of our political rules and institutions is likely to be the last step toward our destination, not the first.

The "Nobody Cares" Obstacle. If the vast moderate middle of American society is increasingly hard to mobilize and often poorly informed about normal policy issues, this is even truer when it comes to proposals for political reform. Despite frequent expressions of political discontent, most voters show little inclination to think about such matters. We recently witnessed a particularly telling demonstration. In 2000, the popular vote loser ascended to the presidency for the first time in more than a century. Non-Americans reacted with extreme puzzlement: How could this happen in the world's oldest democracy? According to polls, Americans showed no great love for the electoral college. But they also showed no great interest in the matter of changing it, and the issue quickly faded from the scene. Proposals to reform politics are so abstract, so removed from the substance of daily life, that they rarely capture sustained public attention.

Rarely doesn't mean never. "Reform" can become a rallying call for political mobilization when abuse or corruption is visible and simple to understand. But it is a tough challenge. And again, it suggests that advocates of change need to think hard about what kind of reform goals provide a plausible basis for mobilizing centrist, nonactivist elements of the electorate. They also need to think about ideas that don't require such mobilization—that rest, at least initially, on effective countermobilization of those who are already engaged and attentive, including active opponents of the currently dominant coalition as well as disaffected elements within it.

The "Half a Loaf Is Worse Than None" Obstacle. Facing such a formidable array of roadblocks, the natural reaction is to advocate piecemeal change at the federal level or to focus on other sites of political power. Indeed, the obvious strategy when national political conditions are inauspicious is to seek reform, at least at the onset, in particular states where reformers can gain a sympathetic ear. This is, of course, in keeping with a hallowed tradition for American political reformers—to treat the states, in Justice Louis Brandeis's famous description, as "laboratories of democracy." Many of the reforms of the Progressive Era of the early 1900s, when Justice Brandeis coined his phrase, were achieved first (and sometimes only) at the state level. Triumphing initially in areas of the country where reformers were unusually strong, advocates of reform were often able to spread their ideas nationally as reform gathered momentum.

This is not, however, the Progressive Era, when most government activity took place at the local or state level. American politics and policy are now much more thoroughly nationalized, as are American political parties. Reforms that do not touch Washington politics are unlikely to achieve the kinds of successes that would lead them to spread or to change the workings of the federal government. In fact, these experiments could even backfire. Many reforms designed to increase political competition at the state level could have the *opposite* effect at the national level. This is because the states where discontent with current affairs is the deepest are precisely those states in which politically influential groups most often find themselves on the losing end of national political battles. In current parlance, it is the "blue" states where the reformers' message is most likely to resonate, not the "red" ones. And that means that many laudable state-level reforms, like nonpartisan redistricting or proportional allocation of electoral votes, could end up being acts of unilateral disarmament. Adopted nationally, these reforms would empower moderate voters, encourage centrist tendencies, and heighten accountability. Adopted disproportionately in blue states, they would increase Republicans' ability to gain representation in states where they are now disadvantaged and further consolidate off-center politics.

At both the state and national levels, many well-intentioned political reforms could end up being counterproductive if they are not done *after* political momentum has shifted against today's dominant conservative coalition. If the opposition party throws away the few weapons it has left while doing nothing to blunt those of its opponents, Tom DeLay, Grover Norquist, and Karl Rove will be the first ones to stand and applaud. Sometimes a half a loaf is worse than none.

The Social Roots of Reform

The lesson is clear—not that reform cannot succeed but that the biggest challenge is generating the momentum needed to bring reform within the realm of the possible. Would-be reformers are typically reluctant to grapple with this topic, either because they risk seeming partisan or because they think that their expertise does not extend to political warfare. But if the goal is to reassert the hold of voters in the center, it is essential to identify political challengers to the governing coalition that could ultimately increase centrist voters' sway. For those concerned about the tilt of American politics off center, who those challengers are is the $64,000 question. The answer is not self-evident. The remarkable resurgence of conservatism in recent decades reflected the merger of many organizational streams. The same will be true for its opponents. But a successful reform push will need to combine the strongest organizational foundations of the past and the best new outreach strategies of the present.

Renewing Labor. Perhaps no single social change would do more to reverse the off-center tilt of contemporary American politics than a revitalization of the American labor movement. The past three decades have witnessed an increase in economic inequality that has no precedent in modern U.S. history or the recent experience of other affluent nations. Over the same period, and not by coincidence, political inequality has also increased dramatically. Today money plays a much larger role in politics than it once did, and other forms of political participation appear to have become increasingly skewed in economic terms, too. In no other rich democracy has the playing field become so sharply tilted against citizens of modest means.

It is also no coincidence that the Republicans' most successful off-center policies have concentrated heavily on economic issues. Time and again in assembling and advancing its agenda, Republican elites 'have placed the interests of business and the most affluent elements of American society at the head of the line. After an election supposedly dominated by security issues and "moral values," each of the three top items in the Bush administration's second term agenda— Social Security privatization, restrictions on tort litigation, and a tax overhaul—focuses on economic matters. Each is receiving strong corporate backing, and each would distribute resources from those lower down on the economic ladder to those at the top. To a striking degree, the business of the contemporary Republican Party truly is business.

In his colorful *What's the Matter with Kansas?* Thomas Frank argues that this should not be a surprise, because these are the issues our country's governing elite truly cares about. What should be a surprise, Frank claims, is that many middle-class Americans are rallying to its cause. Conservative politicians "mobilize voters with explosive social issues, summoning public outrage . . . which it then marries to pro-business economic policies. Cultural anger is marshaled to achieve economic ends." For Frank, it is all an elaborate and masterful bait and switch: "*Vote* to stop abortion; *receive* a rollback in capital gains taxes. . . . *Vote* to stand tall against terrorists; *receive* Social Security privatization."[8]

There is little question that conservatives often use cultural messages to trump economic ones. But as we have seen in this book, Frank's story is misleading on two counts. First, class still matters a great deal in that most ubiquitous of political activities, voting. Indeed, as we have pointed out, voters are more reliably sorting themselves into the two major parties on the basis of their economic standing—below the middle siding with Democrats, above it siding with Republicans.

Second, if the Republican policy agenda tilts much more toward Wall Street than Main Street, this is not simply because the wealthy are often the party's paymasters. It is also because those parts of the GOP agenda that appeal to Wall Street have the greatest chances of success and the smallest prospect of provoking backlash. This is partly because the opportunities for strategic manipulation—whether through rhetoric, agenda control, or policy design—are typically far greater in the witheringly complex and arcane areas of economic and social policy. By contrast, most of the prominent cultural issues are easier to understand (abortion: yes or no), closer to zero-sum (one person's loss is another's gain), and harder to approach with the degree of backlash insurance that Republicans have enjoyed in carrying out their economic agenda.

In addition, and probably more important, Republicans have often faced fiercer and better-organized opposition on the noneconomic aspects of their agenda. In contemporary American politics, opposition to conservatives on cultural and social issues is intense, organized, and well heeled. A major development of the past few decades has been the explosion of liberal advocacy groups around a host of nonmaterial issues, such as abortion and the environment, that resonate with highly educated and better-off voters.[9] On economic matters, however, the story is radically different. For those of modest means, as the political scientist Theda Skocpol has argued, large-scale voluntary organizations no longer have the presence in citizens' lives, or the role in linking politics with everyday life, that they once did.[10]

Much has been made of the general decline in what Robert Putnam calls "social capital"—social skills and institutions that allow people to work together toward common ends.[11] But the drying up of this vital form of social glue has not had equal effects across the economic spectrum. Nor has it been neutral in its political effects. The economically privileged start with plenty of the most traditional sort of capital—namely, money. And they have continued to vote, contribute, and participate in high numbers. The same is not true of less affluent Americans. Precisely because they are disadvantaged with regard to material resources, they need social capital *more* than the well off, and they need organizational backing the most. Faced with limited information, a clamor of competing messages, and a media that does little to help sort things out, relatively inattentive voters often must rely heavily on "cues" they receive from organizations and associates they respect and trust. But the signals that ordinary citizens once received from affiliated organizational networks, and the leverage these associations once provided them to act on these signals, have steadily weakened. And the decline of unions is the most visible and profound reason why.

The hollowing out of the union movement is now almost five decades old. Yet the full extent and repercussions of the decline are not always appreciated. In the decade after World War II, more than a third of wage and salary workers were in unions, placing the United States ahead of its left-leaning northern neighbor, Canada. By 2004, the share had dropped to 13.8 percent, and just 8.6 percent in the private sector—whereas Canada had seen only a slight decline (to around 30 percent in all sectors).[12] In spite of the sharp drop in union rolls, American unions still are far and away the most powerful organizations oriented toward the economic interests of working- and middle-class citizens. But although their influence and reach in American society remain remarkable given the challenges they have faced, both have declined markedly. And as unions represent an ever narrower segment of American workers, their capacity to speak powerfully and effectively to the broad economic concerns of middle America has atrophied as well.

Whether sympathetic or hostile to organized labor's decline, Americans are conditioned to think of it as natural, even inevitable. As globalization spreads and the American workforce shifts from blue-collar manufacturing into new service industries, according to this common view, unions are gradually rendered obsolete. This conventional wisdom is simply false. All affluent democracies are undergoing these large so-cial transitions. Most are actually more exposed to the forces of global-ization than is the United States. But in many of these countries, rates of unionization have declined little if at all. And none has experienced the precipitous decline in unions experienced in the United States.

The scale of union decline in the United States cannot be explained by anything distinctive about the composition of the American workforce or patterns of American economic activity—the United States is not, for instance, more "postindustrial" or "globalized" than other countries. Instead, the dramatic fall of unions most clearly reflects two distinctively American realities. The first is the acute difficulties that American unions have confronted in adapting to a new economic environment given their high levels of fragmentation and their very uneven geographic reach. These features have made it easier for employers to pit one group of workers against another and to move their activities—or threaten to move their activities—to areas where unions are weak or absent, whether inside or outside the United States.

The second reality is more overtly political, and it gets to the heart of the problem. The capacity of unions to organize depends on the rules governing collective bargaining, and these rules have grown steadily less favorable to their cause. Unions organize far more workers in other countries not just because workers there are more sympathetic to unions but also because the law makes it much easier for unions to organize. Over the past twenty or so years, in a wide range of settings, American employers have worked steadily and effectively to tilt the rules of collec-tive bargaining in their favor, and they have received a very sympathetic ear from the Right.

Like Margaret Thatcher in Britain, Ronald Reagan made curbing the power of unions in national politics a central goal, and unlike his attempts to scale back the welfare state, he made significant progress in this area. Contemporary Republicans have not had to do as much as Reagan did to keep America's emaciated union movement in check. As with many other issues of economic reform, they have not had to do much to succeed. Simply blocking actions that counter the economic and state-level shifts that have hurt American unions, or that might weaken employers' hands in union struggles, has usually been enough.

To many Americans, we would guess, the idea that stronger unions would make a major contribution to redressing political inequality in the United States may seem quaint. Even a doubling of unionization rates—an astonishing change—would leave three-quarters of the workforce on the outside looking in. Perhaps conditions for those newly unionized workers would improve. Perhaps all of us would pay a bit more for the products that those workers make. Otherwise, though, would anything really change?

We believe so. It is not the economic changes that unions bring about that inspires our conviction. It is the political check on extreme public policies that stronger unions would provide. The emerging off-center tilt of U.S. public policy exacts a heavy price from the vast majority of Americans, especially on economic matters. Indeed, although we have written about the Republican economic agenda as if it benefits the "well off" universally, the fact is that all but a small slice of the well off are disadvantaged by much of what Republicans have done.

In our signal case of taxes, for example, the Republican agenda has not directed its largesse toward the upper-middle-class or even the run-of-the-mill rich. It has repeatedly advanced the priorities of the super-super-rich. As Yale scholars Michael Graetz and Ian Shapiro note in their book *Death by a Thousand Cuts,* roughly 95 percent of the rich Americans who are likely to pay the estate tax could have gotten off the hook back in 2001 with no prospect that the estate tax would spring back to life when the "sunset" in the 2001 legislation took effect.[13] The Republican coalition rejected compromise and went for the long bomb: total abolition, which required sunset provisions that threatened to undo their efforts entirely. The gamble, as we have argued, was based on the not-unreasonable expectation that the richest of the rich would have the motive and means to keep the estate tax dead. But it was a big gamble, one that was necessary only for the very wealthiest families, with estates in excess of $10 or $15 million. Given the vast potential rewards, the risk was reasonable for them. For everyone else, including virtually all of the ostensible beneficiaries of reform, it was not.

The Republican manipulation of the alternative minimum tax is equally revealing. Over the next few years, millions of well-off Americans who think they are big winners from the Republican tax cuts are going to get a rude shock. Although costly repairs will eventually come, many, many upper-middle-class families will be snared by the net of the AMT before they do. When this happens, most of their anticipated gains from the tax cuts will evaporate. Typically, the losers will be households earning between $100,000 and $200,000 per year. They, like most Americans of more modest means, will suddenly find themselves playing the Homer Simpson role in our tax-cut cartoon, their pocket picked by the same hand that showered cash on them a few years earlier.

In short, union strength is not just an issue for low-wage workers or for the ranks of union members. It is an issue for the great American middle, stretching from working families of modest means into the upper middle class. There is real force to *Times* columnist Paul Krugman's joke that American politics will turn around when corporate vice presidents march on Washington, having finally realized that politicians represent only the economic interests of their bosses. The diminishing role of organized labor has opened a political void, and that void has been filled by the most affluent and extreme elements of the Republican base. On economic issues, Republicans have raced to the base with little concern that they might face an effective, organized, and trusted opposition that could alert and mobilize both core Democrats and less-than-super-rich independents and Republicans. As a result, on these issues backlash insurance has been provided to rank-and-file conservative politicians at bargain-basement prices.

The revitalization of organized labor would make a big difference. But are there any prospects for such a development? Trends of the past few decades give plenty of reason for doubt. At the same time, the "bootstrapping" problem we discussed earlier applies to unions with a vengeance. The playing field of labor-management relations is now so tilted that unions cannot lift themselves up dramatically without major changes to the present legal and institutional context.

Still, in the past decade, unions have worked aggressively to combat their decline. They have, for starters, more energetically sought to organize the service and retail sectors of the economy, which have previously resisted union drives. They have also worked to secure their position in their core sectors, notably, public employment. And at the same time, they have not forgotten about politics. John Sweeney's ascension to the presidency of the AFL-CIO in 1995 was followed by an increased allocation of resources for political activism and organizing. Although union membership has continued to slide on his watch, the share of the electorate made up of union members in recent elections has not. In the past few years, union reformers have pushed to accelerate organizing efforts. Sweeney recently accepted demands to transfer significant resources to unions eager to make a stronger push to recruit new members. The challenges to these efforts are immense, but these new initiatives are impressive as well.

Unions will not come back on their own. They will need assistance at both the state and national levels from sympathetic politicians and friendly judges willing to tilt the legal playing field back in their direction. Here is where the concerted efforts of Republicans to shape the courts and federal agencies over the past twenty years—through appointments, nominees, and policy changes—become truly telling for union advocates. But union-friendly policy changes would not have to be a first priority of reformers. Rather, granting unions greater organizational resources falls into a category of what we would call "second-phase reforms"—changes that are difficult to package politically or implement in the short term but that could be pursued once reformist forces gained a stronger hand. Weakened as it may be, organized labor will need to be part of any opposition coalition seeking a basis for the organizational revitalization of the great American middle. But it will not have to be the only part. In fact, its clout will depend greatly on whether it forms alliances with emerging organizational forces that could become formidable new players in American politics.

Digital Democracy. Winners write history or, at least, capture the ears of journalists. Had John Kerry won the election of 2004, much more discussion would now be centering on a remarkable element of that fiercely contested election. At the beginning of the campaign, it was confidently predicted that the Democratic nominee for president would be doomed from the beginning. Almost a year before the election, the Republican financial juggernaut was already wrapping up its main efforts. The president, long recognized as a fundraising superstar, had shattered all records. Unchallenged within his party, Bush had the luxury of shifting into full-time campaign mode while he sat on his brimming war chest. His potential challengers, by contrast, faced many more months of begging for table scraps, most of which would be expended on their own private food fight. The eventual Democratic nominee would stagger forward, drained and destitute, look up, . . . and find himself buried under a mountain of Republican cash.

It did not turn out that way, of course. Although Bush eventually eked out a narrow victory, John Kerry was able to raise huge sums with unprecedented speed. Against all expectations, the financial playing field was essentially level. In a stunningly expensive campaign, Kerry and allied groups matched the Republicans almost dollar for dollar.

This rapid and unexpected development points to new possibilities for effective countermobilization. Granted, not every aspect of the story is entirely uplifting or universally applicable. Given the present imbalances in American politics, it is not surprising that Kerry's success depended on galvanizing deep-pocketed individuals alarmed by the Republican agenda and Bush personally. Kerry and his allies drew heavily on well-heeled groups that faced political attack (think trial lawyers), as well as a handful of fabulously wealthy individuals who could back up their political beliefs with huge contributions funneled through "527s" (think George Soros and Peter Lewis). And the galvanization of Democrats in 2004 was deep and broad. Nearly every fundraising technique worked more effectively than ever, as established sources of Democratic finance gave and then gave more. Fundraisers reported turnouts and grosses that had no recent parallel and that may not be easily replicable in the future.

Yet alongside the dismaying and distinctive, a new organizational factor also burst into prominence: the Internet. Before 2004, discussions of the political impact of the Internet were long on hype and short on evidence. The evidence came, however, when Howard Dean leveraged the Internet to mobilize an army of volunteers and small contributors to his campaign. Riding this technological and organizational innovation,

Dean's campaign came from nowhere to the brink of victory. Dean raised $20 million over the Internet, passing a startled Kerry campaign that had expected to coast to victory on its vastly larger traditional fundraising base. By the end of 2003, the obscure upstart Dean had raised twice as much money—most in small donations—as the far better known and well-connected Kerry.

When Dean's campaign imploded, Kerry quickly borrowed, refined, and expanded its model of Internet fundraising. Kerry raised $5 million in the two days after the string of primaries known as Super Tuesday and almost $6 million in a single day when he accepted the Democratic nomination. Veterans of the Dean campaign quickly went to work for Kerry, and the Internet became a crucial element in the senator's revitalized campaign organization. The Internet's new significance was symbolized by Kerry's decision to announce his selection of John Edwards as his running mate by e-mail and a posting on his Web site, rather than the traditional news release. Eventually the Kerry campaign raised a remarkable $82 million over the Internet—$30 million more than Gore had raised from *all* sources of individual contributions in 2000.[14]

Nor was the expanded role of the Internet limited to fundraising. In the process of the 2004 campaign, a large number of Americans, across the political spectrum, were brought into a new form of participation—one that allows ongoing and relatively inexpensive, albeit constrained and largely one-sided, communication. The Dean campaign helped lead the way on this front, too. Web-based "meet-ups" brought thousands into engagement with one another and their chosen candidate, often on a moment's notice. Internet technology provided opportunities for hybrid organizations that combined elements of traditional grassroots activity with national reach, instant communication, and turn-on-a-dime flexibility.

In the past few years, not only campaigns but also advocacy groups have exploited this organizational gold mine. The most striking example is the roller-coaster saga of MoveOn.org. Started in 1998 by two Silicon Valley entrepreneurs out of frustration with the unfolding impeachment saga, "MoveOn" referred to the group's position that Congress should censure Clinton and move on. Within two years, however, a simple petition had morphed into a new organizational phenomenon. Skillfully riding reactions to the aftermath of the election of 2000 and the decision to invade Iraq, MoveOn had by 2004 amassed an e-mail list of 2.3 million. Hundreds of thousands of these adherents proved willing to contribute not just money but time and energy. In a matter of months, MoveOn had transformed into an organization able to raise funds and generate phone calls to Capitol Hill faster than traditional advocacy groups ever thought possible.

As the 2004 election approached, MoveOn morphed again. It adopted a strong focus on the media and campaign activity and operated (like many similar groups on the Republican side) in ways intended to complement the efforts of its favored presidential candidate, John Kerry. To fund a range of campaign activities, it raised perhaps $50 million, some of which came from wealthy contributors like Lewis and Soros but most of which came from small contributors. During the summer of 2004, when Kerry's campaign "went dark" to hoard money for the fall, MoveOn maintained a vigorous and costly media effort.

MoveOn's meteoric rise has also been marked by stumbles and confusion. Republicans sought, with some success, to demonize it as extremist. The organization itself has struggled to find a more permanent footing. Although its capacity to fundraise and mobilize is astonishing, the effectiveness with which it deploys these resources is open to question. To some, and not just Republicans, it has developed messages and activities that resonate with Democrats' core voters—in the words of one party activist, that "monetize two million liberals"—but that fail to engage the middle of the country. For all its achievements, MoveOn's record is uneven and its future uncertain.[15]

But the lessons of MoveOn go beyond any of the particular claims it has made or activities it has engaged in. They concern the advantages of the Internet in the current political environment. The Internet can be a powerful mechanism for coordination. Through quick electronic communication, large numbers of widely scattered political participants who share common concerns and interests can rapidly identify one another and act collectively. Consider the remarkable development of Web-logs or "blogs," which have exploded into a major form of online exchange. Blogs facilitate the quick and cheap dissemination of huge amounts of information, and they are growing like Topsy. In October 2004, about twelve thousand new blogs were created every day, a new blog every 7.4

seconds.[16] Most, of course, are apolitical, and many are soon abandoned. Yet a surprisingly large number are centrally concerned with public life and committed to shaping its course.

In the past two years, some of the implications of this new coordination capacity have become evident. Both Left and Right have increased their ability to monitor a wide range of social activity—of allies, opponents, and other relevant actors like the media. They can rapidly share information and exchange ideas about how to respond. In many cases, they are able to settle on collective responses and bring pressure to bear with great speed. Internet-based action played a key role, for example, in the collapse of the CBS News story on Bush's National Guard experience. On the other side of the fence, Internet-based mobilization led to a rapid and effective boycott of Sinclair Broadcasting Corporation's plan to run a blatantly anti-Kerry news program on its local television affiliates just weeks before the November election. Josh Marshall's *Talking Points Memo* Web site has played a unique role in the unfolding debate over Social Security. Marshall, working without a staff, organized a small but far-flung army of amateur reporters to monitor the actions and utterances of every member of Congress. The army's goals: to rapidly identify and put the spotlight on wavering Democrats, and to document and publicize Republican efforts to buy themselves backlash insurance through disingenuous statements about their own stances on Social Security and the Bush administration's proposals.

A second potential advantage of the Internet for organizations is its flexibility. At its most effective, MoveOn sought to fill a yawning gap between the Democratic Party and the spectrum of single-issue groups that populate its base. An umbrella organization like MoveOn can address a wide range of issues. It does not have to commit permanently to a single priority. Instead, it can speak to multiple concerns and issues that many individuals share, and it can adapt its focus as circumstances or popular concerns change. For individuals, the level of commitment is equally flexible. When the organization's attention shifts, individuals within the group can choose to increase or decrease their level of involvement accordingly. In short, these new groups potentially have the capacity to play the kind of "encompassing" role that is so essential for linking broad swathes of average citizens to the political process.

Whether that role will be seized, in what form, and by which side of the political spectrum all remain to be seen (although this appears to be one area of civic life where conservatives actually lag behind). But even though we don't yet know how powerful a factor the Internet will be, there is reason to believe that it is a rapidly building force that could potentially address some of the challenges outlined in this book. Political change often occurs through a combination of new technologies and organizational innovation, married to a reform agenda that mobilizes large numbers of citizens behind appealing and inspiring political figures.

The remarkable rise of contemporary conservatism itself provides a vivid illustration. The rise of direct mail, a field in which Karl Rove was a pioneer, and the concerted conservative effort to build up alternative organizations of intellectual production and political might, such as think tanks and grassroots conservative networks, both helped propel first Reagan and then Newt Gingrich and George W. Bush into positions of power. None of these elements was wholly original, nor did they make the off-center turn of American politics inevitable. But their combination was innovative and consequential, tilting the playing field of American politics sharply to the right, even as most Americans remained largely centrist in their political beliefs.

The Internet may be today's direct-mail technology and grassroots network rolled into one. It creates enormous opportunities for collecting and exchanging information, for combining and coordinating the energies and resources of large numbers of otherwise disconnected individuals who have modest resources and feel excluded from political influence, and for flexibly responding to new issues and demands. To be sure, these are only opportunities. The Internet could be used to organize only the extremes or to reinforce existing political inequalities. It could fail to sustain anything beyond brief bursts of political activity. It could even produce new and unanticipated political pathologies. Technology is not destiny. But the Internet is a tool that could be used by activists and everyday citizens concerned about the drift of American politics off center—at a time when so many other possible tools are firmly in the hands of the dominant Republican coalition. In this sense, it could be a catalyst for creating the momentum for political reform that will be necessary to tackle the broader imbalances in organization and resources that this book documents.

Fissures in the Republican Facade

As reformers gather the social resources needed to mount an effective challenge to governing elites, they must be vigilant in searching for political openings. Cracks in fortresses of political power cannot always be anticipated. What can be anticipated is that these cracks will occur, if sometimes only fleetingly, and that challengers will need to pry them open to reveal true opportunities for change. As Newt Gingrich's success a decade ago demonstrates, challengers must be ready to capitalize on stumbles by the governing coalition when they occur.

And here at last is some good news: Cracks in the Republican fortress are not hard to find. In consolidating and coordinating authority, Republicans have worked against the grain of many embedded and long-standing tendencies of American politics. Indeed, it is precisely the ability of the New Power Brokers to short-circuit strong protections against excessive concentrations of power that makes their achievements so remarkable. The United States remains a highly diverse society, with intensely fragmented institutions that heighten that diversity. Maintaining coordination and unity in this context is an uphill battle, and small setbacks can magnify into large losses—if opponents aggressively exploit them.

The Republican electoral edge, for instance, is extraordinarily thin. Unified control of all branches of government has prompted triumphalist rhetoric that finds easy echo in the media. Yet never in American history has a series of elections revealed such a close balance between the leading parties. Never has a congressional majority rested for so long on such slim margins. Only rarely has a president been reelected so narrowly. By historical standards, it would not take much of a push back toward the center for Republicans to lose their electoral advantage.

The history of American politics also suggests that shifts of this sort are difficult to foresee. The erosion of dominant coalitions often occurs slowly and almost invisibly. Demographic changes undercut sources of electoral strength. Coalitions splinter on the shoals of sustained internal tensions or divisive new issues. Fifteen years ago, few would have predicted the quick collapse of the Democrats' almost fifty-year run as the majority party in the House.[17] In retrospect, the reasons for the reversal are relatively easy to spot: The civil rights movement divided the party, leading white Southern Democrats to leave it in droves. Demographic change accentuated the effects, as the Sunbelt became increasingly prominent in American politics. And House Democrats, seemingly insulated from hostile political winds, grew complacent in their leadership, while House Republicans honed their oppositional tactics and rhetoric.

Given what the New Power Brokers have produced in the past four years, waiting four decades may not sound like a good idea. Fortunately, erosion of political advantage can occur rapidly. As Richard Nixon's experience demonstrates, a major political scandal can have devastating effects. Sustained or dramatic failures of governance can have similar consequences. External events, like an economic crisis, may lead voters to punish the governing party. And politicians may simply overreach, using their power to pursue policies that are so extreme, so corrupt, or so poorly thought out that, even with the full armament of backlash insurance deployed, they provoke public outcry.

None of these possibilities can be predicted with confidence. Republicans have worked assiduously to diminish the threat of scandals— not by becoming a party of choirboys but by tightening their grip over the normal channels for ethics challenges. In January 2005, Republicans first passed and then repealed provisions designed to let their ethically challenged House leader, Tom DeLay, stay in power even if charged with ethics violations. Then, House leaders changed the rules of the Ethics Committee to prevent inquiries from proceeding without support from at least one Republican member. They also removed the committee's chairman, along with any Republican who showed the slightest inclination toward independence. The new head of the committee immediately proceeded to fire the two top members of the committee's staff, notwithstanding the copious praise showered on them by the outgoing Republican chair. Still, Republicans have had only partial success in keeping scandals off the agenda. A few weeks after the assault on the Ethics Committee, House Speaker Dennis Hastert engineered a reversal of the committee rule change (but not the committee shakeup). An aide to the

House GOP leadership candidly explained that it was "impossible to win the communications battle."[18]

Overreach is another looming possibility. As we have documented, Republicans have good reason for self-congratulation. But self-congratulation can lead to hubris, and hubris can lead to overreach. The Bush administration's astonishingly aggressive push on Social Security—which places the president farther from the center than any other major policy foray of his presidency—may turn out to represent such a turning point. If it does, the reversal will not be unprecedented. While FDR's court-packing fiasco and Clinton's health care debacle are often cited as textbook examples of presidential misjudgment, the more chilling example for the Right may well be the demise of one of the most powerful conservatives of the twentieth century, British Prime Minister Margaret Thatcher. At the height of her influence, Thatcher launched a war against the last remaining bastion of leftist strength—local government councils. Her weapon of choice was an astonishingly regressive tax reform, which required that every Briton, prince or pauper, pay the same amount for local services. Designed to bring the wrath of voters down on local governments, the proposal (quickly dubbed the Poll Tax) brought that wrath down on Thatcher instead. Fearing political immolation, her party unceremoniously turned on its most successful leader since Winston Churchill, and threw the Iron Lady overboard.

America's political system, however, looks very different from Britain's. Indeed, it looks very different today from how it looked when Reagan and congressional Republicans retreated from Social Security cuts after the GOP's midterm losses of 1982. The clear lines of political accountability created by the unification of legislative and executive powers in the British prime minister's office have no real parallel in American politics. And, as we have seen, America's more decentralized system of accountability has itself become less effective in recent years. Overreach on the scale of Thatcher's Poll Tax is certainly a possibility—indeed, Bush's campaign to overhaul Social Security is the strongest candidate yet for this dubious honor. But the effects of such overreach are likely to be much less inherently dramatic in the U.S. context. On American soil, effective mobilization will be required to drive home to voters the extent of overreach and the identity of those responsible for it.

Where might such mobilization come from? One place to look might be moderate fringes of the Republican Party itself. GOP centrists, while an endangered breed, are not completely extinct. And in the past few years they have occasionally made bids for recognition. From John DiIulio to Paul O'Neill to Christine Todd Whitman, the occasional cries of "It's my party, too!" stand out as markers of how far the Republican Party has shifted to the right. Unfortunately, these cries are unlikely to prove a harbinger of an incipient GOP rebellion. So far, opposition within the Republican Party has looked a lot like the teenage rebellions of well-schooled youths: noisy but half-hearted, mostly staged, and ultimately short-lived.

Republicans, moreover, still act like a team when it matters, for all the reasons we have outlined. Key interest groups and contributors, core pieces of the conservative media apparatus, and a wide range of networked elites—all would have to experience serious breakdowns of coordination for moderate insurgents to seize the initiative. The well-known story of McCain's bid for the White House in 2000 is instructive. Back then, McCain was much better known nationally than Bush. But he never had the conservative ground troops or the support of key elements of the Republican fundraising and ideological machinery. And even if a reformist figure like McCain were to capture the presidency, he would still have to work with the GOP Congress and the conservative movement more generally. With congressional elites and their allies mostly insulated from the winds of electoral change, the "coattails" of even GOP presidents are short, their power to get things done as dependent on Congress as the other way around.

A similar fate would probably also await an isolated Democratic president. Although a Democratic candidate would be better poised than a GOP moderate to offer an effective reformist challenge, a moment's reflection suggests how limited the scope for reform would be if only the Oval Office changed party hands. Consider the counterfactual scenario of a Kerry presidency. If he had won, Kerry would have faced a relentlessly hostile Congress with little incentive to depart from its base, along with the entrenched conservative movement whose impressive coordination we have documented. Kerry would have blocked GOP policies, and his effect on foreign policy would have been significant. But he would have had little chance of passing major political reforms, even if he had made reform a major campaign goal.

All of which underscores the need for advocates of political change to think beyond the next election and think outside the presidential office. Behind the shift of American politics off center lie large and long-simmering trends. At least some of these will have to be arrested and reversed for political reform to take root and spread. This would not be the political equivalent of waiting for Godot. It would mean developing an immediately attractive reform agenda that could lay the groundwork for a broader set of institutional and policy changes down the road. And this means that serious thinking about what reform should entail needs to occur now.

Exploiting the Potential

Just as Republicans have treated tax cuts as a solution always on the lookout for a problem, reformers need to start thinking ahead. Now is the time to consider which solutions they want to attach to the problems thrown up by continued Republican ascendance. Moments in which the scattered attention of mainstream America fixes on reform are likely to be rare and fleeting; if such windows of opportunity are missed, they will close. Even severe political reversals may not be enough to dislodge the New Power Brokers permanently. They may lay low, waiting for their next opportunity. And if the underlying conditions that facilitate off-center politics are not addressed, these brokers—like monsters in B-grade horror flicks—will spring back to life. In short, when the political winds shift, reformers will need to have ideas in hand to bring about a more competitive and accountable political process.

We do not pretend to have all of these ideas. In strategically responding to moments of Republican weakness, much will depend on the particular circumstances under which a reform window opens. Yet our analysis of what has gone wrong in American politics provides some strong clues about how to proceed. Real reform of the political system must advance three goals: It must increase the political *resources* of the middle; it must make the *votes* of the middle more important; and it must enhance the ability of average voters to make *informed judgments,* so that their expanded resources and more decisive votes can be put to good use. The ordering of these goals reflects our presumptions about which will have the most effect, but it does not necessarily reflect our views about which should come first. In all these areas, we think that there are simple and relatively doable reforms that should be considered now and more complex and challenging reforms that could and should follow.

Increasing the Resources of the Middle. As our discussion of organized labor suggests, a window for reform is unlikely to open without the revitalization of large-scale membership organizations that give average citizens greater leverage over the political process. We have already examined how such revitalization might occur. Essentially, the problem posed by the skewed decline of social capital is how to create large-scale organizations that provide leverage to the middle and that appeal to Americans in an age in which personal volunteerism has taken priority over active participation in large-membership groups.

The Internet provides one useful tool for reconciling these two aims, but it will do so only if a broader array of public supports is in place. Unions need regulations and statutes that give them a fighting chance to organize despite hostility from ever larger and more mobile businesses. Measures to consolidate and strengthen encompassing organizations should be coupled with efforts to expand voter turnout and reduce the sway of money in politics. For skewed turnout and the disproportionate role of money are perhaps the greatest obstacles to translating enhanced organizational strength for average voters into true shifts in the way American politics is run (and whom it is run for).

Getting more people involved in politics is crucial, and it is a goal that sensible reforms could greatly advance. As the political scientist Morris Fiorina has argued, many efforts to expand popular participation in the past thirty years have actually fanned the flames of extremism. Opening the gates a little has allowed only the most energized to squeeze through. These eager participants, however, tend to be the most ideologically extreme.[19]

The solution is to open the gates wider still. Empowering the center requires efforts to enhance low-intensity participation, not just energetic political activism. Reformers need to lower the barriers for those who are unlikely ever to see politics as more than an occasional activity—as a "sideshow in the great circus of life," as Robert Dahl once put it.[20]

Perhaps the most important goal is to increase America's abysmally low turnout rates at elections. Even in presidential elections, turnout of the voting-age population hovers around 50 to 55 percent, compared to norms of between 65 and 80 percent—and sometimes higher—in Europe.

Fortunately, this is something we actually know how to do. Many barriers to voting would be easy to eliminate if the political will to do so existed. Decreasing the frequency of elections, simplifying ballots, and requiring that states permit same-day registration would make a real difference. Restoring the right to vote to ex-felons—close to five million citizens who are currently excluded from full citizenship despite having served their time—would remove another huge obstacle. Simply eliminating the requirement that voters re-register when they move could, by some estimates, increase turnout by almost 10 percent.

Making Election Day a national holiday would also boost turnout. By creating the prospects for a dramatic event that could draw the attention and interest of only sporadically engaged voters, it could also pull moderate citizens back into the process. Harvard economist Richard Freeman has observed that voting rates are much higher among Puerto Ricans in Puerto Rico, where Election Day is a festive holiday, than among Puerto Ricans living on the mainland.[21] Such a reform might also help to reverse the disturbing decline of voting among the young. As Thomas Patterson writes: "A national holiday would . . . impress upon children and teenagers the civic importance of voting, particularly if teachers, as they do now for many holidays, engaged students in holiday-related projects."[22] Nonetheless, getting more voters to the polls is only half the battle. The other half is making those votes count.

Making the Middle Count for More. Under current American electoral rules, huge parts of the electorate are simply written off. This both deflates participation (by making it seem all but pointless to participate for many Americans) and encourages extremism (by leaving the field clear for more partisan and unrepresentative forces). If we take notions of democratic accountability seriously, the overwhelming prevalence of safe seats should be a national scandal. It means that politicians often face little challenge in general elections. For these candidates and representatives, the primary campaign, with its small and heavily skewed electorate, creates the real "accountability moment"—to use President

Bush's description of the election of 2004. The winner-take-all quality of the electoral college means that presidential candidates from both parties often ignore voters in huge swaths of the nation rather than competing for their votes. And the ability of partisan majorities in key states to redraw legislative boundaries almost at will means that, increasingly, politicians are picking voters rather than the other way around.

These are also problems we know how to address. Nor are the potential reforms purely hypothetical. Many are in use in some parts of the country. Iowa's system of congressional districting, for instance, removes the process from partisan auspices and places it in the hands of a nonpartisan civil service commission. As a result, four of Iowa's five congressional districts were competitive in 2002. That year, little Iowa, with 1 percent of the nation's congressional seats, hosted 10 percent of the nation's competitive races.[23]

Taking redistricting away from politicians is not the panacea that many now seem to believe. The evidence that partisan gerrymandering is the root cause of incumbency advantage and growing partisan polarization is weak. The boundaries of Senate districts—that is, state borders—are fixed, but polarization and incumbency advantage have risen in the Senate, too. And the increase in the number of safe districts in the House has occurred in years in which redistricting hasn't taken place. The risk of unilateral disarmament is also real. Redistricting reform is attractive only if it is pursued in states dominated by Republicans as well as Democrats. Otherwise, it merely hobbles the contestant who is already losing the race.

Nonetheless, partisan gerrymandering has grown more sophisticated and ruthless in the recent years, and there is little positive to say for its more extreme manifestations. It is also critical to remember that even a modest rise in the number of truly competitive races could make a big difference. One does not need 435 competitive House elections to empower the center in American politics. Fifty might well do the trick. And this is a goal that is eminently achievable without altering any of the nation's basic political institutions.

The electoral college is another matter. Abolishing it is a classic *there* that cannot be reached from *here*. Still, its lamentable constriction of political competition, with candidates ignoring voters in solidly "blue" or "red" states, could be reduced. Nebraska and Maine currently award electors by a mix of congressional district results and state vote totals, while Colorado recently considered a system for awarding electoral votes in proportion to statewide totals. Either approach would have the effect of opening up states that lean one way or the other to meaningful competition. Adopted across the country—for here again, unilateral disarmament is a concern—such reforms would transform tens of millions of voters from bystanders to participants in the selection of our chief executive. And since turnout is notably higher in battleground states, expanding the battlegrounds will likely generate higher turnout.[24]

Pure open primaries, in which all registered voters can vote to send candidates from either party (usually the top two vote-getters) on to the general election, is another idea that has gained popularity in recent years. The reason for thinking open primaries would produce greater centrism is that primaries would no longer be dominated by partisans on one or the other side of the aisle. Candidates would instead be forced to appeal beyond their respective bases. In theory, moreover, turnout should be higher, both because primary contests are more likely (which increases turnout) and because independents are more likely to have a say in both primary and general elections (and hence an incentive to go to the polls).[25] It has not always worked out this way in practice—in part because true fence-sitters still tend to participate infrequently in primaries. But in a context in which more voters came to the polls, open primaries could well increase the political sway of the middle. In states where one party dominates, they would also allow members of disadvantaged parties to influence political outcomes. (With closed primaries, they merely get to choose their favorite sacrificial lamb.)

The ultimate goal, however, is not greater sway for any particular segment of the electorate; it is more competitive elections. And although open primaries might help produce them, the reality is that the formidable advantages of incumbency are the most significant deterrent to effective political competition today. One successful race for Congress, no matter how closely fought, should not be a ticket to lifetime membership. To say this is not to demand that half or even a third of officeholders lose every election cycle. An occasionally competitive election, if sufficiently common and sufficiently unpredictable, is like a tax audit.

Just as we do not need to catch every tax cheat to strike fear into those who contemplate dropping a few zeros from their tax form, we do not need to vote out of office every member of Congress who egregiously departs from the center. What matters is that the risk of such defeats is real and foreseeable—that at least normal amounts of backlash insurance will not inoculate the feckless and reckless against involuntary retirement.

Undermining incumbency advantage will require, first and foremost, reducing the huge financial advantages that incumbents enjoy. Though political scientists are often dismissive of popular handwringing about the influence of money on politics, the high and rapidly rising levels of spending by deep-pocketed individuals and groups raise some troubling issues for American democracy. Investment—in politics or anything else—is rational only if it brings a return. Although some of that return may be the warm glow of civic participation, we are supremely doubtful that the raging flood of money reflects a sudden surge of patriotism among the well heeled and well organized. The big policy drives that we have discussed—energy legislation, Medicare reform, tax cuts, bankruptcy reform—all strongly indicate that interest groups and other big contributors are getting something besides civic reward for their dollars.

Popular debates over campaign finance, however, frequently conflate means and ends. The real issue isn't that there is too much money in American politics. The real issue is that the returns that well-heeled contributors and deep-pocketed interests receive for their dollars is too high, whereas the return that ordinary Americans received for their nonmonetary political efforts is too low.

When considered in these terms, the problem of money in politics is a lot like the drug problem in the United States. In principle, it can be attacked from either of two directions: the supply side (the giving of money) or the demand side (the desire to receive it). The half-hearted efforts to reform campaign finance of the past thirty years all focus on the supply side. They seek to restrict—within the limits set by political realities and constitutional precedent—the flow of money to candidates and how much they can spend. But the demand side is in many ways a more fruitful target. Making the return on investments of political money *relatively* lower would go much farther toward solving the money problem than clamping down on giving. In politics, money is like water—it flows around any barriers created, finding new ways to trickle into the hands of parties and politicians. Building barriers is much less effective than lessening the incentives for contributors to open the spigot in the first place.

For example, public financing of elections is often seen as a means of enhancing electoral competition. But the idea is a nonstarter at the federal level, and it's a classic "half-a-loaf-is-worse-than-none" reform—since most Republicans will endorse only the half a loaf that hurts Democrats. Yet an equivalent to public financing could be easily supplied with relatively limited cost and disadvantage: free access to the airwaves. The radio and television spectrums are true public goods, belonging to all of us as citizens. But the federal government currently requires strikingly little of users of this precious commodity. Asking all TV and radio stations to provide a minimum of free airtime to all federal candidates who meet basic standards would give challengers a much better shot at getting their names and positions into the public domain.

A similar argument can be made about each of the reforms we have proposed to empower moderate voters. Expanded turnout and organizational capacity among ordinary voters, open primaries, and nonpartisan redistricting—all would cheapen the coin of campaign contributions by making politicians more accountable to voters instead of contributors.

Over the long run, however, additional measures may be needed to ensure that incumbent politicians do not enjoy overwhelming electoral advantages. Some of these involve reform of the congressional process, a subject we take up shortly. But another goal should be to decrease the ability of incumbents to use the power of office to provide special favors that greatly advantage the favor-granters. Such "casework" or "constituency service" is often of real value, but it is not a service legislators need provide. A strong case can be made for moving some of the routine casework duties out of the hands of members of Congress and their offices and placing them under the auspices of "ombudsmen" whose sole role is to respond to special requests.

Admittedly, this is an extreme example of a "second-phase" proposal. It would take tremendous pressure for members of Congress to relinquish such an advantage. The same, however, was said about control over patronage jobs at an earlier stage of American political history. Moreover, there may be other tactics for reducing the perks of incumbency. The

point is that if members of Congress were no longer as capable of showering favors on their districts but instead had to be judged on their
broader positions and achievements, incumbents would have less of an
inherent advantage—especially if other changes we have advocated were
adopted.

Increasing Transparency and Accountability. Reducing incumbency
advantage is the first means of increasing accountability. The second is
making backlash insurance more expensive to provide and less effective
at shielding incumbents. As we have learned, knowledge really is power.
One of the core sources of off-center policies is elites' growing capacity
to mislead voters through agenda setting, procedural gimmicks, and
sophisticated policy design. The world of politics and policy is immensely
complicated, and knowledge of that world is very unequally distributed.
When knowledge is limited and unequal, middle-of-the-road voters have
a hard time holding politicians accountable.

Americans like to believe that more education will solve most social ills.
Yet inequalities of political information are very large, and most voters
have little reason to invest much effort in gaining more information.
Attempts to bolster average voters' political knowledge can only be
applauded. But we are skeptical of proposals that depend heavily for their
success on making voters into ideal consumers of economic theory, much
less ideal citizens of democratic theory.

Fortunately, accountability has never depended on an electorate of
political junkies and policy wonks. If accountability has declined, it is not
because voters were once highly knowledgeable and now are not. It is
because the world of politics and policy has become less transparent and
the role of intermediate organizations has declined. For this reason, the
strengthening of encompassing groups that combine material resources,
social networks, and reputations for trustworthiness can play a central
role in restoring electoral control for ordinary voters. Encompassing
organizations are vital for empowering the vast multitude of citizens who
will never pay more than intermittent and limited attention to politics.

Furthermore, the complexity of today's political world is not an
inevitable consequence of government's expanded role in modern societies. Other countries, for instance, raise the tax revenue they need without anything remotely like our excruciatingly complex tax code. What

government does is indeed complicated. But the lack of transparency of policymaking is very much a result of the growing sophistication and frequency with which backlash insurance is used. In recent years, elites have greatly improved their capacity for political manipulation, and they exercise the art with growing skill. The first step in improving effective political knowledge is to make backlash insurance more costly to provide.

Because backlash insurance thrives in environments where information is scarce, even a relatively small amount of additional knowledge would increase its price tag substantially. It is depressing but true that many voters know little more about candidates for federal office than their party labels. Yet it is also encouraging, because it means that just a small amount of additional information—say, about the relative ideology of competing candidates (moderate versus conservative Republican, moderate versus liberal Democrat)—could empower the middle. In a context in which incumbency advantage is weakened and open-seat elections are fought more fiercely among a wider range of ideological positions, small bits of knowledge could significantly erode the bias of the current system toward extreme partisans.

Where would that information come from? Over the past few decades, Americans have come to view news organizations as the principal watchdogs in our politics. This expectation stems partly from the decline of traditional membership organizations, partly from the media's pervasive presence in modern American life, and partly from the media's effectiveness in trumpeting its own role. But even though the quality of the best reporting remains high, the gap between the media's hypothetical capacity to inform citizens and its actual performance is huge and growing, and we see little reason to expect the trend to reverse. Hectoring the media to fulfill its civic obligations is a dead-end street.

By contrast, there is a relatively simple reform that would cost the federal government little and with which our country already has extensive experience: requiring equal time for competing political views on the airwaves. The Fairness Doctrine, as it was called, was abolished in the late 1980s. That decision now appears fixed in stone. But in fact Congress nearly restored the Fairness Doctrine under President George H. W. Bush, who vetoed a law that would have brought the doctrine back. Since the administration of the first President Bush, the virtue of this simple requirement has become clearer. The airwaves are now flooded with highly partisan statements on matters of national importance, much of it voicing an avowedly right-of-center view. The old argument that cable news and talk radio make the Fairness Doctrine unnecessary turned out to have it exactly backwards. It is precisely the proliferation of new media sources that has fostered a strongly right-wing journalistic presence in talk radio and on cable, while encouraging the established news media to make its reporting on politics so much more vivid and superficial. If the Federal Communications Commission can crack down on every entertainment show that TV networks run because of a few-second flash of a single bare breast in a Super Bowl halftime show, surely it can justify restoring the simple requirement that news include a fair representation of views on controversial public issues and in important electoral races.[26]

Another intriguing possibility for heightening accountability and transparency—focused on the most visible and powerful American politician, the president—would be the introduction of the parliamentary institution of Question Time. Occasional watchers of C-SPAN will be familiar with the political theater of British prime ministers appearing on the floor of the House of Commons while their opponents pepper them with questions and television cameras roll. It is quite a spectacle. (A television critic writing about C-SPAN's footage described Question Time this way: "One part game show, one part sitcom, one part Masterpiece Theatre, this weekly half-hour program is a weird shot of adrenaline in the soma-soaked upper end of the cable dial.")[27] Yet it is also an extraordinary opportunity to push elected officials hard and for those officials to show their mettle. Question Time is a remarkable forum for discussion of important issues. It gives opponents a fighting chance to push alternative agendas onto the political stage. And it is captivating to watch.

Why would any president consent to such scrutiny? The answer is that no elected president would. But the beauty of such an arrangement is that it could start informally—introduced by a single successful reform candidate who committed to start such a practice as part of a campaign vowing increased accountability. Once sustained for a time, this informal institution could become so customary that it would be hard for future officeholders to back out. After all, presidential debates are simply a custom that started out the same way. No candidate is required to participate. Historically, some clearly would rather have not. But the well-established precedent now makes such an evasion politically dangerous. Like it or not, candidates have to appear face to face with their opponents.

A final category of transparency-enhancing reforms concerns government activities. Many of these are second-phase reforms. No current political leader would embrace a major transformation of budget rules and congressional procedure, and many reforms in this category are fairly abstruse. But not all these ideas are hard to grasp, and not all would have to wait for other political changes to take hold.

The basic goal should be to make the government process relatively straightforward to understand—not completely open (indiscriminate "sunshine" often makes legitimate deal-making harder) but accessible in its broad contours to ordinary Americans. Many changes would help, including a restoration of budget rules that require that new spending or tax cuts be paid for. But perhaps the simplest idea is a citizen "prospectus" that describes the federal government's activity in terms that most Americans can understand. Think of it: Less than 60 percent of adult Americans are stakeholders in the stock market, but we are all stakeholders in American government. Yet while mutual funds are required to provide all investors with a prospectus, the only information that most Americans get about the federal government comes from their own experiences or the news. A short prospectus that describes the major activities of government, how much they cost, and how their benefits are distributed would be inexpensive to produce and distribute—it could be attached to tax forms, for example. If this idea seems frivolous, recall that most Americans do not know which programs are most costly or how much is "spent" via special tax breaks, much less how the benefits of these programs are roughly distributed. A reform candidate could easily champion an inexpensive prospectus of this sort as a means of giving people a bit more information about the government they entrust with their tax dollars.

The ultimate aim, however, is not transparency itself. It is curbing the disproportionate influence that the extremes of ideology and wealth have over public policy in the United States. Many of the reforms that we have discussed so far would help in this cause. But if the aim is to make backlash insurance more costly, there is no substitute for changes in how Congress is run. These changes may be the hardest to achieve of all the proposals we have offered. But history provides reason for believing they are possible. The bipartisan Legislative Reorganization Act of 1946, for instance, essentially created the modern congressional committee system, including the routinized practice of conference committees. Congressional reforms in the 1970s (in the name, ironically, of decentralized democracy) established the basis for the remarkable powers wielded by the majority party in the House. Many of the important rules that govern Congress are ones that Congress itself has established over time to accomplish its constitutional role, not rules that are embedded in the Constitution itself. And for this reason, nearly all can be revised—and some must be revised if American politics is to be brought back to the center.

The two features of the contemporary Congress that have most aided the majority party in pursuing off-center policies are closed rules (in which debate is tightly limited to a set of preselected amendments) and House-Senate conference committees (in which a committee consisting of senators and representatives cobbles together differing bills from each chamber). Probably the most effective means of dealing with both closed rules and conference committees is to create safeguards against their abuse by the majority party. In practice, this would mean setting up high hurdles (a two-thirds vote, for example) to departures from certain established procedures designed to ensure that the minority party has a true voice. The ranking Democratic member of the House Rules Committee, Louise Slaughter of New York, has suggested that closed rules be available only on certain days of the week. This would force the majority party to pursue most of its proposals with open debate, but it would still permit occasional closed rules. As for conference committees, they are already governed by a number of rules designed to limit how they can be used for explicitly partisan purposes. But these rules can be waived by a simple majority vote of the Rules Committee, which has used this extraordinary power with increasing frequency. Simply requiring that such "waivers" of the normal rules of the House pass a two-thirds hurdle would make them available only in actual emergencies.

These reforms may seem technical, and they are not changes that will galvanize a popular reform movement. But they are emblematic of the kinds of second-phase reforms that we believe are needed to increase transparency and accountability. Not every aspect of American politics needs to be open to public scrutiny. Sometimes watching the sausage being made, as Otto von Bismarck described the legislative process, is neither edifying nor enjoyable. But a well-functioning democracy requires a minimum level of openness and clarity. It requires that voters know enough about politicians to hold them to account and that politicians are not able to hide their most extreme actions from public view. We have seen that these safeguards are no longer as secure as they once were. But if the resources and votes of the middle regain their rightful place in American politics, the basic institutional protections against off-center policymaking can be reestablished as well.

Looking Back toward the Future

When the Committee on Political Parties published its report in 1950, it began by stating that its recommendations were "a summation of professional knowledge" that rested "on the results of scientific analysis that have come from the research activity of a great number of specialists."[28] This was an unusual position to take, but it was not unprecedented. Another group of analysts—with less formal training but far more hands-on experience—had assumed the task earlier, recommending complex solutions to what they saw as the weightiest political problems of their day. We know these proto-political scientists today as the Founding Fathers.

As anyone who has read the *Federalist Papers* can attest, these designers of American political institutions confronted fundamental issues of political engineering. How could democracy be adapted to a complex and heterogeneous society? How could institutional design be used to keep power from concentrating in the hands of one or a few politicians? How could the inarticulate and often poorly informed preferences of a large number of citizens be translated into clear and considered government action? The Founders' solutions were not perfect, as the passage of time has shown. But their thinking has left a profound legacy for all Americans.

Perhaps their greatest insight was contained in James Madison's observation that mere "parchment barriers" were not sufficient to protect and further democratic freedoms. Rules were not enough. Ambition needed to check ambition. Accountability needed to temper power.

Today, as we have shown in this book, American democracy grapples with striking new challenges. Once again, no simple procedural solution will suffice. Many of our proposals are controversial. Other thinkers and reformers will have their own ideas, perhaps better ones. But the core message of this book is that we need to increase the resources of the center, make elections more competitive, and foster the right kind of transparency in the political process. We already know a good deal about how these things might be done. And we know that the task is less a matter of institutional engineering than of political mobilization. The true challenge is to assemble an effective reform movement to pursue these fundamental goals.

The shift of American politics off center has taken years to unfold, and it will not be undone in a single moment of reform. We have sought to explain why American politics has made a stunning transit to the right, even as the American public has not. This stark disconnect between the public and elites is deeply troubling, for it strikes at widely accepted views about how American politics can and should hold politicians accountable. Yet it also offers encouragement, for it suggests that today's disturbing state of affairs need not last. Most voters don't want their leaders to head off center. They simply need the power to have their voices heard.

Still, the work of creating a more competitive, accountable, and responsive political system will be hard. It will take time. And it will rely on the efforts of many. Our journey of inquiry began with the powerful forces that are pulling political leaders away from the center, traced the impressive strategies that have allowed them to mask their growing extremism, and ended with a consideration of how these forces and strategies could be overcome. The next journey—a journey of action— will have to begin in living rooms and meeting halls across the nation. It will have to begin, as American democracy began, in the once-radical notion that "We the People" are both the mapmakers and the navigators on the great voyage of discovery called democracy.

AFTERWORD

Off Center began with George W. Bush's triumphant State of the Union address. On the heels of his successful bid for reelection, Bush announced his plan to spend some of his "political capital" on a conservative makeover of Social Security, the cornerstone of FDR's New Deal. At a time when the numerical balance between the parties remained exceptionally close, the initiative signaled the administration's hyper-confidence, as well as how aggressive the GOP's policy plans had become.

Few governing majorities in the United States have ever experienced such a rapid collapse of popular support. Bush's ambitious agenda crumbled in a matter of months. In little over a year, pundits were issuing obituaries for his administration. The series of missteps and failures that registered and accelerated the decline can be enumerated in a list of evocative names: Katrina, Terri Schiavo, Harriet Miers, Valerie Plame, Tom DeLay, Jack Abramoff. Beneath these episodic political traumas, deep-seated social concerns also grew, as did a conviction that the Bush administration had either failed to act or made problems worse. The Social Security debacle, high oil prices, large budget deficits, rising economic insecurity, growing concerns over immigration, and, most important, the war in Iraq—all contributed to a widespread sense, held by two-thirds of Americans by late spring 2006, that the country was on the "wrong track." By mid-2006, President Bush had registered a disapproval rate (65 percent) exceeded only by one postwar president: Richard Nixon, a few weeks before his resignation (and even Nixon bested Bush by only a single percentage point).[1]

Yet amid the deep crisis of faith in American governance, many pundits professed to see a new center emerging. Thanks to the exhaustion of rigid conservatism and "temper-tantrum" liberalism, wrote *New York Times* columnist David Brooks in May, "the smartest people in both parties have shifted attention from the past to the future, and a sense of flexibility and promise is in the air."[2] Democrats had failed to offer compelling alternatives in 2004, according to this conventional wisdom, and had paid the price. Republicans had overreached in 2005, and had paid the price. Now the political center was reasserting itself. The pendulum of American politics was swinging back.

Is the political center finally poised to reassert its preeminence? There are certainly greater reasons for hope than when we first wrote *Off Center*. But given all that we have laid out in this book, such a development will require much more than a fall in Republican popular standing, however swift and devastating.

The central message of *Off Center* is that we shouldn't expect any natural, pendulum-like process to revive moderation in Washington, despite the clear and persistent departure of ruling Republicans from the center. Unequal polarization—in which the governing party has moved far to the right of public opinion yet has nonetheless built itself a formidable political position—remains the dominant fact of American political life. And although recent events have certainly highlighted the vulnerabilities of Republican leadership (including some that we insufficiently appreciated when writing *Off Center*), the current political setting also, paradoxically, signals the impressive success of GOP efforts to evade accountability. Over the past dozen years, Republicans have built up formidable floodwalls against electoral tides, and now, with the biggest storm they have ever faced brewing, they are much better protected against backlash than any governing party in memory. The assessment offered in the *Congressional Quarterly*'s survey of the 2006 electoral landscape is telling: "The Republicans have every political advantage going for them except one: popularity."[3]

Congressional Quarterly's astute assessment makes no sense in the pendulum view of politics we have criticized throughout this book. In this view, if politicians are unpopular with middle-of-the-road voters, they should be packing their bags. In this view, elections are contests between two sets of views and candidates, akin to electing the president of a high school class. In this view, the party that wins is by definition giving the people what they want; the party that doesn't, is not.

Our view of politics, by contrast, emphasizes that elections (and governance) are a contest between organizations, drawing on political resources that are very unequally distributed. These organizations compete, moreover, on an institutional terrain that creates particular, often powerful biases. By no means is it a contest in which the party with views and actions closest to those of the electorate on the most salient issues will necessarily prevail. If it were, American politics would not have moved so far off center.

For all the GOP's travails, the playing field of American politics remains heavily tilted in the Republican Party's favor. Moreover, the party still possesses formidable strategic assets, including its extensive coordination and well-developed methods of backlash insurance. *Off Center* chronicled the Republican political apparatus when it was riding high (even as opinion surveys suggested that voters had very different preferences on a host of issues). The crucial question now is what happens to Republican power when public opinion has soured. Under these less favorable circumstances, GOP coordination clearly weakens as a means of pushing through off-center policies. Nonetheless, it still confers on the GOP formidable strengths, including staggering incumbency advantages that leave few seats open to challenge, a big financial edge, extensive control over the political agenda, and the set of techniques that we have laid out in previous pages that allow vulnerable incumbents to posture as moderates and mavericks even as they cast reliable GOP votes when the chips are down.

The sum of these advantages is simple and telling: Even as George W. Bush's presidency implodes and Republican popularity sinks, the GOP grip on Congress and on the reins of American political power remains surprisingly strong. Although the future of the party is more in doubt than in any point since 1994, Republicans retain the ability to recover from blows that would have been mortal to any governing party in the past. The sharp-edged brand of off-center politics perfected by America's Republican majority remains, if not resoundingly healthy, still very much alive.

To see this requires reemphasizing a central point of our book: The core of contemporary Republican rule rests in Congress, not the presidency. The curtain is closing on Bush's presidency, but when it comes to domestic policy, Congress, not the White House, is the keystone of Republican power. And congressional Republicans have always looked a lot stronger than their party's ostensible standard-bearer. After all, when Bush was eking out the narrowest reelection victory of an incumbent president since Woodrow Wilson, most of the very conservative members of the GOP-controlled House and Senate were coasting to reelection without breaking a sweat. Indeed, congressional Republicans have been far to the right of moderate voters since well before Bush entered office. Yet they have still managed to pass big, controversial bills in Congress and easily get reelected, as shown throughout this book.

Republicans have been able to do this, despite their slim margins and public skepticism toward many of their key goals, because they have built a powerful organizational structure—with the congressional party leadership, not the executive branch, as its nerve center—that controls the agenda of politics and protects potentially vulnerable party stalwarts. Since 1994, the GOP's defining characteristics have been its centralization and coordination. Defying all precedent in modern American politics, the GOP has operated as a near-parliamentary party in a constitutional system explicitly designed to thwart such coordinated action. It has given the leadership enormous control over the legislative agenda, the party's message, committee assignments, and the crafting of legislation. These strategies have not only strengthened the ability of GOP leaders to get what they want; they have also allowed the party to use backlash insurance to shield themselves from electoral retaliation for the off-center policies they have pursued.

The cost of backlash insurance is now going up. But it still seems to be insulating Republicans. One of the most striking features of the fall in Republican standing is how disassociated it seems to be from public reaction against specific government policies (or proposed policies, like Social Security privatization). Back in 1994, when Republicans took down a Democratic majority that was in disarray, domestic policy issues—the tax increase of 1993, gun control, President Clinton's failed health plan— were front and center.[4] Not so today. Instead, the reaction against President Bush and congressional Republicans appears to be driven by a few high-profile events and scandals—notably, the botched response to

Hurricane Katrina and the ethical lapses of leading Republicans—as well as a profound loss of confidence in President Bush's handling of the war in Iraq. The many domestic policies of dubious public standing that we chronicled in the book remain beneath the radar screen—a tribute to the effectiveness of Republican efforts to protect themselves against future backlash over these off-center forays. Indeed, one marvels to contemplate how low the GOP would have sunk by now if these policies had become an issue, too.

Nor have Republicans much moderated their stance since the freefall in their standing began, as the pendulum view of politics would anticipate. This suggests that they think backlash insurance remains potent, too. The main consequence of their drop in public support has instead been a return of legislative sclerosis, with key bills either tabled or hung up on intra- and inter-party disputes. Election years often create legislative graveyards, but Republicans have buried more than their fair share of post-2004 aims in the run-up to the 2006 elections. Still, where GOP leaders retained room to maneuver they revealed no hint of moderating their stance.

The absence of a midcourse correction was on clearest display on the budget, where the GOP remained wedded to a set of priorities far removed from those of the public. In May 2006, they managed to eke out victory on a major tax-cut package costing $70 billion—which delivers the vast bulk of its largesse in the form of a continuation of the dividend and capital gains tax cuts of 2003, policies whose benefits flow almost exclusively to the richest of the rich.[5] (The undeniably skewed distribution of the cuts did not prevent President Bush from claiming that failure to extend the tax cuts would be "disastrous" for "all working Americans.")[6] The dividend and capital gains tax cuts had been blocked in the Senate at the loud insistence of Republican moderate Olympia Snowe of Maine, but as everyone expected, these cuts were quietly reinserted into the bill during the conference committee with the House and passed with a four-vote margin in the Senate.[7]

To fund the plan, Republicans said they were cutting spending. And, indeed, their 2006 budget plan reduced outlays for Medicaid, student loans, and other benefits for low- and middle-income families by nearly $40 billion. Republican leaders used every play in their remarkable playbook to get the budget through Congress, as well as a few new moves. For the first time in the history of the modern budget process, they split the tax cuts from the spending part of the bill so that they could talk about a "deficit-reduction" package even as they planned to cut taxes by nearly twice as much. They passed a conservative House spending bill and a more moderate Senate alternative. Then they pulled the bill way to the right in the conference committee, excluding Democrats from the deliberations and adopting most of the House-passed program cuts. And finally, they slammed the bill through the House and Senate.

Lest "slammed" seem too strong a description, in the House they introduced the nearly eight-hundred-page bill at one o'clock in the morning; they held the vote four hours later. To get around the normal requirement that members of Congress have at least a little time to read what they are voting on, they invoked an expedited procedure that is known (without irony) as "martial law"—on a party-line vote, of course. In the Senate, the process was just as dramatic. Vice President Dick Cheney rushed back from a trip to the Middle East to cast the decisive vote, breaking a fifty-to-fifty-vote tie barely forty-eight hours after the conference report was revealed and pressed through the House. And of course, conference reports can't be amended even in the Senate, meaning that all of the dramatic movement toward the conservative House plan could be undone only by taking down the entire bill.

Whatever the merits of cutting programs for the disadvantaged in the wake of Hurricane Katrina, the cuts still left an obvious $30 billion gap, to be made up by yet more deficit spending. Yet the obvious gap is by no means the biggest. In fact, to pass the bill without threat of a Senate filibuster, Republicans larded the tax-cut bill with gimmicks that obscured its true costs. As we discussed in Chapter 2, Senate rules prevent the expedited budget process from being used to pass bills that will increase the deficit beyond the budget period that the bill covers (in this case, 2006–2010). The dividend and capital gains tax cuts, however, were almost certain to run afoul of this rule. So Republican leaders included tax-cut provisions that raise money in the short term but lose money in the long term. Then they insisted that these undeniable long-term costs shouldn't be considered under Senate rules because they fell outside the 2006–2010 budget window. Finally, they moved all the tax cuts they thought they could enact without threat of a filibuster into a separate tax-cut package estimated to cost about $20 billion a year. Not surprisingly, they plan to bring up these additional tax cuts, all of them completely unfinanced, just before the 2006 elections.[8]

Meanwhile, Republicans offered yet another short-term patch for the Alternative Minimum Tax, rescuing upper-middle-class Americans from the AMT for a year or two so that Republicans can come back to rescue them again. The growing reach of the AMT was a problem that, it will be remembered, was vastly worsened by the 2001 tax-cut package, which left out an AMT fix for the simple reason that it allowed Republicans to get greater tax cuts in 2001—and more tax cuts later when they valiantly saved taxpayers from the monster they had helped create. Apparently, for all the public skepticism and blows to other elements of their agenda, Republicans are not ready to give up their tax-cut crusade just yet.

Recall, too, that the Republican tax-cutting strategy was designed to achieve the maximum number of tax cuts in the short term while shaping the future policy agenda to the GOP's favor. There are signs that even amid the Republicans' current crisis, the effect of these past choices remains profound. In January 2006, for example, at a moment of large deficits and pressing competing demands, additional tax cuts estimated to cost $150 billion over the next decade became part of the tax code. Nobody noticed, largely because these were not the result of new legislation but long-delayed "phase-ins" of the 2001 tax cuts. Not coincidentally, 98 percent of the benefits of these phased-in cuts went to households with incomes over $200,000 a year.[9]

The continuing tax-cut steamroll suggests that Republicans still have plenty of tools left in their kit. Yet with the loss of Tom DeLay's leadership and the erosion of popular support for the Republican Party, Republican leadership has certainly become more in doubt. After all, coordination is hard in American politics. A bunch of moving parts have to work together to make it operate effectively. Equally important, keeping those parts working together relies on expectations that are self-fulfilling. If members of the GOP coalition expect coordination to keep working, they will tend to act in ways that produce that result. These self-reinforcing expectations have been especially important in a context in which, as we argue, the conservative movement has been defying the normal operation of American institutions designed to fragment authority and create centrifugal tendencies within any coalition.

If you put together "multiple moving parts" and "expectations" you are in the kind of setting Malcolm Gladwell has popularized in *The Tipping Point*.[10] Even relatively small changes can snowball, altering expectations and sometimes causing a radical shift. In this case, substantial numbers of Republicans might alter their calculations and decide that their best chance of survival is to rebel against their leadership, rather than merely to "put a little daylight" between themselves and the party on peripheral issues or when their votes do not truly matter.

Being able to envision a scenario of collapse doesn't make it certain, or even likely. So far, a good deal of the disunity within the Republican Party has been as much theatrical as real—confined to marginal issues or immaterial to the party's continued power to lead. Indeed, when the chips are down, both party leaders and rank-and-file Republicans can profit from showing a bit of disagreement among themselves. The GOP has used this strategy in previous political storms: When the government shutdowns and impeachment battle of the 1990s proved intensely unpopular, for example, the Republican leadership took its foot off the gas, allowed moderates a little room, and waited for the public outcry to die down. But when the storms passed, it was back to the same old project: building a permanent conservative majority.

Nor does Tom DeLay's departure signal the collapse of GOP unity. Republicans have also had leadership changes before—many of them, in fact. The House GOP majority has repeatedly moved quickly, once it decides to move, to throw a discredited leader overboard and replace him with the person best placed to play a very similar role. DeLay joins the ranks of Newt Gingrich, Dick Armey, Trent Lott, and Bob Livingston as a leader who has capsized without causing a major ripple. The ascension of Jon Boehner, a product and an experienced practitioner of the new GOP politics, signals a change of style more than a change of direction. Although his ties to the K Street Project are less extensive than DeLay's—or than those of his main opponent in the leadership race, Roy Blunt—he is actually a more reliable conservative than DeLay. (The *National Journal* finds that in 2005, Boehner was more conservative on domestic issues than 94 percent of House members; DeLay was more conservative than 77 percent.)[11] As a *Washington Post* news story summed up the change, "Boehner, who has extensive links to lobbyists, hardly represents a radical break from the past."[12]

To be sure, if the GOP's troubles continue to mount, staged disunity could give way to the real thing, and leadership challenges could become more substantial. But we should not mistake greater conflict within the party or between Republicans in Congress and President Bush for an inevitable sign of the party's crack-up. Such conflicts can be a form of backlash insurance as well as a sign of real disunity, a dispute at the margins as well as a fundamental disagreement. And such conflicts can be fleeting—a reflection of fears about the party's electoral future that will be enduring only if the "accountability moment" that President Bush talked about in 2004 truly takes place in 2006.[13] Whether such a moment of accountability is at hand is a surprisingly open question—a fact that provides the strongest confirming evidence of the argument developed in *Off Center.*

The upcoming midterms of 2006 have left vote prognosticators in a quandary. By every survey-based measure—popular dissatisfaction with the country's direction, public disapproval of President Bush, disgust with Congress, generic support for Democrats over Republicans— Republicans are doing terribly, considerably worse than Democrats were doing on the eve of the historic 1994 election, in which Republicans picked up more than fifty seats and both houses of Congress. Yet at the level of individual congressional contests, Republicans still have a substantial edge in races for the House and especially the Senate.

This is not because Republicans enjoy an overwhelming electoral margin. Far from it: To capture Congress in the midterm elections, Democrats need to pick up six seats in the Senate and sixteen in the House—a modest swing by postwar standards, especially in the sixth year of a presidency, when the president's party often loses ground. Yet in late spring 2006 veteran election-watchers still place odds against the Democrats' prospects of regaining control of either chamber.[14] Understanding why a party that is so battered can still be so favored reveals a great deal about how the GOP has insulated itself from the traditional swings of the political pendulum.

Much of the Republicans' advantage reflects the geographic structure of American elections. In the Senate, Republicans have a tremendous built-in edge because small states, which lean Republican, are so overrepresented. As a result, Democrats can win a majority of votes nationwide and still not gain control. Surprisingly, the electoral battlefield is also heavily tilted in the House. Congressional districts are roughly equal in population. But Republicans are helped by the fact that Democratic voters are more tightly packed together. The Republicans could retain control of the House next year even if the majority of voters cast their ballots for Democratic candidates.

Not only do Republicans get more seats per vote; almost all the seats they hold are also very safe. The past two elections have seen the fewest incumbents defeated by challengers in all of American history—four in 2002 and five in 2004. In 2004, the average margin of victory for House incumbents was 40 percentage points.[15] Incumbency advantage is often blamed on gerrymandering, but an equally important cause is money—and money strongly favors the GOP. Over the past decade, Republicans have cultivated close ties to deep-pocketed donors and special-interest groups. They have also developed a highly institutionalized system of intercandidate giving, in which party members and their political action committees donate to other Republicans to keep the majority in power.

The huge advantages incumbents enjoy do not end with bulging campaign war chests. They have an enormous edge in name recognition, as well as the capacity to tailor an appealing (if often grossly distorted) public profile in their district. These advantages seem to have grown more pronounced in recent years even as extremism has grown, and they help to explain why only open seats are typically in play. Once a candidate has won one or two elections, they are usually very safe.

The high level of Republican unity and coordination that we have discussed helps the GOP protect these advantages for *its* incumbents in particular. Unity and coordination facilitate Republican control over the agenda, keeping the focus on issues that cast their members in the best possible light. They also enable Republicans to pursue a whole range of policy tricks and procedural moves that allow their members, especially the vulnerable ones, to appear independent without jeopardizing the party's conservative agenda. We have explored many of these strategies in this book—letting moderates vote against legislation when their votes aren't needed, relying on closed rules or redesigning bills in conference committees so members don't have to vote on specific unpopular changes one by one—but though these strategies are always useful, they become all the more crucial when the GOP is under fire.

It speaks volumes that election watchers have to debate whether Democrats can pick up the small number of seats required to take Congress in 2006. Against the backdrop of nearly unprecedented public dissatisfaction with President Bush and congressional Republicans, any well-functioning system of political accountability would deliver one verdict. Indeed, in a truly parliamentary system, where elections serve as referenda on the party in power, the GOP would undoubtedly be facing electoral disaster. Instead, thanks to the GOP's institutional and organizational advantages, Democrats can hope only for a narrow victory—and six months before the vote most election watchers still believed that even a narrow Democratic victory remained less likely than continued Republican governance.

An alternative interpretation, of course, is that Republican survival rests on the relative unpopularity of Democrats. Indeed, a common critique of our work has been that we should be heaping more blame on Democrats for Republican success. To us, this "Democrats must be at fault" view rests on the naive view of politics as a simple popularity contest fought entirely on the electoral battleground, in which, by definition, the party that loses is not giving the people what they want. This view shifts our attention away from the vital subject of this book: governance, which is key to understanding Republican power (and its limits). It shifts our attention away from what the people running the show in American politics actually *do:* how they coordinate their actions, how they decide on their goals, how they use the levers of power to get what they want and, in recent years, to evade accountability. And even as an account of electoral outcomes, it flies in the face of the strong evidence that, as a rule, incumbents lose office, opposition candidates don't win it—that is, that disapproval of the incumbent, rather than approval of the opposition, drives vote choice.[16]

According to the popularity-contest view, the continuing advantages of Republicans reflect the continuing failure of Democrats to position themselves properly to capture the vital center. In a widely discussed analysis released in October 2005, "The Politics of Polarization," Democratic strategists William Galston and Elaine Kamarack argue that their party needs to quit comforting itself with the myth that turnout efforts or new liberal constituencies will rescue it from its plight and instead move decisively to the center. "One thing is clear," they write, "the polarization of the parties has created an opportunity for a political leader—from either the center-right or the center-left—to capture the hearts and the votes of the vast legion of moderate voters who are not comfortable calling either party 'home.' "[17] This clear prescription implies a clear diagnosis: Both parties have raced away from the center at equal speed. Yet, as we saw in Chapter 1, partisan polarization has in fact been extremely unequal: Republicans have moved much farther to the right than Democrats have moved left. Meanwhile, middle-of-the-road voters have *not* moved sharply right; they may even have moved slightly left. Democrats have surely had problems attracting the median voter, but not because they hold policy stances that are farther from the center than Republican stances.

Nor does the popularity-contest view square easily with the most common historical referent to which commentators reach—namely, the 1994 elections. Republicans did not win in 1994 because voters were enamored of the Contract with America, which Republicans unveiled just weeks before the election. Most voters had never heard of the contract, and political scientists are unanimous in dismissing its importance as a shaper of voter choice.[18] Instead, more than anything else, the 1994 result was vote against Democrats in Congress and against President Clinton, informed only by the most general sense that opposition Republicans were offering a different course. (1994 was also when time finally caught up with many Democrats, who found themselves in highly vulnerable seats as a result of the long, slow realignment of the South in American politics.) Given the current level of public dissatisfaction with Republicans and President Bush, Democrats would under normal political circumstances have little problem doing the same thing the GOP did in 1994, however effectively or ineffectively they presented their own positive case. A pundit recently sniffed, "You can't simply rely on the weakness of your opponents."[19] This may be true today, yet not because this formula hasn't usually worked but because Republicans have so fortified their position.

Indeed, Democrats appear to have responded to this new strategic reality, particularly with regard to their political tactics within Congress. They have centralized their operations and worked with unprecedented success to keep their members in line. During the debate over Social Security, they refused to accept any compromise, fearing—correctly, in our view—that such compromises would be pushed way to the right once they had been made and recognizing that unity in opposition was their greatest strategic asset. On the electoral battlefield, Democrats have fielded better candidates and attempted to contest a wider range of races, although their ground-level operations still remain notably weaker than the Republican Party's and they suffer from all of the other fundamental disadvantages just discussed.

Democrats have been less effective in formulating a coherent alternative philosophy and attractive set of themes for campaigning and governing. Yet even here some progress has been made—and, again, these tasks have not historically been preconditions for winning elections against governing majorities as unpopular as the current Republican Party. As this book shows, the fundamental problem for Democrats when it comes to what consultants call "messaging" is not that they are just as far from the center as Republicans are. The problem is that Democrats have had difficulty unifying the disparate electoral races being fought in 2006. A crucial factor in 1994 was that the elections became nationalized. Many Democrats had long survived by following Tip O'Neill's dictum of keeping politics local, making the elections a referendum on their own personalities and positions, not the image or position of their party. When the 1994 election instead became a referendum on the governing party, dozens of them lost—and those who had grown most of out step with their constituents lost biggest.

The central reality of American politics today, as congressional scholar Sarah Binder observes, is a historically unprecedented combination: "a world of candidate-centered electoral contests conducted within a system of active, nationalized political parties."[20] *Off Center* shows how such an arrangement gives a well-coordinated majority enormous advantages, even when its ambitions are extreme and unpopular. Operating as a team, a cohesive majority can govern as a party, but face the voters, when necessary, as individuals. All of the normal checks and balances—from electoral accountability to routine congressional oversight of the White House and White House discipline of Congress—become short-circuited. (As of May 2006, George W. Bush had yet to veto a bill during his presidency, a virtually unprecedented streak that signals how strong GOP control of the agenda remains.) For ordinary citizens this is, in many ways, the worst of both political worlds. It offers the concentrated political power of parliamentary democracies without that system's clear lines of accountability.

For accountability to work under current conditions, American elections must begin to match the contours of American governance. Individual politicians must be held accountable for what their parties do, not just for their own positions, postures, or personae. Any prospect for 2006 to be a breakthrough for Democrats turns on the upcoming elections becoming effectively nationalized. Moreover, the prospects improve greatly if the elections are nationalized on terms that replicate the uneven mobilization that occurred in 1994, when conservatives were incensed and Democrats demoralized. Given the continuing concentration of power and availability of backlash insurance, however, there remains a limited amount that Democrats can do to produce this result. Again, the GOP retains a significantly greater capacity to set the agenda, and its capacity to do that may well prove to be crucial to its fortunes.

A national election fought over national issues that truly matter to America's embattled political center is something we could only hope for when we wrote the hardcover edition of this book, and it would certainly be an important step toward the renewal of political responsiveness. Yet it would be only a start. The very fact that the GOP's position remains so strong in the face of such widespread disillusionment with its rule suggests the systemic character of the challenges we face today. Ultimately, the restoration of political accountability in America's off-center system will depend on major reforms of the sort that we outline in this book, not on narrow electoral victories or half-hearted measures to correct the most egregious abuses of power.

NOTES

Introduction

1. If the ambit is expanded to foreign policy, a fourth moderate tell-all—eerily similar to the other three in key respects—is Richard A. Clarke, *Against All Enemies: Inside America's War Against Terror* (Chicago: Free Press, 2004).

2. Ron Suskind, "Why Are These Men Laughing?" *Esquire,* 1 January 2003, 96–105.

3. Christine Todd Whitman, *It's My Party, Too: The Battle for the Heart of the GOP and the Future of America* (New York: Penguin, 2005).

4. Ron Suskind, *The Price of Loyalty: George W. Bush, the White House, and the Education of Paul O'Neill* (New York: Simon and Schuster, 2004).

5. David Broder, "The Polarization Express," *Washington Post,* 12 December 2004, B7; Nolan McCarty, "The Policy Consequences of Political Polarization," in Paul Pierson and Theda Skocpol, eds., *The Transformation of the American Polity* (Princeton, NJ: Princeton University Press, forthcoming).

6. E. J. Dionne, Jr., *Why Americans Hate Politics: The Death of the Democratic Process* (New York: Simon and Schuster, 1991).

7. Available at http://www.princeton.edu/~csdp/events/pdfs/ Panel7.pdf.

8. Christopher Jencks, "Does Inequality Matter?" *Daedalus,* Winter 2002, 49–65.

9. See *American Democracy in an Age of Rising Inequality: Report of the American Political Science Association Task Force on Inequality and American Democracy* (Washington, DC: American Political Science Association, June 2004).

10. Norman Ornstein, "GOP's Approach to Continuity: Not Just Unfortunate. Stupid," *Roll Call,* 9 June 2004.

11. James A. Stimson, Michael B. MacKuen, and Robert S. Erikson, "Dynamic Representation," *American Political Science Review* 89 (1995): 543–65.

12. The best work on political manipulation through the crafting of rhetoric is Lawrence Jacobs and Robert Shapiro, *Politicians Don't Pander* (Chicago: University of Chicago Press, 2000).

13. *American Democracy in an Age of Rising Inequality;* Theda Skocpol, *Diminished Democracy: From Membership to Management in American Civic Life* (Norman: University of Oklahoma Press, 2003).

14. These trends are discussed and documented in Chapter 4.

15. The fundraising role of the parties is examined in Chapters 4 and 5.

16. These findings come from a unique database developed by Keith Poole and Howard Rosenthal (and available at http://voteview.com), discussed in Chapter 4.

17. Martin Wattenberg, *The Rise of Candidate-Centered Politics* (Cambridge, MA: Harvard University Press, 1991).

18. Anthony King, ed., *The New American Political System,* 2nd ed. (Washington, DC: AEI Press, 1990); John E. Chubb and Paul E. Peterson, eds., *Can the Government Govern?* (Washington, DC: Brookings Institution Press, 1989).

19. Lawrence C. Dodd and Bruce I. Oppenheimer, eds., *Congress Reconsidered,* 7th ed. (Washington, DC: Congressional Quarterly, 2000); David W. Rohde, *Parties and Leaders in the Post-Reform House* (Chicago: University of Chicago Press, 1991).

20. E. E. Schattschneider, *The Semi-Sovereign People: A Realist's View of Democracy in America* (New York: Holt, Rinehart, and Winston, 1960), 66.

21. Paul Pierson, "When Effect Becomes Cause," *World Politics* 45 (1993): 595–628; Theda Skocpol, *Protecting Soldiers and Mothers: The Political Origins of Social Policy in the United States* (Cambridge, MA: Harvard University Press, 1992); Jacob S. Hacker, *The Divided Welfare State: The Battle over Public and Private Social Benefits in the United States* (Cambridge: Cambridge University Press, 2002); Joe Soss and Suzanne Mettler, "The Consequences of Public Policy for Democratic Citizenship: Bridging Policy Studies and Mass Politics," *Perspectives on Politics* 2 (2004): 1–19.

22. The exact provenance of the "starve the beast" slogan is unclear, though it certainly predates the presidency of George W. Bush. A *Wall Street Journal* article of 1985 quotes a Reagan White House official thus: "We didn't starve the beast. It's still eating quite well—by feeding off future generations." Paul Blustein, "Reagan's Record," *Wall Street Journal,* 21 October 1985, A1.

23. Sheryl Gay Stolberg, "Cut Short: The Revolution That Wasn't," *New York Times,* 13 February 2005, D1.

24. Robert Dahl, *On Democracy* (New Haven and London: Yale University Press, 1998).

25. Joseph A. Schumpeter, *Capitalism, Socialism, and Democracy* (New York: Harper and Brothers, 1942), 269.

26. Thomas Hobbes, *Leviathan* (Cambridge: Cambridge University Press, 1996), 130.

27. Justice Oliver Wendell Holmes to Harold J. Laski, 4 March 1920, in Mark DeWolfe Howe, ed., *Holmes-Laski Letters,* vol. 1 (Cambridge, MA: Harvard University Press, 1953), 249.

28. Jacobs and Shapiro, *Politicians Don't Pander.*

29. *New Republic,* 26 August 2004.

30. Luntz Research Companies, "Growth, Prosperity, and Restoring Economic Security," n.d., 6, available at http://www.politicalstrategy.org/archives/ 001189.php.

31. On the power of public opinion, key works include Dennis Chong, *Rational Lives: Norms and Values in Politics and Society* (Chicago: University of Chicago Press, 2000); John A. Ferejohn and James H. Kuklinski, eds., *Information and Democratic Processes* (Urbana: University of Illinois Press, 1990); Shanto Iyengar, "Shortcuts to Political Knowledge: Selective Attention and the Accessibility Bias," in Ferejohn and Kuklinski, eds., *Information and Democratic Processes*, 160–85; Arthur Lupia and Mathew D. McCubbins, *The Democratic Dilemma: Can Citizens Learn What They Need to Know?* (Cambridge: Cambridge University Press, 1998); Michael B. MacKuen, Robert S. Erikson, and James A. Stimson, *The Macro Polity* (Cambridge: Cambridge University Press, 2002); Benjamin Page and Robert Shapiro, *The Rational Public: Fifty Years of Trends in Americans' Policy Preferences* (Chicago: University of Chicago Press, 1992); and Paul M. Sniderman, Richard A. Brody, and Philip E. Tetlock, *Reasoning and Choice: Explorations in Political Psychology* (Cambridge: Cambridge University Press, 1991). On the power of the "median voter," the seminal analysis is Anthony Downs, *An Economic Theory of Democracy* (New York: Harper and Row, 1957). Reviews of the median-voter framework and its application include Donald Green and Ian Shapiro, *Pathologies of Rational Choice Theory* (New Haven and London: Yale University Press, 1994), and Kenneth Shepsle and Mark S. Boncheck, *Analyzing Politics: Rationality, Behavior, and Institutions* (New York: W. W. Norton, 1997). Recent extensions include David W. Brady and Craig Volden, *Revolving Gridlock: Politics and Policy from Carter to Clinton* (Boulder, CO: Westview Press, 1998), and Keith Krehbiel, *Pivotal Politics: A Theory of U.S. Lawmaking* (Chicago: University of Chicago Press, 1998).

Chapter 1. Off Center

1. Rachel Clarke, "Drawing Up Blueprints for Bush Victory," *BBC News,* 6 November 2004, http://news.bbc.co.uk/1/hi/world/americas/3987237.stm.

2. This discussion of congressional ideology draws on the dataset of Poole and Rosenthal, which is available at http://www.voteview.org. The numbers referred to are d-nominate scores, which can be compared across Congresses (at least within stable two-party periods of Amerian political history) but cannot be compared across the House and Senate. See Keith T. Poole and Howard Rosenthal, *Congress: A Political-Economic History of Roll Call Voting* (New York: Oxford University Press, 1997).

3. Michael Barone, with Richard E. Cohen and Grant Ujifusa, *The Almanac of American Politics, 2004* (Washington, DC: National Journal, 2003), 1287; The Club for Growth, "RINO Watch," 2 October 2003, http://www.clubforgrowth.org/ rino-03.php; description of Conservative Action Team from the Web site of House Republican John Doolittle of California, a founder of the group, http://www.house.gov/doolittle/aboutjtd.htm.

4. Barone, *Almanac of American Politics, 2004*, 1359.

5. Barone, *Almanac of American Politics, 2004*, 1237.

6. David Frum, *The Right Man: The Surprise Presidency of George W. Bush* (New York: Random House, 2003).

7. A search of the headlines and lead paragraphs of top newspapers shows that, in his first four years in office, Bush's name appeared near "conservative" almost twice as often as it did during his father's presidency. The political scientist Jeffery Jenkins has calculated—using a technique similar to that of Poole and Rosenthal—that Bush is to the right of every postwar president except Reagan and that he is roughly in the ideological middle of the current (highly conservative) congressional GOP. Jeffery Jenkins, "Ideologically, Bush Is Right of Center, but Not Extreme Right," *Chicago Tribune*, 7 March 2004, 3.

8. Bill Minutaglio, *First Son: George W. Bush and the Bush Family Dynasty* (New York: Crown Books, 1999).

9. John C. Fortier and Norman J. Ornstein, "President Bush: Legislative Strategist," in Fred I. Greenstein, ed., *The George W. Bush Presidency: An Early Assessment* (Baltimore: Johns Hopkins University Press, 2003), 139.

10. Peter Baker, "Rove Is Promoted to Deputy Staff Chief: Job Covers a Wide Swath of Policy," *Washington Post*, 9 February 2005, A21.

11. Quoted in Joel Havemann, "Some Find Strong Pulse in Social Security," *Los Angeles Times*, 12 December 2004, A1.

12. Laura Blumenfeld, "Sowing the Seeds of GOP Domination: Conservative Norquist Cultivates Grass Roots beyond the Beltway," 12 January 2004, A1. The comments about the Holocaust were made on the National Public Radio program *Fresh Air*, 2 October 2003, available at http://www.npr.org/templates/story/ story.php?storyId=1452983.

13. For an excellent muckraking study of DeLay's career, see Lou Dubose and Jan Reid, *The Hammer—Tom DeLay: God, Money, and the Rise of the Republican Congress* (New York: Public Affairs Press, 2004).

14. John Micklethwait and Adrian Wooldridge, *The Right Nation: Conservative Power in America* (New York: Penguin, 2004), 23.

15. Todd Purdum, "An Electoral Affirmation of Shared Values," *New York Times*, 4 November 2004, A1.

16. Quoted in Bob Woodward, *Plan of Attack* (New York: Simon and Schuster, 2004), 28.

17. Clark Bensen, "Presidential Results by Congressional Districts: Bush Strengthens His Control in the U.S. House," March 2005, http://www.polidata.org/press/ wprec23z.pdf.

18. Hendrik Hertzberg, "Nuke 'Em," *New Yorker*, 14 March 2005, 56.

19. Lawrence R. Jacobs and Benjamin I. Page, "Who Influences U.S. Foreign Policy," *American Political Science Review* 99 (February 2005): 121.

20. Stimson, *Public Opinion in America: Moods, Cycles, Swings*, 2nd ed. (Boulder, CO: Westview Press, 1998). Updated data are at http://www.unc.edu/ ~jstimson/time.html.

21. Morris P. Fiorina, with Samuel J. Abrams and Jeremy C. Pope, *Culture War? The Myth of a Polarized America* (New York: Pearson, Longman, 2004).

22. All of the NES results to follow are available at http://www.umich.edu/~nes/nesguide/gd-index.htm#4.

23. *Los Angeles Times* exit poll, available at http://www.latimesinteractive.com/pdfarchive/state/la-110204poll-513_pdf.pdf; *Newsweek* poll, conducted 22–23 January 2004 (1,233 adults; margin of error +/– 3 percent), available at http://nationaljournal.com/members/polltrack/2004/issues/04socsec.htm.

24. "Bush Inauguration Comes with Nation Still Deeply Divided, Dubious on Iraq, Social Security, Annenberg Data Show," Annenberg Public Policy Center, Philadelphia, 17 January 2004, available at http://www.annenbergpublicpolicycenter.org/naes/2005_03_inauguration_01-17_pr.pdf.

25. Pew Research Center for the People and the Press, 5–9 January 2005 (1,503 adults; margin of error +/– 3 percent), available at http://nationaljournal.com/members/polltrack/2005/issues/05socsec.htm#21.

26. *Newsweek* poll, 3–4 February 2005 (1,000 adults; margin of error +/– 4 percent, available at http://nationaljournal.com/members/polltrack/2005/issues/05socsec.htm#19.

27. Barry C. Burden, "An Alternative Account of the 2004 Presidential Election," *Forum* 2:4, Article 2, http://www.bepress.com/forum/vol2/iss4/art2.

28. Stephen Ansolabehere and Charles Stewart, III, "Truth in Numbers," *Boston Review,* February–March 2005, http://www.bostonreview.net/BR30.1/ansolastewart.html.

29. Fiorina, *Culture War?* 113.

30. Fiorina, *Culture War?* 8.

31. Fiorina, *Culture War?* 80.

Chapter 2. Partying with the "People's Money"

1. "Transportation—DeLay Stands in Path of Proposal to Expand TEA-21 Spending," *CongressDailyPM,* 17 March 2003.

2. William G. Gale and Peter R. Orszag, "Sunsets in the Tax Code," *Tax Notes,* 9 June 2003, 1553–61.

3. Citizens for Tax Justice, "Year-by-Year Analysis of the Bush Tax Cuts Growing Tilt to the Very Rich," 2002, available at http://www.ctj.org/html/ gwb0602.htm.

4. William G. Gale, Peter R. Orszag, and Isaac Shapiro, "Distributional Effects of the 2001 and 2003 Tax Cuts and Their Financing," Urban Institute and Brookings Institution Tax Policy Center, 3 June 2004, http://www.urban.org/UploadedPDF/411018_tax_cuts.pdf.

5. Robert Dahl, *Who Governs? Democracy and Power in an American City* (New Haven: Yale University Press, 1961), 1.

6. Lawrence R. Jacobs and Robert Shapiro, *Politicians Don't Pander: Political Manipulation and the Loss of Democratic Responsiveness* (Chicago: University of Chicago Press, 2000), 3.

7. Larry M. Bartels, "Homer Gets a Tax Cut: Inequality and Public Policy in the American Mind," *Perspectives on Politics* 3 (March 2005): 15–32; Paul Krugman, "The Tax-Cut Con," *New York Times Magazine*, 14 September 2003, 54.

8. The survey findings reported in this chapter were obtained from the following sources: Karlyn H. Bowman, *Public Opinion on Taxes* (Washington, DC: American Enterprise Institute, 2004), available at http://www.aei.org/docLib/20040407_Taxes2.pdf; *National Journal's* Poll Track (http://nationaljournal.com/members/polltrack); and PollingReport.com (http://www.pollingreport.com/).

9. John Mark Hansen, "Individuals, Institutions, and Public Preferences over Public Finance," *American Political Science Review* 92 (1998): 514.

10. Bowman, *Public Opinion on Taxes*, 10.

11. A detailed summary of these surveys is contained in our article, "Abandoning the Middle: The Bush Tax Cuts and the Limits of Democratic Control," *Perspectives on Politics* 3 (March 2005): 39.

12. See the revealing discussion in Clay Chandler, "Will the Republicans Trip over Tax Reform?" *Washington Post*, 13 August 1995, H1.

13. CNN/Gallup/*USA Today*, survey of 9–11 March 2001, retrieved from *National Journal* Poll Track.

14. *Newsweek*, survey of 15–16 March 2001; Penn Schoen Berland, survey of 15–21 February 2001; both available via *National Journal* Poll Track.

15. The memo can be found at http://thepriceofloyalty.ronsuskind.com/thebushfiles/archives/000058.html.

16. Eliza Newlin Carey, "Moore's Club for Growth Causing a Stir in the GOP," *National Journal*, 26 October 2002, 3128.

17. Matt Bai, "Fight Club," *New York Times Magazine*, 10 August 2003, 24; Carey, "Moore's Club for Growth Causing a Stir in the GOP."

18. Americans for Tax Reform, "Questions and Answers about the National Taxpayer Protection Pledge," available at http://www.atr.org/nationalpledge/index.html.

19. Martin A. Sullivan, "The Decline and Fall of Distribution Analysis," *Tax Notes*, 27 June 2003, 1872.

20. Leonard E. Burman, William G. Gale, and Jeffrey Rohaly, "The AMT: Projections and Problems," *Tax Notes*, 7 July 2003, 105–17.

21. Joel Friedman, Richard Kogan, and Robert Greenstein, "New Tax-Cut Law Ultimately Costs as Much as Bush Plan: Gimmicks Used to Camouflage $4.1 Trillion Cost in Second Decade," Center on Budget and Policy Priorities, 27 June 2001, http://www.cbpp.org/5-26-01tax.htm.

22. George W. Bush, statements at Republican Presidential Debate, Columbia, South Carolina, 15 February 2000; the 2004 statement is available at http://www.factcheck.org/article281m.html.

23. Juliet Eilperin and Dan Morgan, "Something Borrowed, Something Blue: Memo Enlists Lobbyists to Trade White Collars for Hard Hats at GOP Tax Cut Rally," *Washington Post*, 9 March 2001, A16.

24. White House, Office of the Press Secretary, "Remarks of the President on Tax Cut Plan," Washington, DC, 5 February 2001, available at http://www.whitehouse.gov/news/releases/20010205.html.

25. Paul Krugman, "Bad Heir Day," *New York Times,* 30 May 2001, A23.

26. Citizens for Tax Justice, "Year-by-Year Analysis."

27. Tod Lindberg, "The Bush Tax-Cut Record," *Washington Times,* 10 June 2003, A17.

28. Burman, Gale, and Rohaly, "The AMT."

29. Burman, Gale, and Rohaly, "The AMT."

30. White House, Office of the Press Secretary, "Remarks by the President in Tax Cut Bill Signing Ceremony," 7 June 2001, available at http://www.whitehouse.gov/infocus/tax-relief.

31. Jim VandeHei and Jonathan Weisman, "GOP Seeks to Change Score on Tax Cuts," *Washington Post,* 6 February 2003, A35.

32. Steve Inskeep, "Tax Bill Congress Passed This Week," *National Public Radio—Weekend Edition,* 24 May 2003, http://www.npr.org/templates/story/story.php?storyId=1273727.

33. V. O. Key, Jr., *The Responsible Electorate* (Cambridge, MA: Harvard University Press, 1966), 7.

34. National Public Radio/Kaiser Family Foundation/Kennedy School of Government, "National Survey of American's Views on Taxes," April 2003, available at http://www.npr.org/news/specials/polls/taxes2003/20030415_taxes_survey.pdf.

Chapter 3. New Rules for Radicals

1. Saul Alinsky, *Rules for Radicals* (New York: Vintage, 1971).

2. For those, see Peter Baker, *The Breach: Inside the Impeachment and Trial of William Jefferson Clinton* (New York: Scribner, 2000); Richard A. Posner, *An Affair of State: The Investigation, Impeachment, and Trial of President Clinton* (Cambridge, MA: Harvard University Press, 2000); Jeffrey Toobin, *A Vast Conspiracy : The Real Story of the Sex Scandal That Nearly Brought Down a President* (New York: Touchstone, 2000); and, of course, Kenneth W. Starr, *The Starr Report: The Findings of Independent Counsel Kenneth W. Starr on President Clinton and the Lewinsky Affair* (New York: Public Affairs, 1998).

3. An excellent compendium of poll results on impeachment is contained in Center on Policy Attitudes, *Expecting More Say: The American Public on Its Role in Government Decisionmaking with a Special Section on the Impeachment Process,* available at http://www.policyattitudes.org/pres.html.

4. Lou Dubose and Jan Reid, *The Hammer—Tom Delay: God, Money, and the Rise of the Republican Congress* (New York: Public Affairs, 2004), 152–55.

5. Center on Policy Attitudes, "Expecting More Say."

6. Baker, *The Breach,* 179.

7. Baker, *The Breach,* 225.

8. Baker, *The Breach,* 17.

9. Dubose and Reid, *The Hammer*, 154–55.

10. Jacob S. Hacker, *The Great Risk Shift: The New Economic Insecurity—And What Can Be Done About It* (New York: Oxford University Press, 2006).

11. Paul Pierson, *Dismantling the Welfare State? Reagan, Thatcher, and the Politics of Retrenchment* (Cambridge: Cambridge University Press, 1994), 64–69; Paul C. Light, *Still Artful Work: The Continuing Politics of Social Security Reform* (New York: McGraw-Hill, 1994).

12. *2005 Annual Report of the Board of Trustees of the Federal Old-Age and Survivors Insurance and Disability Insurance Trust Funds* (Washington, DC: U.S. Government Printing Office, 2005).

13. Steven Teles, *Parallel Paths: The Evolution of the Conservative Legal Movement, 1970–2005* (Princeton, NJ: Princeton University Press, forthcoming); Stuart Butler and Peter Germanis, "Achieving Social Security Reform: A 'Leninist' Strategy," *Cato Journal* 3 (1983): 551–53.

14. The quotations are from Jill Zuckman, "Hastert: Public Not Sold on Social Security Plans," *Chicago Tribune*, 11 February 2005, http://www.chicagotribune.com/news/nationworld/chi-0502110241feb11,1,1729146.story.

15. Elizabeth Drew, "He's Back," *New York Review of Books*, 24 March 2005, 44.

16. Memo from Peter Wehner, President Bush's director of strategic initiatives, on the White House's plans for Social Security, 3 January 2005, leaked to *Wall Street Journal* and available at http://online.wsj.com/article/0,,SB110496995612018199,00.html?mod=home_whats_news_us.

17. Quoted in Joel Havemann, "Some Find Strong Pulse in Social Security," *Los Angeles Times*, 12 December 2004, A1.

18. Frank Luntz, "The Environment: A Cleaner, Healthier, Safer America," available at http://www.luntzspeak.com/graphics/LuntzResearch.Memo.pdf.

19. CBS News, "Dems on Social Security Warpath," 28 January 2005, http://www.cbsnews.com/stories/2005/01/28/politics/main670060.shtml.

20. See the discussion in Mark Schmitt, "The Byrd Rule and Social Security," available at http://markschmitt.typepad.com/decembrist/2005/01/the_byrd_rule_a.html. (Schmitt was Bill Bradley's policy director in the 1990s.)

21. Glen Justice, with assistance by Carl Hulse, "Social Security Fight Begins, over a Bill Still Nonexistent," *New York Times*, 17 February 2005, A26.

22. Elizabeth Warren on *TalkingPointsMemo.com*, available at http://www.talkingpointsmemo.com/bankruptcy/archives/2005/03/index.php.

23. David Broder, "A Bankrupt 'Reform,'" *Washington Post*, 13 March 2005, B7.

24. The classic examination of the disadvantages faced by diffuse interests (and how they can sometimes be overcome) is James Q. Wilson, *Political Organizations* (New York: Basic Books, 1971), building on Mancur Olson, *The Logic of Collective Action* (Cambridge, MA: Harvard University Press, 1965).

25. Frontline, "Blackout," PBS, June 2001, http://www.pbs.org/wgbh/pages/frontline/shows/blackout/traders/power.html; Center for Responsive Politics, "A Money in Politics Backgrounder on the Energy Industry," 16 May 2001, available

at http://www.opensecrets.org/ pressreleases/energybriefing.htm. Overall, Republicans received 78 percent of oil and gas industry donations and 90 percent of coal industry donations.

26. The next three paragraphs draw on Eric Alterman and Mark Green, *The Book on Bush: How George W. (Mis)Leads America* (New York: Viking, 2004), 12–35.

27. NBC News/*Wall Street Journal,* 6–8 March 2004 (surveyed 1,018 adults; margin of error +/− 3.1 percent), available at http://nationaljournal.com/members/polltrack/2004/issues/04environment.htm.

28. Surveys by Gallup Organization, March 2001, 2002, 2003, 2004, 2005. Retrieved 28 March 2005 from the iPOLL Databank, Roper Center for Public Opinion Research, University of Connecticut, http://www.ropercenter.uconn.edu/ ipoll.html.

29. Dubose and Reid, *The Hammer,* 276, 277.

30. The stories are legion: Republicans first resisted a Homeland Security Department, then abruptly switched sides when they sensed defeat, and finally tarred the proposal's original Democratic supporters for holding it up when the Bush administration insisted on inserting "poison pill" restrictions on the rights of civil servants. (The attacks helped Republicans bolster their position in the House and Senate in 2002.) Republicans responded to concerted legal attacks by the European Union over one set of U.S. tax subsidies to pass a bevy of new (and unfunded) tax breaks for U.S. corporations. The resulting legislation—misleadingly titled the American Jobs Creation Act, since most companies indicated they would use the funds for purposes other than new employment—allowed American multinationals to repatriate tens of billions in profits almost tax-free.

31. Jonathan Oberlander, *The Political Life of Medicare* (Chicago: University of Chicago Press, 2003), 183–95.

32. Gail Shearer, *Skimpy Benefits and Unchecked Expenditures* (Washington, DC: Consumers Union, June 2003), available at http://www.consumersunion.org/pdf/medicare-603.pdf.

33. Congressional Budget Office (CBO), "Updated Estimates of Spending for the Medicare Prescription Drug Program," 4 March 2005, available at http://www.cbo.gov/ftpdocs/61xx/doc6139/03–04-BartonMedicare.pdf.

34. General Accounting Office, "Department of Health and Human Services—Chief Actuary's Communications with Congress," 7 September 2004, available at http://www.gao.gov/decisions/appro/302911.pdf.

35. David Blumenthal and Roger Herdman, eds., *Description and Analysis of the VA National Formulary* (Washington, DC: National Academies Press, 2000).

36. Survey by Henry J. Kaiser Family Foundation, Harvard School of Public Health, 4–28 November 2004. Retrieved 29 March 2005 from the iPOLL Databank, Roper Center for Public Opinion Research, University of Connecticut, http://www.ropercenter.uconn.edu/ipoll.html.

37. Robert Pear and Richard A. Oppel, Jr., "Results of Elections Give Pharmaceutical Industry New Influence in Congress, *New York Times,* 21 November 2002, A34.

38. Michael Heaney, "Identity, Coalitions, and Influence: The Politics of Interest Group Networks in Health Policy" (Ph.D. diss., University of Chicago, 2004).

39. We thank Michael Heaney for this quotation.

40. The AARP was also desperately concerned about a business-backed provision of the Senate legislation that allowed firms to offer reduced health benefits to employees eligible for Medicare without violating age-discrimination laws—a provision that was, in fact, struck from the final bill. See Heaney, "Identity, Coalitions, and Influence."

41. H.R. 1, "Medicare Prescription Drug, Improvement, and Modernization Act of 2003," 108th Cong., 1st Sess., 33, available at http://www.cms.hhs.gov/medicarereform/MMAactFullText.pdf.

42. CBO, "Updated Estimates of Spending."

43. A good compendium of polling on Medicare is available at http://www.polling report.com/health2.htm#Medicare.

44. ABC News/*Washington Post* poll, 9–13 October 2003 (1,000 adults; margin of error +/− 3 percent), available at http://nationaljournal.com/members/polltrack/2003/issues/03healthcare.htm#2.

45. Thomas R. Oliver, Philip R. Lee, and Helene L. Lipton, "A Political History of Medicare and Prescription Drug Coverage," *Milbank Quarterly* 82 (2004): 284–85.

46. Survey by Henry J. Kaiser Family Foundation, Harvard School of Public Health, 6–12 August 2003, and Survey by Pew Research Center and Princeton Survey Research Associates, 14 July–5 August 2003. Retrieved 29 March 2005 from the iPOLL Databank, Roper Center for Public Opinion Research, University of Connecticut. http://www.ropercenter.uconn.edu/ipoll.html.

47. Survey by NBC News, *Wall Street Journal,* and Hart and Teeter Research Companies, January 19–January 21, 2003. Retrieved March 29, 2005 from the iPOLL Databank, The Roper Center for Public Opinion Research, University of Connecticut, http://www.ropercenter.uconn.edu/ipoll.html.

48. Survey by Henry J. Kaiser Family Foundation, Harvard School of Public Health, 25 April–1 June 2003. Retrieved 29 March 2005 from the iPOLL Databank, Roper Center for Public Opinion Research, University of Connecticut, http://www.ropercenter.uconn.edu/ipoll.html.

49. On the partisan use of conference committees, see Robert Parks Van Houweling, "An Evolving End Game: The Partisan Use of Conference Committees in the Post-Reform Congress" (Paper presented at the History of Congress Conference, University of California, San Diego, 5–6 December 2003).

50. The evolution of Smith's story is well chronicled by Timothy Noah in the online magazine *Slate.* See his "Defendant DeLay? Nick Smith's Bribery Accusations Land in the Majority Leader's Lap," 1 October 2004, and related stories, at http://slate.msn.com/id/2107623/. The official Ethics Committee report—a study in whitewashing, if ever there was one—is available at http://www.house.gov/ethics/Medicare_Report.pdf.

51. Edward Epstein, "Democrats Decry Republican Tactics in Marathon Vote," *San Francisco Chronicle,* 9 December 2003, A17.

52. Sara Fritz, "Medicare Ads Called Political," *St. Petersburg Times Online,* 10 February 2004, http://www.sptimes.com/2004/02/10/news_pf/Worldandnation/Medicare_ads_called_p.shtml.

53. Some of the ads were even developed by a Virginia-based firm, National Media, that was working for Bush's reelection.

54. David Barstow and Robin Stein, "The Message Machine: How the Government Makes News; Under Bush, a New Age of Prepackaged News," *New York Times,* 13 March 2005, A1.

55. Jim Drinkard, "Report: PR Spending Doubled under Bush," *USA Today Online,* 26 January 2005, http://www.usatoday.com/news/washington/2005-01-26-williams-usat_x.htm.

56. Richard E. Neustadt, *Presidential Power and the Modern Presidents: The Politics of Leadership from Roosevelt to Reagan* (New York: Free Press, 1991), 29, emphasis in original.

57. Kenneth R. Mayer, *With the Stroke of a Pen: Executive Orders and Presidential Power* (Princeton, NJ: Princeton University Press, 2001); William G. Howell, *Power without Persuasion: The Politics of Direct Presidential Action* (Princeton, NJ: Princeton University Press, 2003).

58. Cited in Council for Excellence in Government, "Case Study: Building a New OHSA," n.d., http://www.excelgov.org/usermedia/images/uploads/PDFs/Case_Study_-_Building_a_New_OSHA.pdf.

59. Survey by Council for Excellence in Government, February 20–February 24, 1997. Retrieved 29 March 2005 from the iPOLL Databank, Roper Center for Public Opinion Research, University of Connecticut, http://www.ropercenter.uconn.edu/ipoll.html.

60. Survey by the Marlin Company, Conducted by the Gallup Organization, July 6–July 27, 1999. Retrieved 29 March 2005 from the iPOLL Databank, Roper Center for Public Opinion Research, University of Connecticut, http://www.ropercenter.uconn.edu/ipoll.html.

61. The Center for American Progress and OMB Watch, *Special Interest Takeover* (Washington, DC: Citizens for Sensible Safeguards, May 2004), 37.

62. The memo was divulged by the Economic Policy Institute, which opposes the overtime changes. Excerpted text is available at http://www.epinet.org/content.cfm/overtime_2003.

63. These changes are meticulously documented in the Center for American Progress and OMB Watch, *Special Interest Takeover.*

64. A multimedia presentation of the series, "When Workers Die," is available at http://www.nytimes.com/ref/national/WORK_INDEX.html. The quotation is from David Barstow, "U.S. Rarely Seeks Charges for Deaths in Workplace," *New York Times,* 22 December 2003, TK.

65. Christine Todd Whitman, *It's My Party, Too: The Battle for the Heart of the GOP and the Future of America* (New York: Penguin, 2005).

66. CBS News/*New York Times* poll, 20–24 November 2002 (996 adults; margin of error +/– 3 percent), available at http://nationaljournal.com/members/polltrack/2002/issues/02environment.htm#4.

67. General Social Survey, 1972–2002 Cumulative Data File, Question: GRNECON, 1993, 1994, 2000, available at http://webapp.icpsr.umich.edu/GSS/.

68. *Special Interest Takeover,* 11.

69. Whitman, *It's My Party, Too,* 173–74.

70. Environmental Integrity Project, "Newly Uncovered Memo from Former EPA Administrator Whitman to Vice President Cheney Warned That Proposed Rule Change Would Undercut Clean Air Act Enforcement Cases," 15 October 2003, http://www.environmentalintegrity.org/pubs/Press_Release_Whitman_Memo.pdf.

71. "Statement of Senator Jim Jeffords, Reaction to Administration's New Source Review Proposal," 13 June 2002, http://www.senate.gov/~jeffords/press/02/06/06132002nsr.html.

72. Whitman, *It's My Party, Too,* 185.

73. Center for American Progress and OMB Watch, *Special Interest Takeover,* 7.

74. Jeff Claassen, Scott Streater, and Seth Borenstein, "Is the EPA Doing Enough," *Star-Telegram,* 18 July 2004, http://www.dfw.com/mld/dfw/ news/9184148.htm.

75. Peter Bachrach and Morton S. Baratz, "Decisions and Nondecisions: An Analytical Framework," *American Political Science Review* 57 (1963): 632–42.

76. R. Kent Weaver, *Automatic Government: The Politics of Indexation* (Washington, DC: Brookings Institution Press, 1988).

77. Brady Campaign to Prevent Gun Violence, "The Assault Weapons Ban: Frequently Asked Questions," http://www.bradycampaign.org/facts/faqs/?page=awb.

78. David Lee and Bob Cusack, "Minimum Wage Hike," *Hill,* 14 April 2004, 1; Milt Freudenheim, "Bush Health Savings Accounts Slow to Gain Acceptance," *New York Times,* 13 October 2004, C1; Elizabeth Fulk, "Unions Insulted by Bush Minimum Wage," *Hill,* 18 November 2004, 6; Craig Garthwaite, "Affleck Is 'Dazed and Confused' over Kennedy's Minimum-Wage Bill," *Hill,* 13 May 2004, 17; Emily Heil, "New Chairmen Would Push Plan to Boost Minimum Wage," *CongressDaily,* 26 October 2004, 15.

79. Pew Research Center poll cited in Diane E. Lewis, "Election Drives Minimum-Wage Proposals," *Boston Globe Online,* 13 June 2004, http://bostonworks.boston.com/globe/articles/061304_wages.html.

80. "On the Job: Minimum Wage as Election Year Issue," *Seattle Post-Intelligencer,* 17 May 2004, http://seattlepi.nwsource.com/business/ 173484_onthejob17.html.

81. U.S. Census Bureau, *Income, Poverty, and Health Insurance Coverage in the United States* (Washington, DC: Department of Commerce, 2004), available at http://www.census.gov/prod/2004pubs/p60–226.pdf.

82. Kaiser Family Foundation/Harvard School of Public Health Survey, "Health Care Agenda for the New Congress," January 2005, http://www.kff.org/kaiserpolls/loader.cfm?url=/commonspot/security/getfile.cfm&PageID=50263.

83. *Budget of the United States Government, Fiscal Year 2004* (Washington, DC: U.S. Government Printing Office, February 2003); *Budget of the United States Government, Fiscal Year 2005* (Washington, DC: U.S. Government Printing Office, February 2004); *Budget of the United States Government, Fiscal Year 2006* (Washington, DC: U.S. Government Printing Office, February 2005); Cindy Mann, Melanie Nathanson, and Edwin Park, "Administration's Medicaid Proposal Would Shift Fiscal Risks to States," Georgetown University and Center for Budget and Policy Priorities, 22 April 2003, http://www.cbpp.org/4-1-03health.pdf.

84. David Maraniss and Michael Weisskopf , *Tell Newt to Shut Up: Prize-Winning "Washington Post" Journalists Reveal How Reality Gagged the Gingrich Revolution* (New York: Simon and Schuster, 1996); Paul Pierson, "The Deficit and the Politics of Domestic Reform," in Margaret Weir, ed., *The Social Divide: Political Parties and the Future of Activist Government* (Washington, DC: Brookings Institution Press, 1998), 126–78.

85. Chuck Muth, "Commentary: More Tax Cuts Please," United Press International, 17 August 2001.

86. Thomas M. Keck, *The Most Activist Supreme Court in History: The Road to Modern Judicial Conservatism* (Chicago: University of Chicago Press, 2004).

87. Cass R. Sunstein, "The Rehnquist Revolution," *New Republic,* 27 December 2004, 32–36.

Chapter 4. The Race to the Base

1. Maurice Carroll, "Job Fulfills Expectations of New Representative," *New York Times,* 23 July 1981, B2.

2. Lou Dubose and Jan Reid, *The Hammer—Tom Delay: God, Money, and the Rise of the Republican Congress* (New York: Public Affairs, 2004), 273.

3. Carroll, "Job Fulfills Expectations of New Representative," B2.

4. Tip O'Neill and Gary Hymel, *All Politics Is Local: And Other Rules of the Game* (New York: Crown, 1993).

5. Richard S. Dunham, with Lee Walczak and Lorraine Woellert, "Commentary: When Courting the Right Turns Off the Middle," *Business Week Online,* 9 July 2001, http://www.businessweek.com/magazine/content/ 01_28/b3740061.htm.

6. *American Democracy in an Age of Rising Inequality: Report of the American Political Science Association Task Force on Inequality and American Democracy* (Washington, DC: American Political Science Association, June 2004).

7. Congressional Budget Office (CBO), *Historical Effective Federal Tax Rates: 1979 to 2002* (Washington, D.C: CBO, March 2005).

8. Thomas Pickety and Emmanuel Saez, "Income Inequality in the United States, 1913–1998," *Quarterly Journal of Economics* 118 (2003): 1–39. Their tables have been updated through 2002 at http://emlab.berkeley.edu/users/saez/.

9. Edward N. Wolff, *Top Heavy: The Increasing Inequality of Wealth in America and What Can Be Done About It,* 2nd ed. (New York: New Press, 2002).

10. *American Democracy in an Age of Rising Inequality.*

11. Richard B. Freeman, "What, Me Vote?" NBER Working Paper no. W9896, August 2003.

12. All expenditure data in this chapter are from the Federal Election Commission (http://www.fec.gov). Those uninterested in navigating the commission's strikingly unhelpful site can find much of the data at the Center for Responsive Politics' well-oiled Web site: http://www.opensecrets.org/bigpicture/index.asp.

13. The average cost of running for an open Senate seat was $16.7 million in 2000, up from $2.3 million—again, adjusted for inflation—in 1980.

14. *American Democracy in an Age of Rising Inequality,* 7.

15. Andrea Louise Campbell, "Parties, Electoral Participation, and Shifting Voting Blocs," in Paul Pierson and Theda Skocpol, eds., *The Transformation of the American Polity* (Princeton, NJ: Princeton University Press, forthcoming).

16. Larry Bartels, "Economic Inequality and Political Representation," November 2002, http://www.princeton.edu/~bartels/papers.

17. David Brooks, "One Nation, Slightly Divisible," *Atlantic Monthly,* December 2001, 53–65.

18. Jeffrey M. Stonecash, *Class and Party in American Politics* (Boulder, CO: Westview Press, 2000).

19. *American Democracy in an Age of Rising Inequality,* 8.

20. U.S. Census Bureau, *Statistical Abstract of the United States, 2004–2005* (Washington, DC: U.S. Government Printing Office, 2004), 419.

21. Theda Skocpol, *Diminished Democracy: From Membership to Management in American Civic Life* (Norman: University of Oklahoma Press, 2003), 125.

22. *American Democracy in an Age of Rising Inequality;* the full report, along with related research memoranda, is available at http://www.apsanet.org/section_256.cfm.

23. Recent instructive analyses of the role of the South in American politics include Daniel J. Balz and Ronald Brownstein, *Storming the Gates: Protest Politics and the Republican Revival* (New York: Little, Brown, 1996); Earl Black and Merle Black, *The Rise of Southern Republicans* (Cambridge, MA: Harvard University Press, 2002); and Michael Lind, "The Southern Coup," *New Republic* 19 June 1995, 20–29.

24. Sean M. Theriault, "The Case of the Vanishing Moderates: Party Polarization in the Modern Congress," 2 May 2004, available at http://www.la.utexas.edu/~seant/.

25. The two poles are represented by, on the party power side, Gary Cox and Mathew McCubbin, *Legislative Leviathan: Party Government in the House* (Berkeley: University of California Press, 1993), and, on the parties as creatures of the members (indeed, as nothing more than like-minded members), Keith Krehbiel, "Where's the Party?" *British Journal of Political Science* 23 (1993): 235–66. A thoughtful middle ground is developed in Eric Schickler, *Disjointed Pluralism: Institutional Innovation and the Development of the U.S. Congress* (Princeton, NJ: Princeton University Press, 2001).

26. Michael Barone, with Richard E. Cohen and Grant Ujifusa, *The Almanac of American Politics, 2004* (Washington, DC: National Journal, 2003), 1042.

27. The expectation that Roukema would be replaced by a moderate Democrat is ably voiced in John Judis, "The Hunted," *New Republic,* 17 April 2000, http://www.tnr.com/041700/judis041700.html.

28. Liz Marlantes, "Patriotism Becomes Nasty Campaign Issue," *Christian Science Monitor,* 5 July 2002, 2; Maria Newman, "Effort to Oust Republican Falls Short, but Not Far," *New York Times,* 8 June 2000, B6; Ivan Peterson, "Moderate Republican's Foe Is Back, Aided by Conservatives," *New York Times,* 23 May 2000, B2.

29. Available at http://www.clubforgrowth.org/video/garrett-script.php.

30. Marlantes, "Patriotism Becomes Nasty Campaign Issue."

31. Mark Gersh, "The Republicans' Great Gerrymander," *Blueprint* 3 (2003), online at http://www.ndol.org/ndol_ci.cfm?kaid=127&subid=177&contentid =251791.

32. Federal Election Commission, "A Closer Look: House Open Seat Races," n.d., http://www.fec.gov/press/press2005/acloserlook1.shtml.

33. Carol M. Swain, *Black Faces, Black Interests: The Representation of African Americans in Congress* (Cambridge, MA: Harvard University Press, 1993); David Lublin, *The Paradox of Representation* (Princeton, NJ: Princeton University Press, 1999).

34. Jeffrey Toobin, "The Great Election Grab," *New Yorker,* 28 December 2003, 63–68.

35. Ronald Keith Gaddie, "The Texas Redistricting, Measure for Measure," *Extensions* (Fall 2004), http://www.ou.edu/special/albertctr/extensions/fall2004/ Gaddie.htm.

36. Clark Bensen, "Presidential Results by Congressional Districts: Bush Strengthens His Control in the U.S. House," March 2005, http://www.polidata.org/press/ wprec23z.pdf

37. Bensen, "Presidential Results by Congressional Districts."

38. Michael P. McDonald, "Drawing the Line: Redistricting and Competition in Congressional Elections," *Extensions* (Fall 2004), http://www.ou.edu/special/ albertctr/extensions/fall2004/McDonald.htm.

39. Michael Lind, "75 Stars: How to Restore Democracy in the U.S. Senate (and End the Tyranny of Wyoming)," *Mother Jones,* January–February 1998, http:// www.motherjones.com/news/feature/1998/01/lind.html.

40. Reelection rates are from the Center for Responsive Politics, http:// www.opensecrets.org/bigpicture/reelect.asp?cycle=2002.

41. Data on Thune contributors from the Center for Responsive Politics, http://www.opensecrets.org/races/contrib.asp?ID=SDS1&cycle=2004&special=N; a profile of Volunteer PAC is also available from the center at http://www. opensecrets.org/pacs/lookup2.asp?strID=C00341743.

42. Barry C. Burden, "Candidate Positions in U.S. Congressional Elections," *British Journal of Political Science* 34 (2004): 211–27.

43. E. J. Dionne, Jr., "Room Left to Govern?" *Washington Post,* 2 July 2004, A15.

44. Endorsement information is available at Project Vote Smart, http://www.vote-smart.org/issue_rating_category.php?can_id=BS022393.

45. Kimberly H. Conger and John C. Green, "Spreading Out and Digging In: Christian Conservatives and State Republican Parties," *Campaigns and Elections,* February 2002, http://www.findarticles.com/p/articles/mi_m2519/is_1_23/ai_82757259.

46. Conger and Green, "Spreading Out and Digging In."

47. Quoted on the Web site of People for the American Way, http://www.pfaw.org/pfaw/general/default.aspx?oid=4307&print=yes.

48. Matt Bai, "Fight Club," *New York Times Magazine,* 10 August 2003, 24.

49. Helen Dewar, "GOP Club for Growth Shows Limited Clout," *Washington Post,* 23 May 2004, http://www.washingtonpost.com/wp-dyn/articles/A48378-2004 May22.html.

50. Americans for Tax Reform, "Questions and Answers about the National Taxpayer Protection Pledge," available at http://www.atr.org/nationalpledge/index.html.

51. Michael J. Malbin and Anne H. Bedlington, "Members of Congress as Contributors: When Every Race Counts" (paper prepared for the Annual Meeting of the American Political Science Association, 29 August–1 September 2002, Boston).

52. Thomas B. Edsall, "Corporate PACs Favor GOP: Decisive Shift from Bipartisan Giving Began in 1995–96," *Washington Post,* 25 November 2004, A6, available at http://www.washingtonpost.com/wp-dyn/articles/A11073- 2004Nov24.html.

53. Malbin and Bedlington, "Members of Congress as Contributors."

54. Dubose and Reid, *The Hammer,* 271.

Chapter 5. The Republican Machine

1. John F. Padgett and Christopher K. Ansell, "Robust Action and the Rise of the Medici, 1400–1434," *American Journal of Sociology* 98 (1993): 1259–319.

2. Sheryl Gay Stolberg, "After Ethics Rebukes, DeLay's Fortunes May Lie with His Party's," *New York Times,* 8 October 2004, A22.

3. Quoted in Richard E. Neustadt, *Presidential Power: The Politics of Leadership* (New York: Free Press, 1960), 9.

4. Martin P. Wattenberg, *The Rise of Candidate-Centered Politics* (Cambridge, MA: Harvard University Press, 1991).

5. Isaiah J. Poole, "Party Unity Vote Study: Votes Echo Electoral Themes," *Congressional Quarterly Weekly,* 11 December 2004, 2906–8.

6. Steven Teles, *Parallel Paths: The Evolution of the Conservative Legal Movement* (Princeton, NJ: Princeton University Press, forthcoming).

7. Jeffrey H. Birnbaum, "Many Lobbyists Work the Hill with Kith and Kin," *Washington Post,* 14 June 2004, E1.

8. Chafee quoted in Elizabeth Drew, *Showdown: The Struggle between the Gingrich Congress and the Clinton White House* (New York: Simon and Schuster, 1996), 106. Shays quoted in Linda Killian, *The Freshmen: What Happened to the Republican Revolution* (Boulder, CO: Westview Press, 1998), 133–34.

9. Drew, *Showdown*, 116, emphasis added.

10. David Maraniss and Michael Weisskopf, "Speaker and His Directors Make the Cash Flow Right," *Washington Post*, 27 November 1995, http://www.washington post.com/wp-srv/politics/special/campfin/stories/cf112795.htm

11. Nicholas Confessore, "Welcome to the Machine," *Washington Monthly*, July–August 2003, http://www.washingtonmonthly.com/features/2003/0307. confessore.html.

12. Charles Babington, "Ethics Panel Rebukes DeLay: Majority Leader Offered Favor to Get Peer's Vote," *Washington Post*, 1 October 2004, A1.

13. Louis Jacobson, "The DeLay Factor on K Street," *National Journal*, 4 January 2003, 45.

14. Mary Jacoby, "House Divided," *Salon*, 25 May 2004, http:// www.salon.com/ new/feature/2004/05/24/armey/.

15. This is the paraphrase of a "Republican lobbyist" provided by Jacobson, "The DeLay Factor," 44.

16. Confessore, "Welcome to the Machine."

17. Michael Heaney, "Partisanship and the Leadership of Interest Group Coalitions," typescript, Yale University, 2004.

18. Lou Dubose and Jan Reid, *The Hammer–Tom Delay: God, Money and the Rise of the Republican Congress* (New York: Public Affairs, 2004), 177.

19. Internal Westar e-mail cited in Democracy 21, *DeLay, Inc.: A Democracy 21 Report on House Majority Leader Tom DeLay and His Money Machine*, 22 July 2003, available at http://www.democracy21.org.

20. Gebe Martinez, "DeLay's Conservatism Solidifies GOP Base for Bush," *Congressional Quarterly Weekly*, 12 July 2003.

21. On the weakening of committee chairs, see John H. Aldrich and David W. Rohde, "The Transition to Republican Rule in the House: Implications for Theories of Congressional Politics," *Political Science Quarterly* 112 (1997–98): 541–67. On the new selection process, see Karen Foerstel, "Choosing Chairmen: Tradition's Role Fades," *Congressional Quarterly Weekly*, 9 December 2000, 2796–801; Jonathan Allen, "Effective House Leadership Makes the Most of Majority," *Congressional Quarterly Weekly*, 29 March 2003, 746–50.

22. Nicholas Thompson, "Attacks on Fiscal Moderates Fuel Battles within the GOP," *Boston Globe*, 18 May 2003, http://www.newamerica.net/index.cfm?pg= article&DocID=1232.

23. E. J. Dionne, Jr., "Will the Moderates Speak Up," *Washington Post*, 16 November 2004, A25.

24. Philip Gourevitch, "The Fight on the Right," *New Yorker*, 12 April 2004, 34–40.

25. David Stockman, *The Triumph of Politics: Why the Reagan Revolution Failed* (New York: HarperCollins, 1986), 193.

26. R. Kent Weaver, *Ending Welfare as We Know It* (Washington, DC: Brookings Institution Press, 2000), 177–86.

27. Larry Bartels, "Is Popular Rule Possible?" *Brookings Review* 21 (Summer 2003): 12–15.

28. Davis memo, http://thepriceofloyalty.ronsuskind.com/thebushfiles/archives/000058.html; Luntz Research Companies, "Growth, Prosperity, and Restoring Economic Security," n.d., 6, available at http://www.politicalstrategy.org/archives/001189.php.

29. Robert van Houweling, "Legislators' Personal Policy Preferences and Partisan Legislative Organization" (PhD. diss., Harvard University, 2003).

30. Jonathan Allen and John Cochran, "The Might of the Right," *Congressional Quarterly Weekly*, 8 November 2003, 2761–62.

31. Allen and Cochran, "The Might of the Right."

32. Lawrence Jacobs and Robert Shapiro, *Politicians Don't Pander: Political Manipulation and the Loss of Democratic Responsiveness* (Chicago: University of Chicago Press, 2000).

33. R. Douglas Arnold, *The Logic of Congressional Action* (New Haven and London: Yale University Press, 1990).

34. Paul Pierson, *Dismantling the Welfare State? Reagan, Thatcher and the Politics of Retrenchment* (Cambridge: Cambridge University Press, 1994); R. Kent Weaver, "The Politics of Blame Avoidance," *Journal of Public Policy* 6 (1986): 371–98.

35. Ron Suskind, "Why Are These Men Laughing?" *Esquire*, January 2003, 96–105.

36. Alan I. Abramowitz, Brad Alexander, and Matthew Gunning, "Incumbency, Redistricting, and the Decline of Competition in U.S. House Elections" (paper presented at the Annual Meeting of the Southern Political Science Association, New Orleans, La., January 2005).

37. David R. Mayhew, *Congress: The Electoral Connection* (New Haven and London: Yale University Press, 1974).

Chapter 6. The Center Does Not Hold

1. Michael X. Delli Carpini and Scott Keeter, *What Americans Know About Politics and Why It Matters* (New Haven and London: Yale University Press, 1996); Samuel L. Popkin and Michael A. Dimock, "Cognitive Engagement and Citizen World Views," typescript, University of California at San Diego, February 1995, available at http://www.bsos.umd.edu/pegs/popkin.txt; Michael J. Towle, *Out of Touch: The Presidency and Public Opinion* (College Station: Texas A&M University Press), 2004, 11; Dean Baker, "Numbers before Politics," *In These Times*, 26 April 2005, http://www.inthesetimes.com/site/main/article/2076/; Larry M. Bartels, "Is 'Popular Rule' Possible?" *Brookings Review* 21, no. 3 (2003): 12–15.

2. Key works include John Ferejohn and James Kuklinski, eds., *Information and Democratic Processes* (Urbana: University of Illinois Press, 1990); Shanto Iyengar,

"Shortcuts to Political Knowledge: Selective Attention and the Accessibility Bias," in Ferejohn and Kuklinski, eds., *Information and Democratic Processes,* 160–85; Arthur Lupia and Mathew McCubbins, *The Democratic Dilemma: Can Citizens Learn What They Need to Know?* (Cambridge: Cambridge University Press, 1998).

3. Benjamin Page and Robert Shapiro, *The Rational Public: Fifty Years of Trends in Americans' Policy Preferences* (Chicago: University of Chicago Press, 1992); Michael B. MacKuen, Robert S. Erikson, and James A. Stimson, *The Macro Polity* (Cambridge: Cambridge University Press, 2002).

4. Stephen J. Rosenstone and John Mark Hansen, *Mobilization, Participation, and Democracy in America* (New York: MacMillan, 1993), 248.

5. Philip E. Converse, "Popular Representation and the Distribution of Information," in Ferejohn and Kuklinski, eds., *Information and Democratic Processes,* 369–90.

6. Larry M. Bartels, "Homer Gets a Tax Cut: Inequality and Public Policy in the American Mind," *Perspectives on Politics* 3 (2005): 15–31.

7. Robert Dahl, *Polyarchy* (New Haven: Yale University Press, 1971).

8. Jonathan Chait, "When Democrats Join the Dark Side," *Los Angeles Times,* 4 March 2005, A13.

9. Cited in David Brock, *The Republican Noise Machine: Right-Wing Media and How it Corrupts Democracy* (New York: Crown, 2004), 218.

10. Ronald Brownstein, "Democrats Are Lost in the Shuffle While GOP Holds All the Cards," *Los Angeles Times,* 4 April 2005, http://www.latimes.com/news/politics/la-na-outlook4apr04,1,2637751.column?coll=la-utilities-politics.

11. Leonard Downie, Jr., and Robert G. Kaiser, *The News about the News: American Journalism in Peril* (New York: Knopf, 2002), 8.

12. David Croteau, "Examining the 'Liberal Media' Claim: Journalists' Views on Politics, Economic Policy, and Media Coverage," *International Journal of Health Services* 29 (1999): 627–55.

13. Downie and Kaiser, *News about the News,* 65, 125.

14. Downie and Kaiser, *News about the News,* 138.

15. Downie and Kaiser, *News about the News,* 240.

16. These findings are based on a content analysis of all news stories on the tax cuts in the first six months of 2001. Articles were coded for their primary and secondary news frame, based on methods used in similar analyses (such as "Media Coverage of Health Care Reform: A Final Report," *Columbia Journalism Review* 33 [March–April 1995]: 1–7). Reliability tests were done on twenty-one randomly selected articles (or 10 percent of the total, including both *USA Today* and the *New York Times*). Percent agreement—calculated on all numerical variables using the PRAM computer software package, found at http://www.geocities.com/skymegsoftware/pram.html—was an excellent 96.4 percent.

17. Pew Research Center Biennial News Consumption Survey, Pew Research Center for the People and the Press, 9 June 2002.

18. David C. Barker, *Rushed to Judgment: Talk Radio, Persuasion, and American Political Behavior* (New York: Columbia University Press, 2002).

19. Cited in Howard Kurtz, *Hot Air: All Talk, All the Time* (New York: Crown, 1996), 251.

20. Quoted in Brock, *Republican Noise Machine,* 51.

21. Brock, *Republican Noise Machine,* 11.

22. Albert O. Hirschman, *Exit, Voice, and Loyalty: Responses to Decline in Firms, Organizations, and States* (Cambridge, MA: Harvard University Press, 1970).

23. Downie and Kaiser, *News about the News,* 30–31.

Conclusion

1. Report of the Committee on Political Parties, "Toward a More Responsible Two-Party System," *American Political Science Review* 3 (1950): suppl: 17, 19.

2. As Morris Fiorina notes, drawing on the work of Denise Baer and David Bositis, a surprisingly high proportion of the reforms proposed by the Committee on Political Parties have in fact taken place during the past half century. Morris P. Fiorina, "Parties, Participation, and Representation in America: Old Theories Face New Realities," in Ira Katznelson and Helen V. Milner, eds., *Political Science: The State of the Discipline* (New York: W. W. Norton, 2002), 521–22.

3. Report of the Committee on Political Parties, v, 21.

4. Report of the Committee on Political Parties, 20.

5. Robert A. Dahl, *How Democratic Is the American Constitution?* (New Haven and London: Yale University Press, 2002), 161.

6. Dahl, *How Democratic Is the American Constitution?*

7. Thomas Patterson, *The Vanishing Voter: Public Involvement in an Age of Uncertainty* (New York: Vintage, 2003), 191.

8. Thomas Frank, *What's the Matter with Kansas? How Conservatives Won the Heart of America* (New York: Metropolitan, 2004).

9. Jeffrey M. Berry, *The New Liberalism: The Rising Power of Citizenship Groups* (Washington, DC: Brookings Institution Press, 1999).

10. Theda Skocpol, *Diminished Democracy: From Membership to Management in American Civic Life* (Norman: University of Oklahoma Press, 2003).

11. Robert B. Putnam, *Bowling Alone: The Collapse and Revival of American Community* (New York: Simon and Schuster, 2000).

12. U.S. Census Bureau, *Statistical Abstract of the United States, 2004–2005* (Washington, DC: U.S. Government Printing Office, 2004), 419; data on Canada are available at Statistics Canada's Web site: http://www.statcan.ca/english/Pgdb/econoind.htm#lab.

13. Michael J. Graetz and Ian Shapiro, *Death by a Thousand Cuts: The Fight over Taxing Inherited Wealth* (Princeton, NJ: Princeton University Press, 2005).

14. Glen Justice, "Kerry Kept Money Coming with the Internet as His ATM," *New York Times,* 6 November 2004, A12.

15. For discussions of MoveOn, see Gary Wolf, "Weapons of Mass Mobilization," *Wired* magazine, September 2004, http://www.wired.com/wired/ archive/12.09/

moveon.html; Chris Nolan, "MoveOn.org: No Longer a Start-up or an Upstart," Personal Democracy Forum, 22 December 2004, http://www.personaldeomcracy.com/node/218; Associated Press, "MoveOn.org Moves on to New Battles," 2 December 2004, http://abcnews.go.com/US/wireStory?id=297264; CNN.com, "MoveOn.org Becomes Anti-Bush Powerhouse," 13 January 2004, http://www.cnn.com/2004/TECH/ internet/01/12/moveon.org.ap/.

16. The size of the "blogosphere" is estimated by Technorati, a search engine company that tracks blogs, at http://www.sifry.com/alerts/archives/000387.html.

17. In 1994, just before the Republican sweep of Congress, the political scientists William Connelly and John Pitney published *Congress's Permanent Minority?* (New York: Rowman and Littlefield, 1994) on the House GOP.

18. Mike Allen, "GOP to Reverse Ethics Rule Blocking New DeLay Probe: January Change Led Democrats to Shut Down Panel," *Washington Post*, 27 April 2005, A1.

19. Morris P. Fiorina, with Samuel J. Abrams and Jeremy C. Pope, *Culture War? The Myth of a Polarized America* (New York: Pearson, Longman, 2004).

20. Robert Dahl, *Who Governs?* (New Haven: Yale University Press, 1961), 305.

21. Richard B. Freeman, "Fighting Turnout Burnout: Why Europeans Turn Out at Higher Rates and How to Improve American Participation," *American Prospect Online, Special Report: Political Inequality,* June 2004, http://www.thirdworldtraveler.com/Election_Reform/Turnout_Burnout.html.

22. Patterson, *Vanishing Voter,* 181.

23. Jeffrey Toobin, "The Great Election Grab," *New Yorker,* 8 December 2003, 63–68.

24. Patterson, *Vanishing Voter;* George C. Edwards, III, *Why the Electoral College Is Bad for America* (New Haven and London: Yale University Press, 2004).

25. Kristin Kanthak and Rebecca Morton, "Primaries and Turnout, 9 July 2003," available at http://www.nyu.edu/gsas/dept/politics/faculty/morton/KanthakMort.pdf.

26. Hugh Carter Donahue, *The Battle to Control Broadcast News: Who Owns the First Amendment?* (Cambridge, MA: MIT Press, 1989); Thomas G. Krattenmaker and Lucas A. Powe, Jr., *Regulating Broadcast Programming* (Washington, DC: AEI Press, 1994).

27. Mary Elizabeth Williams, "The Ministry of Silly Talks," *Salon,* 9 May 1996, http://archive.salon.com/media/media960509.html.

28. Report of the Committee on Political Parties, v.

Afterword

1. Susan Page, "Bush Approval Rating Hits New Low," *USA Today,* 8 May 2006, available online at http://www.usatoday.com/news/washington/2006-05-08-bush-approval_x.htm; historical data available at Roper Center Web site at the University of Connecticut: http://www.ropercenter.uconn.edu/cgi-bin/hsrun.exe/Roperweb/PresJob/PresJob.htx;start=HS_index.

2. David Brooks, "Don't Worry, Be Happy," *New York Times,* 11 May 2006, A37.

3. Bob Benenson, "Playing Defense: GOP Strives for Continuing Majority in '06," *Congressional Quarterly Weekly,* 24 April 2006, 1078.

4. Gary C. Jacobson, "The 1994 House Elections in Perspective," *Political Science Quarterly* III (1996): 203–23.

5. Nonpartisan experts calculated that the bill would result in an average tax cut of $20 for middle-income Americans, who would receive less than 1 percent of the benefits. Meanwhile, millionaires would receive an average tax cut of $42,776, accounting for more than a fifth of the benefits. Joel Friedman, "Reconciliation Tax Cuts Would Average $43,000 for Households with Income over $1 Million, but Only $20 for Middle-Income Households," Center for Budget and Policy Priorities, Washington, DC, 12 May 2006, available online at http://www.cbpp.org/5-4-06tax.htm.

6. "President Urges Senate to Pass Tax Cut Legislation," White House Release, 10 May 2006, available online at http://www.whitehouse.gov/news/releases/2006/05/20060510-9.html.

7. Responding to Democratic claims that conferees should be bound by the Senate bill, Republican senator Trent Lott declared, "I hope to be a conferee. Do you think I am going to pay attention to any attention to any motions to instruct me. Baloney." David Welna, "Congress Wrangles over Tax-Cut Measure," NPR Morning Edition, 15 February 2006.

8. Joel Friedman and Aviva Aron-Dine, "Tax Reconciliation Agreement Distorted by Obsession with Capital Gains and Dividend Tax Cuts," Center for Budget and Policy Priorities, Washington, DC, 11 May 2006, available online at http://www.cbpp.org/5-10-06tax.htm.

9. Robert Greenstein, Joel Friedman, and Aviva Aron-Dine, "Two Tax Cuts Primarily Benefiting Millionaires Will Start Taking Effect January 1," Center for Budget and Policy Priorities, Washington, DC, 28 December 2005, available online at http://www.cbpp.org/12-28-05tax.htm.

10. Malcolm Gladwell, *The Tipping Point: How Little Things Can Make a Big Difference* (Boston: Little, Brown, 2000).

11. Rankings are available online at http://www.vote-smart.org.

12. Jim VandeHei and Shailagh Murray, "Post-Abramoff Mood Shaped Vote for DeLay's Successor," *Washington Post,* 3 February 2006, A1.

13. Jim VandeHei and Michael A. Fletcher, "Bush Says Election Ratified Iraq Policy," *Washington Post,* 16 January 2006, A1.

14. See, for example, Charles Cook, "The Winds of Change," *Cook Political Report,* 6 May 2003, available online at http://www.cookpolitical.com/column/2006/050606_cookprev.php.

15. FairVote, "2004 Facts in Focus," available online at http://www.fairvote.org/?page=1471.

16. See, for example, Robert S. Erikson, "Economic Conditions and the Presidential Vote," *American Political Science Review* 83 (1989): 567–73; and Douglas A. Hibbs, "Bread and Peace Voting in U.S. Presidential Elections," *Public Choice* 104(2000): 149–80.

17. William A. Galston and Elaine C. Kamarck, "The Politics of Polarization," Third Way, Washington, DC, October 2005, 4.

18. See Jacobson, "The 1994 House Elections."

19. John Dickerson, "Democratic Daydream: Can the Party Match the GOP Takeover?" *Slate*, 8 March 2006, available online at http://www.slate.com/id/2137685/.

20. Sarah A. Binder, "Elections and Congress's Governing Capacity," *Extensions*, Fall 2005.

ACKNOWLEDGMENTS

Many people have helped us make sense of the transformations in American politics that we chart in this book. We could not have written this book without their generous assistance. Yet we would be remiss if we did not emphasize up front that none of these friends, colleagues, and loved ones should be assumed to endorse our claims or prescriptions. Indeed, the most heartening aspect of writing this book—besides the happy realization that even after seventeen drafts, we still liked each other—was how much help we received from people who had reservations about all or part of our thesis, and who weren't afraid to tell us how to make it better. Maybe bipartisanship has a future, after all.

We must begin by thanking a small handful of very dedicated friends and colleagues who took on the daunting task of reading various drafts of the entire manuscript: Tracey Goldberg, Danny Goldhagen, Oona Hathaway, Michael Heaney, David Mayhew, Sid Milkis, Kit Pierson, Rick Vallely, Theda Skocpol, and Steve Teles. Anybody who knows the folks on this list knows just how much collective intellectual firepower we had on our side. Anybody who knows them also knows that only our own obduracy can account for any errors or missteps that somehow made it past their friendly fusillade.

Many other friends and colleagues helped us with key aspects of this project, either by reading and commenting on parts of the manuscript, or by discussing elements of our argument with us. So numerous are our debts in this regard that we know that any listing will invariably be incomplete. Nonetheless, we want to thank deeply Akhil Amar, Chris Ansell, Larry Bartels, Chris Boas, Barry Burden, Dan Carpenter, Peter Hall, Jennifer Hochschild, David Karol, Richard Kogan, Taeku Lee, Ted Marmor, Andy Martin, Nolan McCarty, Bruce Nesmith, Peter Orszag, Mike Pierson, Eric Schickler, James Stimson, Robert van Houweling, and Joe White. We owe a special debt to two scholars who generously provided us with evidence from their own ongoing explorations of American politics: Sean Theriault of the University of Texas (whose work on changes in the ideology of members of Congress we report in Chapter 4), and Michael Heaney of the University of Florida (whose work on interest groups and health policy we discuss in Chapter 5).

Various institutions also deserve thanks (but, again, no blame or responsibility) for their support of this book: Yale University, for a year of leave on a Junior Faculty Fellowship and research funds; the New America Foundation in Washington, D.C., for additional research assistance and financial support; and the University of California at Berkeley, for financial support and research funds. The support of these institutions allowed us to hire a truly stellar group of up-and-coming scholars to provide assistance: Zahreen Ghaznavi, Rachel Goodman, Hannah Hubler, Nicole Kazee, Rachel Kravetz, Pearline Kyi, Joanne Lim, Christine Mathias, Swati Pandey, Emily Scharfman, Alan Schoenfeld, and Shannon Stockdale. These young researchers were not simply indispensable; they also give us great hope for the future of political science—and American politics more generally.

At Yale University Press, we were fortunate to have two wonderful, committed editors: Lara Heimert, who started us off on the project; and Jonathan Brent, who shepherded us to its conclusion. We were also fortunate to benefit from the stellar skills of everyone at the Press, including John Donatich, Molly Egland, Jessie Hunnicutt, Sarah Miller, and Tina Weiner. Our manuscript editor, Laura Jones Dooley, was an author's dream—speedy, professional, and genuinely enthusiastic. The same can be said of our agent, Sydelle Kramer, who knew what we wanted to do in this book even before we did. Writing can be a lonely business—short on praise and long on criticism. Sydelle made sure we remembered why we were doing it, how we were doing it well, and how we could do it better.

It's customary for acknowledgments to end with heartfelt thanks to the spouses and kids who stuck by the author (or authors) as he (or they) toiled away on the magnum opus now in readers' hands. In the old days, these acknowledgments thanked wives—and they were almost always wives—for holding down the household fort, and sometimes even for typing the magnum opus itself. Thanks to feminism and word-processing, we gratefully do not have to offer these particular words of thanks (though we do have to acknowledge that more than a fair share of fort-holding was done by our wives as we completed our mini opus). But we still have an un-repayable debt to acknowledge. Our wives, Oona and Tracey, have been true intellectual partners in this project from the beginning. They read and responded to our ideas. They urged us on. And perhaps most important, they tolerated us even when we were not always at our most tolerable—which may well be the truest measure of their love.

Our children, Ava and Owen, Sidra and Seth, tolerated us, too. But they also gave us something far greater. With their simple wonder and unfiltered joy, they reminded us why our nation's future is so precious.

INDEX

AARP, 77, 88, 247n40

abortion, 42–43, 68, 81, 105, 121, 127, 175, 195. *See also* moral issues

Abramoff, Jack, 87–88, 143

accountability, 16–18, 47, 48, 65, 159, 164, 166, 174–75, 187–88, 212–13, 217–22. *See also* backlash insurance; center, political; democracy; elections

ACU. *See* American Conservative Union

adaptation, ideological, 118, 120. *See also* base, Republican; replacement, electoral

advertising, 10, 17; elections and, 122, 131, 138, 149; indirect lobbying and, 141; prescription drug coverage and, 92, 248n53; Social Security and, 77, 149; tax cuts and, 53, 57–58. *See also* campaign finance; interest groups

advocacy groups. *See* interest groups

AFL-CIO, 200

agenda setting, 7–8, 12–13, 70, 72–85, 120, 136–37, 151–53; bankruptcy law and, 80–82; Democrats and, 85, 72–75, 170; energy policy and, 82–85; media and, 178–81; obstruction and, 99, 100–103; Social Security and, 75–80; tax cuts and, 49, 64, 103. *See also* *individual policies;* backlash insurance; manipulation; policy design; Republicans

Ailes, Roger, 180

Alinsky, Saul, 70

Allen, George, 66

Alternative Minimum Tax (AMT), 56, 61–62, 91, 199

American Conservative Union (ACU), 33, 129

American Enterprise Institute, 31–32, 120

American Federation of Labor and Congress of Industrial Organizations. *See* AFL-CIO

American Jobs Creation Act, 246n30

American Political Science Association, 116, 185

Americans for Tax Reform (ATR), 10, 12, 33, 54, 121, 129–30, 139–40; anti-tax pledges and, 33, 54, 130. *See also* interest groups; tax cuts

AMT. *See* Alternative Minimum Tax

Anheuser-Busch, 95

Annenberg Public Policy Center, 41

Ansolabehere, Stephen, 42

anti-tax pledges, 33, 54, 130. *See also* Americans for Tax Reform; interest groups; tax cuts

Arctic National Wildlife Refuge, 84

Armey, Dick, 110, 119, 130